Music, Electronic Media and Culture

About the volume:

There has never been greater public exposure to the musical products of electronic technology than there is today. Pubs, clubs, restaurants, banks and shops offer new environments for the experience of musical sound, in addition to the conventional concert hall. There are now many different ways to make music, and, thanks to the loudspeaker, many different ways of listening.

This new world of musical sound and the questions it poses are explored in the nine essays that comprise this volume. At the heart of the collection is the myriad of confusing and exciting possibilities that are raised by sound that we hear but whose source we cannot see – the acousmatic. Part One of the book challenges the received wisdom of generations of writing on the acousmatic, providing new perspectives including an ecological view of human perception. The essays in Part Two explore the ways in which the history and plurality of culture has itself become the object of musical creativity in the form of sampling or plundering. In Part Three the potential fields of sound perception offered by the imagination are probed and given a 'textual' voice in Katharine Norman's concluding essay to the volume. This uses the text itself as a medium for expressing the multi-layered reflections that a listener may have to 'the work' of music.

About the editor:

Simon Emmerson is Reader in Music at City University, London. A composer and writer, he was first prize winner at the Bourges Electroacoustic Awards in 1985 for his work *Time Past IV*. He is the editor of *The Language of Electroacoustic Music* (Macmillan, 1986) and has contributed to the *Journal of New Music Research* and *Organised Sound*.

Music, Electronic Media and Culture

Edited by

SIMON EMMERSON

ASHGATE

Published by
Ashgate Publishing limited
Gower House
Croft Road
Aldershot
Hampshire GU11 3HR
England

Ashgate Publishing Company
Suite 420
131 Main Street
Burlington, VT 05401-5600
USA

Ashgate website: http://www.ashgate.com

British Library Cataloguing in Publication Data

Music Electronic Media and Culture.
1. Music—Social aspects. 2. Electronic music.
I. Emmerson, Simon.
306.4'84

Library of Congress Cataloging in Publication Data

Music, electronic media and culture/edited by Simon Emmerson.
p. cm.
Includes bibliographical references and index.
ISBN 0-7546-0109-9 (alk. paper)
1. Electronic music—History and criticism. 3. Music —
20th century—History and criticism. 3. Music technology.
ML1380.M86   2000
786.7—dc21   00-59415

0 7546 0109 9

Reprinted 2003

Typeset in Sabon and Arial by Manton Typesetters, Louth, Lincolnshire, UK and printed in Great Britain by Biddles Limited, Guildford and King's Lynn.

Contents

Notes on contributors

Chris Cutler, born in 1949, a prolific composer, interpreter and improviser, first became known in the early 1970s as a member of English avant-garde rock group Henry Cow; this was followed by projects with Art Bears, News from Babel, Aqsak Maboul and Les Quatre Guitaristes. In the early 1980s he co-founded the Anglo-German quartet Cassiber. Other collaborations include productions for radio, theatre and dance. He is editor and publisher of the ReR Sourcebook and numerous articles (some collected in his book *File under Popular*). He founded and still runs the celebrated label and distribution service ReR/Recommended.

Simon Emmerson, born in Wolverhampton, 1950, studied Natural Sciences and Music Education at Cambridge, including work with Roger Smalley and Tim Souster. He taught music and physics at secondary school level before pursuing postgraduate studies at City University, London, where he subsequently joined the staff to direct the Electroacoustic Music Studio. He gained a doctorate at the University in 1982 and is now a Reader in the Music Department. In recent years he has received commissions, all including electronics or tape, from Lontano, Shiva Nova, Philip Mead, Nicola Walker Smith, Jane Chapman, the *Groupe de Musique Expérimentale de Bourges*, the Smith Quartet and Inok Paek. He was first prize winner at the Bourges Electroacoustic Awards, 1985, for his work *Time Part IV* (soprano and tape). He is editor of *The Language of Electroacoustic Music* (Macmillan, 1986); he has edited two issues of *Contemporary Music Review* and is a contributor to the *Journal of New Music Research* and *Organised Sound*. He is currently a director of Sonic Arts Network. A CD of his works appeared on the Continuum label in 1993.

Ambrose Field's compositional output includes electroacoustic music for tape, music education works and community music projects. After gaining a first-class degree from the University of York, he undertook postgraduate studies at Cambridge University. In 1993 he was awarded a British Academy studentship to study for a PhD in Electroacoustic Composition with Denis Smalley at City University, London. In 1996 he became a Lecturer at the University of York, where he teaches courses in Electroacoustic Composition, Postmodernism and Music Education. He was a director of Sonic Arts Network from 1995 to 1997. His research has been published in *Organised Sound* and he received a commission from the International Computer Music Association for the International Computer Music Conference 1999.

Kersten Glandien, born in 1953 in Germany, studied Philosophy, Aesthetics and Art History at the University of St Petersburg, Russia. She worked at the University and the Music College in Dresden and as a senior research fellow at the Institute of Aesthetics and Art Theory of the Academy of Science in Berlin. In 1989 she moved to England, lecturing currently at the American International University in London and working freelance as a writer, researcher and curator in the field of new music.

Katharine Norman, Senior Lecturer, Director of the Stanley Glasser Electronic Music Studios at Goldsmiths College, graduated from Bristol University before being awarded a Fulbright scholarship and a Wingate fellowship to study composition and computer music at Princeton University where she received her doctorate in 1993. From 1994 to 1997 she was Lecturer in Composition at Sheffield University. Her 'digital soundscape' *London* (NMC) was voted a critics' choice for 1996 by *The Wire* and she has works recorded on Discus (Sheffield), Empreintes Digitales (Canada) and Sonic Circuits (USA). Her research interests lie in the field of computer and electroacoustic music, in particular the use of recorded 'real world' or documentary sources as musical material. She has contributed to *Contemporary Music Review* and was issue editor for volume 15 ('A Poetry of Reality: composing with recorded sound'). She was also responsible for the extended article on Electronic Music for the world-English edition of Microsoft's Encarta CD-ROM encyclopaedia (1996–97) and for entries in *The New Grove Dictionary of Music and Musicians*. She has also been a board member of Sonic Arts Network and the International Computer Music Association, editing the ICMA newsletter, *Array*.

Simon Waters is a composer. He studied Music at the University of Nottingham before gaining MMus and PhD degrees in Electroacoustic Music at the University of East Anglia. His many residencies for composition and research projects include: 1986–90: Course Leader (with Sarah Rubidge) for Rambert Dance Company Education Unit and the South Bank Centre Education Unit; 1988–90: Research Associate of KACOR (Kineto-Audiologic Communication Research Group) at the Royal Technical University, Stockholm. From 1991 to 1993 he was South West Arts Research Fellow in Interactive Arts at Bath College of Higher Education with a remit to research the interrelationship between different arts practices, particularly music and visual art. In 1994 he returned to the University of East Anglia as Lecturer and Director of the Electroacoustic Music Studio. He has published papers in *Contemporary Music Review*, *Leonardo*, *Sonus* and *ex tempore*, and has presented papers at international conferences such as ISEA, 1998 (The Hague) and ICMC, 1990 (Glasgow).

Luke Windsor has a BSc (Music), MA (Music Psychology) and a PhD (Music Analysis) from City University, London. Since 1994 he has been a Research Assistant at the universities of Sheffield and Nijmegen (Netherlands Institute for Cognition and Information). He is currently a lecturer at the University of Leeds. The results of his research have been published in *Contemporary Music Review*, *Psychology of Music*, *Music Perception* and in 'Song and Signification' (edited by Monelle and Gray), and have been reported at a number of international conferences (psychological and musicological).

Robert Worby is a composer (mainly of electroacoustic music), broadcaster, writer and teacher. In addition to occasional, one-off appearances on radio and television he has produced and presented two series for BBC Radio 3: *Cacophony Now* was broadcast in 1996 and *Ambience: Music and Spaces* in May 1997. His writings appear sporadically in *The Independent*, *The Sunday Times* and *The Gramophone*. His music is composed for the concert hall, dance companies, television and film, and he often produces sound works drawing on non-musical traditions.

For Professor Malcolm Troup
on the occasion of his seventieth birthday
with gratitude for his inspiration,
energy and vision.

Introduction

Simon Emmerson

The death in August 1995 of the founder of *musique concrète*, Pierre Schaeffer, coincided with a groundswell of interest in his ideas and the works of those who had developed the field – often in ways in which he would not have approved. This wave of interest, however, crossed boundaries in unexpected ways, for example, highlighting the growing contact of the popular (Dance) music world with the pioneers of 'high modernist' electronic music. Stockhausen, Xenakis and Henry have, amongst others, all been the subject of 'cross-over' projects.

But claims for the imminent abolition of boundaries between music art forms, 'popular' and 'classical' have not so simply materialised. Each may plunder the other's materials, but an unease and distance still prevails. Indeed the term 'classical' has given way to the term 'academic' used in a pejorative sense to mean élitist, out of touch and self-consciously 'arty', requiring considerable education to 'understand'. While, indeed, public perception of a large part of electroacoustic music is that it has 'retreated' into academic and other specialist institutions, there has never been greater public exposure to the musical products of electronic technology. This contrast of 'common means but non-common ends' throws both challenges and life-lines to the 'art music' composer, offering possibilities in 'applied art' unheard of a generation ago. But the question whether this is a compromise or a challenge, whether to defend 'sound for sound's sake' or to go along with multi-media or commercial forces, are questions which can no longer be avoided by practitioners at any level as public funds for so-called 'art music' diminish.

Behind these contradictions and paradoxes lie fundamental shifts in listening habits. Shifts not revolutions: Christopher Small has recently pointed out (Small, 1998) that what we perceive as the decline of undistracted and concentrated listening, allied to music becoming a more integrated part of social exchange, is but a return to a behaviour quite common before the late romantic era in Europe.

For a considerable time now there has been music in all our spaces, from pubs and clubs to banks and shops. There has always been a corresponding variety of listening habits, from 'background' to 'concert hall'. But these are perpetually shifting their relationships. Superficially the 'style' of listening spaces is changing, but more importantly how we evaluate and work within them is shifting radically. Pubs and clubs have been centres of music for centuries, but the move to seeing these as alternatives to concert halls for the presentation of 'the new' in art and culture, suggests a profound shift in focus – 'where it's at' has quite literally changed.

The fixed seat proscenium becomes but one space and time of many. If in the twentieth century 'art music' was nearly always confined (in live instrumental performance, at least) to the concert hall, electroacoustic music has been evangelical in its search for new spaces to utilise – new to it, but old to the traditions of our social exchange. Of course it is still performed in concert halls, but one somehow senses a yearning to break free of the constraints, to allow the listener to move through the imaginary spaces it creates unfettered by old divisions of performer and audience.

What unites the themes in this book is the loudspeaker: a magical object that is as much creator as recreator. It remains the one link in the recording chain of which the technology (after electrification in the 1920s) has not fundamentally altered. In drawing the parallel to Pythagoras's curtain, behind which he lectured to his followers and which gives us the unenviable term 'acousmatic', Pierre Schaeffer confronted that essential drive in the human psyche – already prefigured in radio art well before the birth of *musique concrète* – to recreate imaginary sources of what we hear but cannot see: 'the pictures are better on radio'. We would not have survived had we not associated the snap of a twig behind us with potential danger, the sound of water at a distance with potential survival.

Now Schaeffer chose to banish, or at least keep at bay, the consequences of this propensity. Many of his followers did not. In the literature of electroacoustic music much has concentrated on assuming the 're-duced listening' that was Schaeffer's ideal. Do not listen with intent to gain real-life information! In such a view the play of sound-forms, addressing the deepest essence of the human spirit – its desire for balance, drama and resolution – need have no recourse to the crudity of recognising the 'real'.

Many of the essays in the present volume try to redress this balance, examining the consequences of re-opening the doors of perception to real or imagined sources which refer to the world outside the listening space, to events, stories and narratives. Some such references go beyond 'mere' representation to symbolism and even myth, while others prey on culture itself plundering the wealth of sounds already made into music to recycle into new work. Several contributions to this book address the 'sampling of history' and its consequences.

This volume is divided into three parts. Part I ('Listening and interpreting') challenges much of the received wisdom of earlier generations of writing on the subject of the 'acousmatic' (in both French and English traditions). Luke Windsor's chapter 'Through and around the acousmatic: the interpretation of electroacoustic sounds' introduces us to an ecological view of human perception, applying principles from evolutionary biology and psychology to the perception of sound and strongly situating the idea of a sound's 'meaning' in a negotiation between objective and subjective worlds. Ambrose Field examines the new resources which result when composers allow the sounds to carry into the work the references and meanings they held in the 'non-musical' world outside the listening space. In 'Simulation and reality: the new sonic objects' he goes beyond the simple 'surrealist' metaphor to further kinds of 'outside music' reference. Finally Simon Waters's chapter 'Beyond the acousmatic: hybrid tendencies in electroacoustic music' explores the contexts within which electroacoustic art has traditionally been placed. Technology at first helped establish new art-forms but has moved on to allow us to subvert, to hybridise, to challenge accepted authorities who define 'meaning' (not only in art).

The second part is titled 'Cultural noise'. Here the history and plurality of culture itself becomes the object of creativity. The inclusion of Chris Cutler's classic essay 'Plunderphonics' introduces us in depth to the history of 'sampling culture'. Appropriation is as old as culture itself, of course, but recording has unique and special qualities; the technology has both created and fed the demand for a radical acousmatic approach which challenges both the ownership and identity of the artwork. My own essay 'Crossing cultural boundaries through technology?' poses more questions than it could possibly answer. There are those who might argue that intercultural exchange should be left to happen 'naturally' – in some sort of global jam session which will produce new hybrids, some doomed to die, others to form the basis of 'new species'. But some attempts at deeper understanding of composition and performance practices might be allowed and developed through new technology. Robert Worby's chapter 'Cacophony' concludes this section. From the Futurists, Schaeffer and John Cage, we have had calls for the return of noise to an active role in music. Noise cannot just be described in acoustic terms but must be related strongly to a social and cultural infrastructure, of conflict between groups and generations. Cacophony articulates at once violence and exuberance, celebration and obliteration.

In the third part, 'New places, spaces and narratives', the new places and spaces tend to be those of the imagination – I have never been happy with the word 'virtual' as all such spaces are real enough, although in a different sense, sometimes metaphoric. Kersten Glandien contributes one of the first in-depth discussions in English about that genre of acousmatic art that predates *musique concrète*. In 'Art on air: a profile of new radio art' she brings together a wide variety of sources in a synthesis to present an art form which will surely inform the web-art of the future. I hope that this chapter stimulates an evidently dormant interest in this field in Britain. My own contribution '"Losing touch?": the human performer and electronics' takes as its starting point a clear split which I hear emerging in recent electroacoustic music between gestures that can still be related to human action and those increasingly divorced from bodily experience; this sometimes corresponds to a separation between the clean and clear, and the (deliberately) noisy and chaotic. I have attempted to extend Denis Smalley's notion of the 'indicative field' to include sounds which are themselves heard nowadays primarily through the ubiquitous loudspeaker and to relate these to life experiences (often urban and industrial) which are strongly indicative. Finally, Katharine Norman has contributed an experimental piece of writing which examines the layers of reality and human reaction to music (specifically the works *Things she carried* by Paul Lansky and Luc Ferrari's *Presque rien avec filles*). 'Stepping outside for a moment: narrative space in two works for sound alone' uses the script itself as a medium for expressing the multilayered reflections that a listener (and the author) has to 'the work' of music.

It has been difficult to choose a group of nine contributors from the enormous wealth of authors now writing on contemporary music. I wanted to feature British-based work, to include younger contributors and to present material which challenges orthodoxies as soon as they appear to be 'settling in'. I also wanted to include genres not usually deemed to be at the centre of electroacoustic music's concerns. I see *Music, Electronic Media and Culture* as a first contribution to a reappraisal of the position of the electroacoustic arts whose effective half-century celebration in 1998 was at a *fin de siècle* in so many senses.

Reference

Small, Christopher (1998), *Musicking*, Hanover: Wesleyan University Press.

PART ONE

Listening and interpreting

CHAPTER ONE

Through and around the acousmatic: the interpretation of electroacoustic sounds

Luke Windsor

Introduction: electroacoustics and the acousmatic

It has become common practice to use the term 'electroacoustic music' to describe a wide variety of musical praxes involving the mediation of loudspeakers. Music created using all kinds of sound synthesis, music using recorded sounds and music which uses amplification all fit into this broad category. Such music varies in its reliance upon technological mediation. One can, for example, imagine a performance of Tchaikovsky's *1812 Overture* with or without sound diffusion and amplification, and in both live or recorded execution. However, one cannot say the same of Henry's *Variations pour une porte et un soupir* (Henry, 1987), nor of Stockhausen's *Kontakte* (Stockhausen, 1992): these pieces require diffusion by loudspeakers for their realisation. Nor could one say this of the music of Motorhead, which although often performed live, relies extensively on the use of amplification for its musical effect. This is not to suggest that some music is more inherently electroacoustic than others, but it does serve to illustrate that for certain pieces and kinds of music electroacoustic mediation is technically essential.

In this chapter I will interrogate the perceptual and music-theoretical consequences of music which not only requires this kind of mediation but also denies a visual source for its constituent sounds. Such music has been termed *acousmatic*, reflecting the theoretical ideas of Pierre Schaeffer (1966). In its broadest sense acousmatic music might be said to be all music which is presented for which we are unable to see the sources of the constituent sounds. A concert performed by musicians seated behind an opaque screen, directly mimicking the pre-Socratic concept of aurally transmitted *akousmata*, would fit into this category, as would an audio-only recording of an acoustic concert. A concert of amplified live musicians or a multimedia presentation in which the sources of sounds were visible would not.

Schaeffer's view of the acousmatic was a complex one, but it is clear that his conception of acousmatic music was a music in which the composer attempted to ignore the physical causation of his or her source materials. The acousmatic was intended not just as a description of how listeners would perceive sounds, but of an attitude composers should develop towards their material. The phonograph, closely followed by analogue tape recording, made it possible to create a technical separation between sound source and sound which had hitherto been impossible. The two terms *objet sonore* and *écoute réduite* (Schaeffer, 1966) had particular importance in delineating this approach. 'Sound objects', isolated and repeated on tape, and 'reduced listening', the manner with which composers were exhorted to analyse them both took their place within a larger and highly prescriptive endeavour to propose a *recherche musicale* (Schaeffer, 1966). These terms point towards the development of new compositional listening strategies rather than toward an attempt to propose a method for either describing or prescribing how music should be perceived by an ordinary listener. Schaeffer himself stresses the varieties of aural experiences available to listeners in his etymological and structuralist notion of *les quatres écoutes* (Schaeffer, 1966, pp. 103–28). He distinguishes between an indexical mode of listening, concerned with the identification of the events that are responsible for the emission of sound (*écouter*), and listening as a symbolic mode, to do with sounds as signs, the relationship of sounds as signifiers to signifieds that are *extra-sonores* (*comprendre*). An example of the former would be the recognition by a listener that a sound was caused by a gong being struck, whereas the latter type of listening would involve the interpretation of this gong sound, perhaps as signalling the beginning of a meal. Similarly, he identifies two other modes of listening which do not refer beyond the sound itself; *ouir*, the naïve reception of a sound's occurrence ('I heard something'), and *entendre*, attention to certain qualities of a sound itself, without reference to its source or significance ('it sounded "vibrant"').

Schaeffer proposed a programme of musical research which aimed to develop the everyday (*banale*), active, yet non-referential listening of *entendre* into a specialised (*praticienne*) semiotic system, equivalent to pre-existing musical and linguistic systems in its relational and abstract nature, yet wholly different in its development of 'natural' listening (Schaeffer, 1966, especially pp. 360–85). Unlike *écoute traditionelle*, the traditional musical model, where a 'repertoire of timbres' (*écouter*) and a system of musical values (*comprendre*) leads to the types of listening appropriate to a traditional sound-world, *la recherche musicale* would ideally be derived from the development of a system of musical values and structures based upon a return to the sound itself, mostly through the type of listening Schaeffer identifies as *entendre*. For this reversal of musical practice Schaeffer proposes a radical and specialised form of listening: *l'écoute réduite*, or reduced listening (Schaeffer, 1966, pp. 261–79, 349–59) in order that familiar sources and semiotic systems should not play any part in this research. The *objet sonore* as an 'in-itself' is to be explored while placing significations and causes in 'brackets'.

Hence one might think of 'acousmatic music' (as opposed to music that is acousmatic) as a kind of music in which the listener would be drawn into an acousmatic approach to listening. One might assume that, like the composer, the listener should attempt to concentrate upon listening to the non-referential, non-symbolic aspects of sounds. In this chapter I will argue that although such a view is far from realistic, the concept of the acousmatic in music is important to our understanding of how we listen to and interpret both *intentionally* acousmatic music and music that is more *coincidentally* acousmatic. By doing so, it will become clear that for the listener at least, attempts to break through the acousmatic 'screen' in order to ascribe causation to sounds are an important facet of musical interpretation. I will begin by showing how a consideration of the relationship between action, perception and meaning can provide a more perceptually relevant analysis of the acousmatic situation. This will be done by exploring the relevance of an 'ecological' acoustics. I will then apply this approach to the perception of acousmatic music, and provide some analyses of pieces by György Ligeti, Pierre Henry and Fred Frith to show how a more subtle and perceptually motivated view of the acousmatic has important aesthetic consequences.

Ecological acoustics and the aesthetic consequences of acousmatic presentation

Gaver (1993a) notes that the concentration upon 'musical' sounds in acoustics, psychoacoustics, and latterly music perception, can be seen as a primary factor in our 'ignorance' regarding 'everyday listening':

> an account of hearing based on the sounds and perceptions of musical instruments often seems biased and difficult to generalise. Musical sounds are not representative of the range of sounds we normally hear. Most musical sounds are harmonic; most everyday sounds inharmonic or noisy. Musical sounds tend to have a smooth,

relatively simple temporal evolution; everyday sounds tend to be much more complex. Musical sounds seem to reveal little about their sources; while everyday sounds often provide a great deal of information about theirs. Finally, musical instruments afford changes of the sounds they make along relatively uninformative dimensions such as pitch or loudness, while everyday events involve many more kinds of changes – changes that are often musically useless but pragmatically important. Our current knowledge about sound and hearing has been deeply influenced by the study of a rather idiosyncratic subset of sounds and sources (Gaver, 1993a, p. 3).

A growing body of research is attempting to study the perception of sounds which do not resemble traditional speech or music in a manner that takes account of the perception of sound sources and their potential to us as active (rather than passive) organisms. Within the field of ecological acoustics, sounds are not viewed as being perceived as abstract entities related only one to another, as 'tone colours' or timbres, nor are they perceived as standing for concepts or things, as signs. Instead they are seen as providing unmediated contact between listeners and significant environmental occurrences. In an ecological framework, sounds provide an organism with information that allows it to locate, identify and successfully interact with food sources, predators or members of its own species with which it may mate, collaborate or challenge for territory. It is within such a context, I will argue, that the concept of the acousmatic begins to make fresh sense. Before applying such a theory to acousmatic presentation, however, I will describe the ecological approach and outline its application to auditory perception.

The ecological approach to perception

According to Gibson (1966; 1979), perception does not require the mediation of mental representations of the external world. This is contrary to the dominant view of perception in which the processing, storage and manipulation of information by the mind is primary (see Costall and Still, 1991). Rather than assuming that the sensations passed from the sense organs to the central nervous system represent a chaotic source of information that mental processes organise and store in the form of meaningful percepts and memories, the ecological approach assumes that the environment is highly structured and that organisms are directly 'sensitive' to such structure. If this were the sum of Gibson's approach accusations of naïve realism would indeed be justified. How could such a view 'explain' the way in which human beings utilise language, mental imagery, knowledge and memories in their experience of the world? Merely stating that an organism is 'sensitive' to environmental structure seems to beg too many questions. Gibson's work is much subtler than this. He does not claim that memory, language and other symbolic systems play no role in our experience of the world. However, he is keen to distinguish between perception itself and the symbolic systems that facilitate the mediation, storage and communication of perceptions (Gibson, 1966; 1979; Reed, 1991).

Action, perception and affordances

The core of Gibson's contribution to psychology lies in the way in which perception is seen as the result of a dynamic relationship between organism and environment. Organisms and species evolve, both phylogenetically and ontogenetically, to become sensitive to information that will increase their chances of survival. Moreover, the dynamic relationship between a perceiving, acting organism and its environment is seen to provide the grounds for the direct perception of meaning. Gibson's term for this kind of meaning is 'affordance'. Objects and events are related to a perceiving organism by structured information, and they 'afford' certain possibilities for action relative to an organism. For example, a cup affords drinking, the ground, walking. For different organisms, affordances will differ; for a human being an open body of water might afford swimming or immersion, but for a water bug the same stimulus information, picked up by different perceptual systems and relative to different organismic structure, would afford support (Gibson, 1979, p. 127). Moreover, affordances are fluid relative to individual perceptual development: for a surfer, certain patterns of waves afford surfing, whilst to a non-surfer they might afford drowning. Affordances 'point both ways' (Gibson, 1979, p. 129) in that they can neither be explained purely in terms of the needs of the organism, nor in terms of the objective features of the environment. The affordance is a relationship between a particular environmental structure and a particular organism's needs and capacities.

As each organism, or species, evolves it will develop certain effectivities (possible actions) and its perception of an environment will reflect those features of the environment that allow for, constrain or demand such actions. Conversely, as an environment develops it will offer certain affordances, features of survival value to an organism. An organism can be said to exhibit an *effectivity structure*, a complex of actions that reflects its relationship to the affordance structure of an environment.

Event perception: the primacy of source recognition

Event perception attempts to identify the invariant properties of events that specify both the permanent and changing features of the environment that are significant to an organism. The aims of this approach are neatly encapsulated by Shaw, McIntyre and Mace (1974, p. 280):

> By analyzing the organism's context of physical stimulation into events with adaptive significance, we have a means of conceptually distilling from the ambient flux of stimulation those aspects most relevant to the maintenance of equilibration in the organism's ecosystem.

Any event will be perceived in terms of its affordance structure, its potential to evoke adaptive behaviour. The affordance structure of an event will vary according to the particular effectivities of an organism, its potential for performing adaptive behaviour. The properties of events that make up a particular affordance structure are termed invariants and may be divided up into two classes, those that specify styles of change and those that specify persistence, or permanence (Warren and Shaw, 1985). An event can be defined as a process that leaves some physical properties unchanged and transforms others. The identification of the styles of change and persistent features of events that are ecologically significant is a primary motive in studying event perception. For example, the perception of facial growth seems to be the result of specific geometrical functions that transform certain elements of facial structure whilst leaving others permanent (Shaw, McIntyre and Mace, 1974; Mark, Todd and Shaw, 1981). Such geometrical functions can be termed transformational invariants, whilst those features left unchanged can be termed structural invariants.

In summary, events can be described in terms of their adaptive significance to an organism and are the result of the coevolution of the perceptual systems of organism and an environment. Within such a perspective, an event's 'meaning' is determined directly, not by mental processes or representation: an event produces structured information that affords further perception or action.

Auditory event perception

Gibson's discussion of invariances is largely dominated by the visual (Gibson, 1979), despite some preliminary work on audition (Gibson, 1966). As the concern here is with a primarily auditory phenomenon, it seems reasonable to move straight to work in audition although other sources of information will prove relevant when we return to the 'acousmatic' listening context itself. Moreover, the research cited will betray a concentration (maintained throughout this chapter) upon invariants that specify sound producing objects, leaving aside work upon sound localisation. The motivation for adopting an ecological approach in this context is to redress the balance between abstract approaches to musical structure and those that take into account the connections between sounds and the environment that produces them.

Heine and Guski (1991) point out that although research in 'ecological acoustics' is as yet an underdeveloped area within ecological psychology, the concern with studying real sounds in realistic situations has a considerable history. Psychoacoustic research in many domains has consistently shown our ability to identify sources despite complex and noisy signals (for example, Solomon, 1958; 1959a and b; Howard and Ballas, 1983) and the influence of source classification and the semantic interpretation of individual sounds upon the syntactic parsing of sound sequences (Howard and Ballas, 1980; 1982). It seems that our ability to identify the causation of sounds depends upon our ability to classify certain acoustic attributes and that, even when we are not explicitly asked to perform such classifications, these acoustic structures tend to be hard to ignore:

> the order of transient components within a pattern is not arbitrary, but rather reflects the temporal structure of the generating events. In an everyday example, one would expect to hear the garage door open before hearing the car being driven out. On the other hand, a car door opening could either precede or follow the sound of the engine being shut off. Although the temporal or syntactic structure which exists in patterns of this sort is clearly less rigid and well specified than that encountered in the grammars of language, some temporal structure does exist (Howard and Ballas, 1982, p. 158).

Whereas psychoacoustic research tends to focus upon noticeable differences in pitch, spectral structure or duration, ecological research attempts to identify the transformations in acoustic structure which inform the listener of some important change in the environment. For example, Warren and Verbrugge (1984) discovered that the distinction between 'breaking' and 'bouncing' glass is made by subjects on the basis of specific temporal invariants, rather than differences in global spectral information. These changes in organisation are specified by the physical natures of the contrasting events; it is hence possible to synthesise convincing *virtual* breaks and bounces by starting from a mechanical description of the masses, densities, elasticities and forces involved (Gaver, 1993b). In this sense Warren and Verbrugge (1984) are involved in what might be described quite accurately as an 'ecological' acoustics where salient and invariant properties of the sound are directly and lawfully related to the physical properties of the causal event. It is this lawfulness and predictability which specifies the event for the perceiver:

> sound in isolation permits accurate identification of classes of sound producing events when the temporal structure of the sound is specific to the mechanical activity of the source (Warren and Verbrugge, 1984, p. 705).

A number of related studies (Spelke, 1976; 1979; Warren, Kim and Husney, 1987) have demonstrated that structured auditory information can be used to predict the movements of objects due to there being lawful relationships between such auditory information and patterns of movement. For example, predicting the bounce height of a ball (from its elasticity) can be achieved just as well by *hearing* the duration of a single bounce as it can be by *seeing* it (Warren, Kim and Husney, 1987). In the domain of sound classification, Freed (1990) has investigated the acoustical and perceptual correlates of 'perceived mallet hardness' using real mallet sounds. Reliable judgements of mallet hardness could be predicted on the basis of the spectral energy distribution of the different mallet sounds. Here, spectral invariants seem to specify the interaction of materials according to the physical nature of the event. Similarly, Repp (1987) has discovered that hand claps are consistently yet incorrectly categorised by gender. Although classifications into male and female clappers are consistent across subjects they do not reliably predict gender. Instead, they predict the physical configuration of the hands and the tempo and intensity of the clapping. Low frequencies in the spectra seemed to correlate with palm to palm clapping; high frequencies with palm to fingers. The perception of gender differences seemed to rely upon the classification of higher, softer, faster claps as being female, according to a cultural stereotype. One must interpret this as providing evidence for lawful and invariant relationships between physical actions and judgements of causation, rather than the matching of stored representations of 'male' and 'female' clapping sounds with acoustic stimuli.

It is one thing to show how we are sensitive to such lawful auditory structures, but many researchers have begun to stress the primacy of such 'causal' listening (see, for example, Vanderveer, 1979; Jenkins, 1984; Gaver, 1993a and b) over more qualitative styles of perception. As Kendall notes:

> In everyday life, sound events arise from action, in fact, from the transfer of energy to a sounding object. The auditory system provides

us with perceptual characterizations of the energy transfer and of the internal structure of the objects involved. Early in childhood one learns to recognize the occurrence of sound events and to relate them to physical events (Kendall, 1991, p. 71).

Moreover, as we have seen, sounds specify events or objects that *afford*. For example, striking a hollow object may produce a sound that informs the perceiver that the object affords 'filling' or 'the carrying of water', just as the perception of the elasticity of a bouncing ball allows a catcher to predict how high a ball will bounce given a certain input of energy (Warren, Kim and Husney, 1987). The transformational invariants which specify a bottle breaking (see Warren and Verbrugge, 1984) also specify its change in morphology and the transformation of one fillable object into a number of un-fillable fragments which precludes that object's potential as a fluid-carrying vessel. A change in structure is not behaviourally neutral: the affordance structure has changed and this change may be directly specified by the event perceived. In this sense it is misleading to portray the perception of 'breaking' as some ecologically neutral classification of this event. It is perceived in so far as it changes the relationship between listener and environment: the bottle no longer affords filling. Within this perspective, the knowledge that the bottle is 'broken' does not explain why we do not attempt subsequently to fill it with water and drink from it. We might describe the bottle as broken in order to communicate this change in structure and its behavioural consequences but such a labelling cannot explain our actions. On the contrary, the representation of an object as broken, and hence useless for its task, relies upon a change in its affordance structure.

Additional support for the hypothesis that the structure of events is lawfully related to auditory perception is to be found in the literature on physical modelling in sound synthesis. Gaver (1993b), for example, has demonstrated the success of using physical models of vibration, and single and multiple collisions between objects, for synthesising the contrasting sounds of scraping surfaces and hitting wooden or metal objects. Cadoz, Florens and Luciani (1984; see also Cadoz, Lisowski and Florens, 1990) have also exploited the synthesis algorithms based upon physical models of objects (or instruments) with gesture transducers.

Such research has led Gaver (1993a; 1993b; and personal communication) to propose that both synthetic and real events may be perceived in terms of their probable causation, whether or not this causation is actual. A 'real' source is not necessary for the perception of a physical cause. Since the invariant structures which specify a particular event may be modelled, presented and controlled in synthesised sounds, it is clear that the notion of 'true' causal correspondence is of limited importance: although events are specified by certain invariants this is not to say that these invariants have to be produced by any actual physical interaction of materials. It would be absurd to argue that controlling an algorithmic 'string' via a gesture transducer relies upon the perception of a causal relationship between player, 'bow' and 'string' in any physical sense. Rather it is the transaction between player and a set of familiar invariant haptic and auditory structures which forms the link between action and perception. In the following sections the consequences of this will be shown to be extremely important for understanding the relationship between sounds and their perceived sources in acousmatic music.

Event perception in acousmatic music

The ecological perspective described above does not imply that sounds cannot be described as having 'qualities' such as those provided by Schaeffer (1966) or that they cannot be used as signs, whether culturally convened or more directly motivated. It does imply, however, both that such mediated concepts are unnecessary for sounds to inform us about our environment and that the sources of sounds may be harder to ignore than one might hope.

This approach may seem at first peculiarly unsuited to describing the perception of music. However, as will become clear, acousmatic music, both due to its avoidance of conventional musical structures and its mode of presentation, benefits from exploring this most direct level of perception. The materials of the acousmatic composer are often precisely those sounds excluded from a traditional view of musical sounds and sources. More importantly it is these 'non-musical' sounds and sources that are perceived by listeners: the parameters of pitch and rhythm are often hard to find in acousmatic music and instrumental and vocal sources no more likely than the sounds of the everyday environment. Gaver's description of the distinction between musical and everyday sounds (Gaver, 1993a), despite his assertion that noisy sounds and pragmatic listening have no musical role to play, could almost be translated into a description of the distinction between the sounds of traditional and acousmatic music. Similarly, when Jenkins (1984, pp. 129–32) notes that 'Music seems to belong in a space or world of its own' and emphasises 'the special status that music may have in the realm of acoustic events' he is quick to discriminate between 'sound effects' which often rely upon contact with the more familiar 'everyday' world and perception in such a specialised context as music.

Within this context acousmatic music seems often to resemble the practice of sound effects in radio broadcasts more than it does conventional music.

Although the appropriateness of choosing an everyday level of description may seem to have its most obvious benefits for understanding the use of recorded 'concrete' sounds in acousmatic music, this chapter proposes more than this. A concrete sound may be edited or processed in such a way as to conceal its original source, just as a synthetic sound with no corresponding environmental cause may specify an unambiguous, yet 'surrogate' (see Smalley, 1986), environmental origin. Moreover, such matters may or may not be under compositional control. Just as a composer might attempt to exclude any connections between his or her piece and familiar events whilst a listener might still hear such connections, so also a composer's intentional 'narrative' of familiar sounds might be misapprehended where a listener fails to perceive the 'correct' sound sources. Just as physical models of sound-producing events may create virtual instruments and events (see above) through modelling invariant acoustic information, such invariances may be perceived regardless of their actual causation.

This discussion can be clarified by a distinction between *real* and *virtual* events. Both real and virtual events are specified in the same way, by acoustic invariances that are lawfully related to the physical interactions that produce sound. In the latter case of virtual events, however, perception is not veridical: the listener hears an event that has not occurred. In a sense all the events of an acousmatic piece are virtual, since they do not inform the listener about his or her real environment. An acousmatic piece destroys the direct and continuous relationship between acoustic invariants and the surroundings of the listener through its fixed artefactual nature. Although one can 'explore' such a piece through repeated listening, one cannot do much more than this to 'explore' the acoustic scene. Moreover, the acousmatic piece prevents the listener from exploring the environment in an intermodal fashion: the 'acousmatic' prevents the listener from using his or her other perceptual systems (vision, touch, smell, taste) and intimately relating the events perceived with one's actions. Neither are the sounds of an acousmatic piece directly relevant to the listener: the sounds clearly originate from a number of loudspeakers and, despite all the efforts of research in modelling spatial perception (see, for example, Kistler and Wightman, 1992), one cannot forget that a listener to an acousmatic piece is already inhabiting an environment within which an impoverished 'virtual' environment is presented. Noble (1981, p. 68; also see Gibson, 1966, pp. 233–4) notes the same limitations for film projection.

Here, since the visual image is, amongst other things, insufficiently wide to fill our visual field, it is this, not our head and eyes, which constrain looking and hence perceiving. As Noble points out, although visual displays that fill the field of view can produce physiological reactions that suggest greater 'realism', such reactions are not generally *interpreted* by the perceiver as being 'real'.

In another sense, however, such events are just as 'real' as any to be found outside acousmatic music. The ability of listeners to identify a recording of an oboe, or for that matter a synthesised oboe, is not significantly different from their ability to identify a water sound, whether produced by granular synthesis techniques or through an actuality recording. The recorded and diffused acoustic structures may be impoverished to a certain extent but this does not mean that listeners may not exploit their sensitivity to invariances in the perception of individual sounds or the structural relationships between them. The differences between listening to an acousmatic piece and listening to the environment are important and unavoidable, yet should not obscure the importance of event perception.

Given that our perceptual systems have evolved to pick up invariant acoustic structures that specify everyday events it is reasonable to suggest that where these invariant structures occur in acousmatic music a listener will be able to perceive the events and objects which would normally and lawfully give rise to such structures. It is sometimes all too easy to confuse the sounds of an acousmatic piece with the 'accidental' sounds that often intrude into listening environment. Given that most acousmatic pieces eschew more familiar 'musical' events such as discrete pitch structures, relatively hierarchical or periodic rhythmic structures and familiar instrumental sources, more often than not the only familiar structures available to the listener, are those that specify everyday events. Moreover, since such familiar events may be directly specified, it follows that any longer term sequence of sounds is liable to be perceived in terms of these events. As Howard and Ballas have shown, the 'syntactic' structure of a sequence of sounds interacts with the 'semantic' structure formed through the events that they may specify (see Howard and Ballas, 1980; 1982). Any structural description of acousmatic music *must* take into account the possibility that listeners are sensitive not only to temporal and frequency relationships as such but as information for events. Moreover, it is suggested that event perception most often dominates more abstract structures. This argument is as important for synthesised sounds and heavily processed sounds as it is for raw samples or more extended actuality recordings. This can work both ways: certain synthesis techniques betray their real causation to those familiar with them, whilst those unfamiliar with the technical processes and resulting sounds of computer music hear one or more virtual events of more general specificity. Frequency modulation, additive and subtractive sound synthesis or the use of a phase vocoder are all quite easily, even unavoidably, heard by practitioners in the field and early electronic music is generally easily identifiable for this reason alone. For a naïve listener, however, many FM sounds tend to specify bells through their inharmonic frequency structure; the sounds of early electronic music might specify the sound track of an early science fiction movie and its attendant 'futuristic' technology which makes bleeps and bloops, because of their steady state or artificially filtered spectra; and many other synthetic sounds are heard as having percussive, or vibrating sources. For example, Louis and Bebe Barron's music for the film *Forbidden Planet* (Barron, 1978) manages to blur the distinction between sound effects and music through the use of identifiably 'synthetic' sounds: here the synthetic nature of the sounds is dominant and seems to occupy a strange position: the sounds are virtual in the sense that their sources are supposedly from the future but quite real in the sense that they correspond to the operation of the machinery in the film *and* in that their real sources (oscillators and noise generators) are perceived. The two types of listener (specialist and naïve) may describe what they hear in different ways and may focus upon different aspects of the auditory structure, but the links between such structure and the source event are lawful and 'out there' waiting to be discovered.

It could be argued at this point that by prioritising the perceived events that give rise to sound, such a perspective denies the 'musicality' of acousmatic music, reducing listening to the identification of sound sources and events. On the contrary, it is proposed that by assuming that abstract structuring principles might be identified which are independent of event perception, one runs the risk of missing the most important facet of acousmatic music. The undoubted ability of listeners to perceive sources, even where such perceptions are non-veridical, suggests that it is precisely the gap between 'everyday' listening and 'musical' listening which is important.

Affordances, interpretation and the aesthetics of the acousmatic

The approach to perception thus far suggested is in stark contrast to Schaeffer's conception of the acousmatic (Schaeffer, 1966). Rather than providing a method for concealing sound sources, the recording, synthesis, processing and rediffusion of sounds over loudspeakers becomes a source of structured acoustic stimulus information about events for the perceiver. Such stimulus information may be structured in such a way as to specify events, regardless of a composer's intentions, and is perceived contextually. This context is provided in two ways. First, context is provided by the fact that any listener has coevolved with a structured environment. Second, context is provided by the combination of stimulus information across the perceiver's perceptual systems. The result of this first kind of context is that the listener is especially sensitive to invariants that specify familiar environmental events. The result of the second is that the listener is not just a listener but perceives acoustic structure originating from the loudspeakers along with a multitude of other informative sources. The result of this, discussed in more detail below, is that the perception of an acousmatic piece may be radically different from the perception of real events, but is not just *acousmatic listening*. The listener inhabits an environment rich in stimulation, rich in structure, and will perceive affordances not only through the pick up of structured auditory information from the piece but from the environment as a whole, whether acoustic or not.

In order to describe the consequences of this view consider my analysis (Windsor, 1996a) of a fragment from Wishart's *Red Bird* (Wishart, 1992). Here, a perceptual and semiotic isomorphism was described between two sounds (book and door) which might lead to a number of interpretations. The listener must here be assumed to perceive structured acoustic information specifying the sources of these two sounds, two familiar everyday events. However, the objects specified cannot be seen or explored in the same way as a real door and book. In this sense listening is indeed acousmatic. The diffusion of the sounds over a loudspeaker system precludes such direct exploration. The objects are simply not available to be explored through touch or vision. The perception of these objects is impoverished but only in relation to the everyday environment. The actual environment of our hypothetical listener is not, however, impoverished to such a great extent. Loudspeakers may be perceived both visually and acoustically (Smalley, 1994), other listeners may be perceived, the programme note may be read and the listener may perceive all these and other available sources of information. The affordances of this environment will depend upon the interaction of all these sources of information whether perceived acoustically or not: perhaps the information may afford the production of a coded, symbolic set of linguistic utterances, perhaps a more subtle change in the listener's actions. However, the difference between the listener's present environment and that specified by the book and door sound is of importance here. The stimulus information specifying these two objects has remained constant: what has changed is the environment of the listener. Within the acoustic structure of the piece and within the surroundings of the listener, a pair of untouchable, invisible objects are specified which are acted upon in a familiar fashion. Whatever this affords, the listener is exposed to an artefact that cannot be 'correctly' perceived. The available information neither confirms nor denies the 'reality' of the sounding objects. However, one must be careful not to overplay the 'illusory' nature of the objects that are perceived. The book and door are only illusory in that they are perceived within a context that affords a deferral of exploratory action. Editing out the book sound and playing it on a high quality sound system behind the head of an unsuspecting subject in a quiet library completely alters the actions that one might expect to result.

The example from *Red Bird*, where clear specification of everyday events is constantly afforded, tells us little about acoustic information which seems not to specify any familiar causal event. Such situations are, however, more common than a naïve application of ecological theory would propose. As Gibson himself states in response to the question of what happens in cases of 'inadequate information': 'the perceptual system *hunts*.' (Gibson, 1966, p. 303). Where the immediate information from a particular source is insufficient the human being not only hunts for additional information from the 'natural' environment but also from the social and cultural environment. By observing the actions of others, exploring cultural artefacts, by involvement in discussion with others, information may be gathered which supplements that provided by the event or object in question. In the case of a sound or sequence of sounds which fails to specify clearly an event, the human listener attempts nonetheless to make sense of these sounds in relation to the environment. Such sounds *do* afford exploration of that environment. They afford behaviour that is social, where the involvement of others is used to provide supplementary information, cultural, where culturally relative affordances are perceived, and aesthetic, in that their affordances may be so far removed from 'everyday' behaviour that they appear functionless.

Acousmatic music, although it may 'afford' raises *aesthetic* issues. It is tempting to see aesthetics as something divorced from everyday experience, something relying upon the disconnection of experience from reality. Whether in terms of 'disinterest', the 'sublime', or 'immanent critique' much philosophical aesthetics suggests that the artwork remains in some sense autonomous or divorced from the concerns of the everyday world. Within an ecological approach such dislocation is always viewed as partial and contingent, relative to the perceptions and actions of an organism within a structured environment.

It seems at first quite odd to discuss the affordances of an artwork. One might assert that a book provides stimulus information which makes sense of our surroundings, however distant; but it is more difficult to consider the distinction made between a technical manual and a copy of Joyce's *Ulysses*. In the same way, an actuality news broadcast seems quite distinct from Wishart's *Red Bird* (Wishart, 1992), let alone François Bayle's piece *Grande Polyphonie* (Bayle, 1992) in which many (but by no means all) of the sounds eschew everyday specificity or obvious denotative and narrative significance. This gap, however, does not serve to diminish the relevance of the ecological approach. On the contrary, only by taking such an approach does it become clear why music in general and acousmatic music in particular might be considered aesthetic at all. In the everyday environment, as has been proposed, sounds are not usually perceived independently from their sources and the activities they afford. Moreover, where events are specified by acoustic invariants, these invariants allow the organism to perceive affordances that are intimately connected to survival. In acousmatic music such direct links between sounds and our survival seem tenuous, if not illusory. Despite the obvious specificity of many of the sounds in acousmatic music, and their more extended ecological relationships, this specificity does not afford everyday behaviour. As described earlier, the contextual information available to a listener affords actions which are socially and culturally appropriate, but this does not help to explain why such cultural norms develop. There is no clearer information for the cultural nature of an acousmatic piece than opening a CD case, reading the liner notes and then playing the CD, but this does not explain why the subsequent listening is 'aesthetic'.

Why then are acousmatic pieces 'meaningful' in a way that an actuality recording is not? The answer, it is proposed, lies in the simultaneous perception of two kinds of structured information. No dualism is intended here, rather a continuum between two poles. On the one hand the acousmatic piece presents structure of an everyday kind, on the other such structure is contradicted. The first kind of structure may be perceived relative to the lawfulness of the environment, the second may contradict this lawfulness or supplant it with novel structures whose lawfulness emerges only in relation to that piece or a specialised context. The acousmatic piece affords 'interpretation' because its affordances must be manufactured, to a large extent, by the interpretative activity of the listener. Such affordances are not however, arbitrary, any more than are the affordances of a football, typewriter or technical manual. 'Interpretation' is merely a term used to describe the production of signs and relationships between signs which provide the structure necessary for developing some form of relationship with an environment. In the case of an acousmatic piece, such symbolic structures may not result in a consistent and lawful state of affairs. The piece may afford an infinite number of interpretations, none of which exhausts or defines its potential affordances. Nonetheless, the piece seems to demand an *attempt* to find an affordance structure. The listener perceives that some of the sounds specify events or the manipulation or juxtaposition of sounds that *should* specify events but fail to do so. The aesthetic nature of the acousmatic piece lies in its position between the demands of everyday perception and its contradiction of the specificity which provides for a structured and relatively unambiguous relationship with the world (see Windsor, 1996b for a discussion of this in the terms of its implications for philosophical aesthetics). The acousmatic piece, however impoverished and unlawful it may be in relation to the *real* environment, is not necessarily impoverished in relation to its intrinsic structure, its *virtual* environment. This interplay between real and virtual, intrinsic and extrinsic, everyday and musical will be briefly explored in the following analyses.

The interpretation of acousmatic music: examples

The three following analyses represent an attempt to describe how musics deriving from different cultural positions make use of the acousmatic. Only one of these pieces was composed within the Schaefferian tradition yet all three, wittingly or otherwise, show how acousmatic presentation both focuses and distracts our attention towards the sources of the sounds.

György Ligeti: Artikulation *(Ligeti, 1988)*

The now famous aural score of *Artikulation* (Ligeti and Wehinger, 1970) can be seen as an attempt to delimit the potential interpretations of Ligeti's electronic piece. In more specific terms, the score reifies the composer's intentions and the means by which the sounds were created at the expense of the listener's imagination. Within the framework developed above it is possible to suggest some alternative analytical interpretations of this piece. Rather than fixing the meaning of the acoustic structure within the context of its manufacture, its actual sources (oscillators, filter banks, etc.), the analysis proposed here attempts to show how the uncertainty in attribution of source events is itself a component in possible interpretations. Within such a view, the actual causes of the sounds are at issue but only insofar as they are available to listeners through structured information and in relation to the listener's environmental context.

It is suggested that in perceptual terms this piece creates a tension between virtual and real sources, between its status as a piece of *elektronische Musik* and as information for possible events. It does provide information for 'electronic' events with which many listeners will be familiar. In combination with a familiarity with the history of electronic music, it would also be possible to suggest an interpretation based upon this work's position within such a history. One might for example 'hear' this piece in relation to Stockhausen's early electronic studies, *Gesang der Jünglinge* (Stockhausen, 1991) or *Kontakte* (Stockhausen, 1992). The environmental context in this case is a highly specific one and its specificity is relative to two sources of structured information. The first is that of the piece and its particular acoustic structures and listening context, the second, familiarity with the acoustic structures of a number of other pieces in combination with their listening contexts, which include information regarding their manufacture.

This piece, however, cannot be seen merely as the result of the technical and historical processes perceived. Just as one might hear 'electronic' source events, and indeed, in combination with the information provided by the 'score', the 'imitation' of speech sounds, one also hears 'metallic' sounds, sounds that specify flowing and bubbling fluids, wind, and changes in spatial structure which suggest events occurring within a number of virtual spaces. These latter interpretations are no less valid than those made in relation to the real sources identified through perceiving the piece in relation to studying the score or listening to other instances of electronic music. Indeed, one might argue that a distinction between real and virtual sources is only possible with reference to the particular 'real' environment of the electronic studio. For the listener no such context should be assumed to be relevant to interpretation nor should it be proposed as providing some form of necessary ground against which other interpretations are to be contrasted. The tension between interpreting this piece as 'electronic music' and as a montage of sounds that more closely resembles occurrences outside the electronic studio is not to be dismissed lightly.

Whatever prescriptive motivations might be given for attempting to ignore the alternative environments which may have produced the sounds of this piece, it is clear that a perceptual approach must embrace all such possible contexts and resulting interpretations: just because the sources of the sounds are well documented does not mean that we are constrained to interpret the piece according to such documentation.

Indeed for most listeners, despite their familiarity with the environment of electronic sound sources, an environment impossible to ignore in contemporary western life, the precise provenance of the sounds will remain contingent unless emphasised through a programme note or the score. For listeners and for analysts whose interests lie beyond the actual manufacture of the piece, an everyday interpretation of the events involved in the piece is no more or less 'true' or 'objective' than one which accounts for sounds in relation to their actual production and status within the historical context of electronic music.

Take, for example, the opening of the piece: is it not possible to interpret the events one hears as drips of water and the impacts of various solid objects? Moreover, as the extract develops one might perceive a growing conflict between such an interpretation and the more clearly artefactual sounds that occur. This contrast between two possible environments creates the possibility not just of interpreting the piece as referring intrinsically within an abstract timbral or gestural framework and extrinsically in relation to the 'environment' of electronic music, but also as an interplay between the electronic (or synthetic) and the 'natural'. Moreover, within the 'natural' domain one could suggest an interplay between solid and liquid events, a kind of proto-narrative interpretation wholly independent of the axis between real and virtual source environments. Such interpretative axes are as important for electronic music as they are for acousmatic pieces that more unambiguously combine recorded and synthesised sounds. Indeed, as argued above, the perception of any acousmatic piece always occurs within the broader context of the familiar environment. Through the mismatch between everyday perception and acousmatic perception, informed by the inability of the listener to explore the perceived events in an unconstrained and cross-modal fashion, the listener is placed in a position where perception is impoverished or misleading in relation to the immediate listening environment, yet meaningful in a less direct but no less informative fashion.

Although the virtual nature of an acousmatic environment may constrain the listener from intervening directly in the events that might be perceived, this does not mean that such events cease to be meaningful in an ecological sense. Although the affordances of such events are undoubtedly transformed by their unusual context or by processes of electronic production or transformation – or indeed by a tension between their status as information as such and information for events – such processes lead to new affordances. The electronic sounds can be heard as impoverished information for everyday events and the tension between everyday and electronic contexts literally affords a search for some kind of social or cultural explanation. That this search may be open-ended in terms of its direct consequences for the future actions of the listener does not reduce the importance of viewing an aesthetic response within the broader context of human actions. By *actively* attempting to produce discourse which 'makes sense' of what we hear as a cultural object, as 'communication' or as 'art', the listener acts in such a way as to replace an everyday interpretation (which is clearly contradicted not only by the structure of the piece but by the structure of the environment in which it is perceived) with one which is consistent with a view of the environment as a *human* environment. Moreover, viewing this piece in such a way, as a structure which affords interpretation in relation to the human environment, avoids reducing musical experience to the discovery of any sole structuring principle by portraying interpretation as an active process which momentarily fixes the piece within the context of human behaviour and the human environment. Such a momentary and contingent view is in direct contrast to that of attempting to define a neutral level of analysis for acousmatic music (Nattiez, 1990) whether through the observation of documentary evidence which supports particular views of analytical pertinence or through empirical research which takes as its starting point the abstract and self-referential nature of musical structure. On the contrary, meaning is here seen as arising from the mutual relationship between listener and piece.

This need not lead to an extreme relativism in which all interpretations have equal status: in the case of Ligeti's *Artikulation* it is clear that by describing available information, an interpretation of the piece may be shown to be grounded within particular informational contexts. The analyst's role within such an approach is to identify such contexts and how they constrain and inform interpretation at any given time, not to discover any more general and coherent view of the 'work'. Such a perspective may not result in the kinds of structural insights desired by traditional models of analysis, but serves instead to emphasise the shortcomings of viewing acousmatic music as a coherent analytical object. Whereas Wehinger's 'listening score' (Ligeti and Wehinger, 1970) attempts to explain how the piece is constructed and to direct our aural attention to acoustic features which relate to the explanation (or confirm it), the approach developed here offers no such certainty. However, it is hoped that what is achieved is a view of the relationship between a piece, the human environment and human perception. In this vein, *Artikulation* is not seen as an analytical object but as structured information which, combined with other sources of information, may result in interpretation. The 'work' is seen not as an object but as a *relationship* between listener and the environment – a relationship which is dynamic, yet open to analysis. Similarly, any division of the work into smaller units must always take into account these units' contingency. *Artikulation* is not its score, nor is it just an acoustic trace, nor indeed is it merely something which resembles everyday events yet fails to specify them unambiguously. It is a combination of sources of information and can be analysed accordingly. These sources of information may include Wehinger's aural score (Ligeti and Wehinger, 1970) but may also include sources of information available only to a particular listener. Some sources of information, such as the real environment, must be regarded as having more stability and generality than others but none should be discounted as having relevance to an analysis. Moreover, interpretation itself should be seen within its social and cultural context as a means of actively constructing affordances where these are ill-defined through perception of the immediate structure of the environment. In the case of *Artikulation* it is clear that there is a distinction to be drawn between awareness that acoustic information is available, and an attempt to understand this acoustic information in relation to the human environment as a whole.

Pierre Henry: Variations pour une porte et un soupir: Comptine
(Henry, 1987)

Comptine, the eighth 'movement' of Henry's *Variations* illustrates the tension between intrinsic and extrinsic structures in acousmatic music in an extreme, yet subtle fashion. Disregarding the titles of the piece and this specific movement for the moment and focusing upon what may be heard, it is notable that the acoustic structures of this piece have multiple environmental specificities. These specificities serve to articulate the virtual environment in a number of ways. First, despite the differences between the individual sounds it is apparent that a single type of source is responsible for the acoustic structures, some form of 'squeaking'. However, in contrast, this 'squeaking' is differentiated according to a number of possible events. Some of these seem to specify a familiar instrumental source, a single reed instrument, perhaps a saxophone, some a more 'accidental' event such as friction between two surfaces. The sounds, whatever their precise sources, all suggest the gestural intervention of a 'player' in the broadest sense. One could suggest that a continuum between a familiar musical source and a familiar everyday source is present here but, notwithstanding this continuum, some form of manipulation of the events concerned seems likely. Two motivating factors can be suggested. First, the 'instrumental' nature of some of the sounds serves to motivate an interpretation based upon a musical environment. Second, within this interpretation, the improvisatory quality of this 'performance', whilst challenging any traditional models of musical structure, is clearly not an actuality recording of a 'natural' event. On the other hand, if we are hearing an instrumental performance, it is clear that, whatever familiar instrument might be perceived, many of the sounds provide information which challenges this perception.

Contextual information helps provide a less ambiguous interpretation here. The title of the piece, and any sleeve notes available might tell us that these sounds are in fact derived from a recording of a particular door. Regarded in a traditionally acousmatic sense the transformations that have occurred between the resultant sounds and the original recording distance the piece from the original events. Although it is not suggested that such a result was intended, it is clear that the virtual environment is not independent from the real environment which was recorded, nor from the real environment with which the listener is familiar. Whether or not the listener 'hears' an instrumental source, a door squeak or fails to hear any source for the sounds at all, perception occurs within such contexts. Indeed, it is suggested that it is the interplay between the virtual environment and the real environment which provides this piece with its focus. The acousmatic does not serve to conceal sources here but serves simultaneously to challenge and conform to the lawfulness of the real environment. The sounds are not a squeaking door, nor are they a saxophone, but they preserve certain invariant features of these sounds in such a way as to present a perceptual conflict. Herein, it is argued, lies the aesthetic component of this piece, a tension between the real and the virtual.

Before moving on, it is important to note that there is a further and more subtle level of specificity here. The 'quality' of the sounds employed, their texture, should not be regarded as a purely abstract, auditory phenomenon. This textural aspect is closely related to the possible causes of such sounds and hence plays a role not only in specifying particular events but providing a link between the piece and the environment of real events. The structure of the sounds specifies causation in a direct yet general fashion: we hear some form of contact between two surfaces or the supposed vibration of a reed between the lips of a player. Moreover, the possibility of hearing a player provides the basis for perceiving a human body as direct instigator of the events. The quality of the sounds is far from abstract, however abstracted from specific events our perceptions may become. Even familiarity with the 'real' sources of the sounds in this piece or conversely an attempt to banish such considerations cannot wholly disturb this virtual environment. Indeed, attempting to follow such listening strategies tends to increase the tension between the 'real' and virtual environment: on the one hand it does not sound as if all the sounds are best interpreted as *merely* a door squeak, on the other they do not seem to be an abstract set of structures. A virtual environment is suggested which is at once a performance, a recording and an exploration of acoustic quality. The latter aspect, however, should not be divorced from the events which produce sounds. A play of timbres may be a good description of this piece in one sense but only when this description is related to source specificity does it take on its full interpretative significance. In order to hear this piece in an abstracted form, one must disregard all the information which richly specifies causal events, an interpretative course which implies a *negation* of this specificity. Such a course is in no way invalid as an interpretation but must be seen within the context within which it takes place. Whether or not the environmental contexts suggested here are perceived, it is clear that these sounds may inform the listener about more than just themselves, and it would be misleading to suggest otherwise.

Fred Frith: Guitar Solos: Alienated Industrial Seagulls *(Frith, 1993)*

The electric guitar, despite its versatility, has a familiarity in the latter part of the twentieth century which is undeniable. Although electronic transformation is very much a part of its identity and playing styles differ considerably, it is generally an easily identifiable instrument. Here however, the 'history' of the electric guitar is challenged through the acoustic structures available from the virtual environment. What we hear is hardly recognisable as a guitar at all: we hear rattles, scrapes, bangs, and very few sounds which clearly specify either the playing styles with which we are familiar (blues, jazz, rock) or the instrument itself. The most important source of information identifying this as guitar playing at all is the information provided through familiarity with Fred Frith as a particular player and, connected to this, the information available through the cover of the CD which conveniently provides a photograph of Frith with a subtly modified guitar in conjunction with the overall title 'guitar solos'.

In the case of this piece the relationship between real and virtual *events* is a subtle one. The virtual environment is one which provides information for a number of events which seem to have little to do with guitar playing. Indeed, it is clear that if one wishes to interpret this piece as a 'guitar solo', rather unusual playing techniques must be involved. Without the extrinsic context of 'guitar solo' the piece could be an actuality recording of any number of sources and any interpretation arrived at would likely leave out the real component of the guitar as a factor. Is the guitar and its player then a virtual or a real source for the acoustic structures which result? In one sense the guitar is a real source, despite its interaction with unusual materials and some degree of electronic manipulation, in another it is a virtual source, specified only through familiarity with the cultural environment, especially the linguistic specificity provided by the sleeve of the CD and any contact a listener may have had with Frith's playing. Not taking this duality into account leads to a situation in which this piece remains either a guitar solo or (perhaps) an improvisation using everyday objects. It is not suggested that either of these interpretations is of less value than the other but it is proposed that the conflict between them leads to an added layer of significance. Only by considering the differing sources of information available to the listener does it become clear that both interpretations may be motivated simultaneously through dual extrinsic contexts (guitars or the everyday sounds of colliding, scraping and rattling 'objects') thus providing an interpretative tension between our familiarity with guitars and the information for events provided by the sound of the piece. Moreover, it is proposed that interpretative action is itself afforded by the conflicting structures available to the listener. Conflict between sources of information, just like insufficient information, affords interpretation whether through a perceptual search for additional information (which may never be definitive) or through the production of interpretative statements which purport to explain the piece. To give one such 'interpretative statement', this piece seems to provide information which both challenges perceptions of what a guitar itself might afford and what might be afforded by a virtuoso instrumental technique. The important point to note here is that such a statement only makes sense in relation not only to what is heard but also to what is available from the context in which it is heard.

One should also note that any clear distinction between culture and nature here is naïve. Frith's playing is 'naturally' lawful in that it is the result of actions which conform to the possibilities provided by the relationship between his body, an instrument and the information provided by his perceptual systems, but equally the results of these actions are cultural in that they challenge the more contingent laws a listener relies upon in making sense of these actions. That these cultural constraints are just as dependent upon the perception of other players' relationships with their resources and are hence far from arbitrary emphasises not the differences between cultural and natural environmental structures but their common source: the activity of human beings in relation to their environment. Viewed from another perspective, one might equally state that Frith's own playing results from his own actions within the context provided by his 'cultural' knowledge of guitar playing: likewise, this cultural knowledge is derived from familiarity with the environment and is far from arbitrary. Neither natural nor cultural lawfulness can be examined independently from the organism that perceives and acts.

The acousmatic curtain revised

I have attempted to show in this chapter that the acousmatic curtain does not merely serve to obscure the sources of sounds. Indeed, it can be seen to intensify our search for intelligible sources, for likely causal events. That it makes this search a personal one, to do with interpretation rather than any one-to-one semiotic mapping is no surprise given the active nature of perception. What I would like to stress is that although it provides a means to re-open potentially closed meanings, the acousmatic does not do away with the constraints upon perception provided by our interactions with the environment.

One way of summing up this concept is through notions of lying and error. The acousmatic provides opportunities for a breakdown in channels of communication between composer and listener: the composer may attempt to lie and the listener may hear something other than the actual cause of a sound. Once these two processes become entwined the result becomes rather unpredictable, but not wholly unpredictable. The notion of real and virtual causation is helpful here since truth is really not the issue: sometimes we hear real sources and sometimes virtual sources. The point is that neither composers nor listeners are fully in control of what will be perceived. The acousmatic, therefore, creates a highly contingent listening context in which both composers and listeners are simultaneously forced into attending to auditory structures and prevented from using their other senses to corroborate the information they gain.

The ecological approach to perception made use of here has many limitations, especially the difficulties it presents for understanding how more culturally convened, semiotic processes operate (see Windsor, 1995). However, through the idea of affordances and the importance it places upon the perception of events and objects, ecological perception provides a useful basis for explaining how sonic meaning is both constrained by our intimate knowledge of the real world and yet extremely flexible. When sounds are presented acousmatically, we are both drawn to and freed from literal perception and where such tension is exploited by the musician, an aesthetic begins to emerge which plays with our relationship with the 'real' world. Such exploitation need not be conscious, potentially playing a role wherever the loudspeaker usurps the acoustic sound source; but where it is witting it seems best to remember that whether one's intentions are narrative or not, the acousmatic can be *heard through*, even if it is visually opaque. Whether a real or virtual 'stage' is heard will depend on the context but we cannot expect the listener to ditch millions of years of perceptual development in the face of a tantalising curtain between sound source and perceiver.

References

Cadoz, Claude, Florens, Jean-Loup and Luciani, Annie (1984), 'Responsive input devices and sound synthesis by simulation of instrumental mechanisms: the CORDIS system', *Computer Music Journal*, 8(3), pp. 60–73.

Cadoz, Claude, Lisowski, Leszek and Florens, Jean-Loup (1990), 'A modular feedback keyboard design', *Computer Music Journal*, 14(2), pp. 47–51.

Costall, Alan and Still, Arthur (1991), 'Cognitivism as an approach to cognition', in Costall, Alan and Still, Arthur (eds), *Against Cognitivism: Alternative Foundations for Cognitive Psychology*, pp. 1–5, London: Harvester Wheatsheaf.

Freed, Daniel J. (1990), 'Auditory correlates of perceived mallet hardness for a set of recorded percussive sound events', *Journal of the Acoustical Society of America*, 87, pp. 311–22.

Gaver, William W. (1993a), 'What in the world do we hear? An ecological approach to auditory event perception', *Ecological Psychology*, 5(1), pp. 1–29.

Gaver, William W. (1993b), 'How do we hear in the world – explorations in ecological acoustics', *Ecological Psychology*, 5(4), pp. 285–313.

Gibson, James J. (1966), *The Senses Considered as Perceptual Systems*, London: Unwin Bros.

Gibson, James J. (1979), *The Ecological Approach to Visual Perception*, New Jersey: Lawrence Erlbaum.

Heine, Wolf-D. and Guski, Rainer (1991), 'Listening: the perception of auditory events?' an essay review of *Listening: An Introduction to the Perception of Auditory Events* by Stephen Handel, *Ecological Psychology*, 3(3), pp. 263–75.

Howard, James H. and Ballas, James A. (1980), 'Syntactic and semantic factors in the classification of nonspeech transient patterns', *Perception and Psychophysics*, 28, pp. 431–9.

Howard, James H. and Ballas, James A. (1982), 'Acquisition of acoustic pattern categories by exemplar observation', *Organisational Behaviour and Human Performance*, 30, pp. 157–73.

Howard, James H. and Ballas, James A. (1983), 'Perception of simulated propeller cavitation', *Human Factors*, 25(6), pp. 643–55.

Jenkins, James J. (1984), 'Acoustic information for places, objects and events', in Warren, William H. and Shaw, Robert E. (eds), *Persistence and Change: Proceedings of the First International Conference on Event Perception*, pp. 115–38, New Jersey: Lawrence Erlbaum.

Kendall, Gary S. (1991), 'Visualisation by ear. Auditory imagery for scientific visualisation and virtual reality', *Computer Music Journal*, 15(4), pp. 70–73.

Kistler, Dorothy J. and Wightman, Frederic L. (1992), 'A model of head-related transfer functions based on principal components analysis and minimum-phase reconstruction', *Journal of the Acoustical Society of America*, 91(3), pp. 1637–47.

Ligeti, György and Wehinger, Rainer (1970), *Artikulation. An Aural Score by Rainer Wehinger*, Mainz: Schott.

Mark, Leonard S., Todd, James T. and Shaw, Robert E. (1981), 'Perception of growth: A geometric analysis of how different styles of change are distinguished', *Journal of Experimental Psychology: Human Perception and Performance*, 7(4), pp. 855–68.

Nattiez, Jean-Jacques (tr. Abbate, Carolyn) (1990), *Music and Discourse. Toward a Semiology of Music*, Princeton: Princeton University Press.

Noble, William G. (1981), 'Gibsonian theory and the pragmatist perspective', *Journal of the Theory of Social Behaviour*, 11(1), pp. 65–85.

Reed, Edward (1991), 'James Gibson's ecological approach to cognition', in Costall, Alan and Still, Arthur (eds), *Against Cognitivism: Alternative Foundations for Cognitive Psychology*, pp. 171–97, London: Harvester Wheatsheaf.

Repp, Bruno H. (1987), 'The sound of two hands clapping', *Journal of the Acoustical Society of America*, 81, pp. 1100–1109.

Schaeffer, Pierre (1966), *Traité des objets musicaux*, Paris: Editions du Seuil.

Shaw, Robert E., McIntyre, Michael and Mace, William (1974), 'The role of symmetry in event perception', in Macleod, Robert B. and Pick, Herbert L. (eds), *Perception: Essays in Honour of James Gibson*, pp. 276–310, Ithaca: Cornell University Press.

Smalley, Denis (1986), 'Spectro-morphology and structuring processes', in Emmerson, Simon (ed.), *The Language of Electroacoustic Music*, pp. 61–93, London: Macmillan.

Smalley, Denis (1994), 'Defining timbre – refining timbre' in Emmerson, Simon (ed.), *Timbre Composition in Electroacoustic Music, Contemporary Music Review*, 10(2), pp. 35–48.

Solomon, Lawrence N. (1958), 'Semantic approach to the perception of complex sounds', *Journal of the Acoustical Society of America*, 30(3), pp. 421–5.

Solomon, Lawrence N. (1959a), 'Search for physical correlates to psychological dimensions of sounds', *Journal of the Acoustical Society of America*, 31(4), pp. 492–7.

Solomon, Lawrence N. (1959b), 'Semantic reactions to systematically varied sounds', *Journal of the Acoustical Society of America*, 31(7), pp. 986–90.

Spelke, Elizabeth S. (1976), 'Infants' intermodal perception of events', *Cognitive Psychology*, 8, pp. 553–60.

Spelke, Elizabeth S. (1979), 'Perceiving bimodally specified events in infancy', *Developmental Psychology*, 15(6), pp. 626–36.

Vanderveer, Nancy J. (1979), *Ecological Acoustics. Human Perception of Environmental Sounds*, Doctoral Thesis, Dissertation Abstracts International, 40/09B, 4543 (University Microfilms No. 8004002).

Warren, William H. and Shaw, Robert E. (1985), 'Events and encounters as units of analysis for ecological psychogy', in Warren, William H. and Shaw, Robert E. (eds), *Persistence and Change: Proceedings of the First International Conference On Event Perception*, pp. 1–27, New Jersey: Lawrence Erlbaum.

Warren, William H. and Verbrugge, Robert R. (1984), 'Auditory perception of breaking and bouncing events: A case study in ecological acoustics', *Journal of Experimental Psychology: Human Perception and Performance*, 10(5), pp. 704–12.

Warren, William H., Kim, Elizabeth E. and Husney, Robin (1987), 'The way the ball bounces: visual and auditory perception of elasticity and the bounce pass', *Perception*, 16, pp. 309–36.

Windsor, W. Luke (1995), *A Perceptual Approach to the Description and Analysis of Acousmatic Music*, Doctoral Thesis, City University, London.

Windsor, W. Luke (1996a), 'Perception and signification in electroacoustic music', in Monelle, Raymond and Gray, Catherine T. (eds), *Song and Signification*, pp. 64–74, Edinburgh: Edinburgh University Faculty of Music.

Windsor, W. Luke (1996b), 'Autonomy, mimesis and mechanical reproduction in contemporary music' in Norman, Katharine (ed.), *A Poetry* of *Reality: Composing with Recorded Sound, Contemporary Music Review*, 15(1–2), pp. 139–50.

Recordings

Barron, Louis and Bebe (1978), *Forbidden Planet*, GNP Crescendo: GN100.
Bayle, François (1992), *Grande Polyphonie*, Magison: MGCB 0392.
Frith, Fred (1993), *Guitar Solos*, RecRec Music: RecDec 904.
Henry, Pierre (1987), *Variations pour une porte et un soupir*, Harmonia Mundi: HMC 905200.
Ligeti, György (1988), *Artikulation*, Wergo: WER 60161–50.
Stockhausen, Karlheinz (1991), *Gesang der Jünglinge*, Stockhausen Verlag: CD 3.
Stockhausen, Karlheinz (1992), *Kontakte*, Wergo: WER 6009–2.
Wishart, Trevor (1992), *Red Bird*, October Music: Oct 001.

Acknowledgements

The research which forms the basis of this article was carried out whilst a doctoral candidate at City University, London, supported by a studentship from the British Academy and is elaborated upon in my doctoral thesis. Many thanks to my friend and former supervisor Eric Clarke, and to Alan Costall and Simon Emmerson for their encouragement and discussions during the course of my research.

CHAPTER TWO

Simulation and reality: the new sonic objects

Ambrose Field

Introduction

Pierre Schaeffer left a legacy of *sonic objects* and *reduced listening* strategies to help composers and theorists bring order and creativity to sounds. However, electroacoustic aesthetics have so often redefined Schaeffer's terminology to fit prevailing compositional trends that it is now easy to forget that sonic objects were considered simply to be sounds that could be used *objectively* within a composition.

It is now evident that we need to develop a discourse which can encompass the compositional use of real world sounds that includes the possibility for extra musical signification in addition to timbral manipulation. It is the purpose of this chapter to set-out methods and compositional devices that might be used by composers who manipulate recorded sounds. The discussion focuses on the role of recorded representations of 'reality' within compositional practice, and includes an examination of how extra musical information can be packaged in the form of sonic rhetoric. The chapter closes with a brief assessment of transcontextuality – when applied to electroacoustic music transcontextual working is a method by which the extrinsic meanings of a sound can have a profound impact on their musical surroundings.

Schaeffer's original definitions of what constituted 'objective' were indeed quite strict: a sound would qualify as a *sonic object* if it could be divorced from any extramusical associations it might have. *Reduced listening* was the means by which this could be accomplished, and involved a tacit agreement between composer and listener that the extramusical implications of what a sound is, or what it might represent in reality were to be bracketed out. These implications were not to be the primary focus of the music. It is also easy to forget that Schaeffer himself identified that sound sources can also have *subjective* elements, and that listeners could employ *several* listening strategies, of which reduced listening was only one (Schaeffer, 1966, pp. 114–17).

The developing electroacoustic aesthetic, fostered by early compositional experiments at what was later to become the *Groupe de Recherches Musicales* (GRM), largely adopted the *objective* view proposed by Schaeffer. This is perhaps no accident as the objectivity displayed in the music of Pierre Henry and Schaeffer was mirrored in their contemporary social environment. Outside the GRM's doors in Paris, radical new building programmes were instituted by a succession of political leaders determined to make a lasting impression on the city. These developments were not merely a tool for civic beautification, but a means of endowing post-war social change with a quantifiable and lasting objectivity.

For composers seeking to 'prove' their new art of electroacoustic composition, the legitimacy afforded by connecting their novel approaches to structures and reference points that were not too dissimilar to those of western classical music, was perhaps too hard to avoid. Thus by compartmentalising real world sound into objects and suggesting that listeners might focus their attention solely on the timbral activity within a sound, Schaeffer had effectively invented the electroacoustic equivalent of the note. Rational composition, he thought, could take place once the perceptual qualities of the sonic raw materials had been carefully classified.

Today, many electroacoustic composers use sounds recorded from the real world as the raw materials for their pieces exploiting some of the undefined and ambiguous characteristics that these sounds often exhibit. Electroacoustic music is uniquely powerful in this respect – reality can be directly alluded to, represented or subverted by the composer. The representation of reality is now a compositional parameter that can be found at the heart of many contemporary electroacoustic approaches, be they *acousmatic, soundscape/ecological,* or even *musique concrète.* There is no longer any need for composers or listeners to ignore the extramusical connotations of electroacoustic sounds.

This chapter analyses ways in which these ideas can co-exist within a composition medium extensively concerned with timbral manipulation. The compositional possibilities afforded by *hyper-real environments* (where it is not possible for the listener to tell the difference between a recording of reality and a simulation of reality) and those that are *virtual* (environments that appear overtly simulated in some way) are investigated here. A rhetorical communication system of *soundscape codes* is suggested to assist composers in defining the listener's extramusical responses to their music. These codes can be embedded into both hyper-real and virtual environments, and are a means of applying structural organisation to sounds that have real world connotations without directly proscribing extramusical meanings or interpretations.

Identifying the real

Current theory suggests that it is the *source-cause*[1] of a sound that is of primary importance in determining how 'real' that sound is. Roughly summarised, this source-cause theory suggests that real world sounds often carry survival connotations for the human race. For example, the sound of animals approaching could mean either the potential for food or extreme danger. Source-cause theory assumes that we seek to relate a sound that we hear to the physical cause that brings that sound into being. As that physical cause is deeply rooted in reality, it would be easy to presume that this source-cause connection is employed by listeners to assess the 'reality' of a sound.

Smalley (1992a, p. 535) proposes the concept of *agency* to differentiate between sources that require a physical initiation to come into being and those that do not. It is tempting to use this distinction to delineate sounds that are produced in real environments (such as a recording of natural sounds) from those that are the product of simulation. But it is important to retain a sense of perspective when applying these distinctions to sounds that are unfamiliar: if we cannot detect an agency aurally, it does not necessarily follow that a sound is simulated.

Bernard Parmegiani's *De Natura Sonorum* (Parmegiani, 1990) uses this process of agency detection as part of the formal identity of the work. In his music, Parmegiani appears to have acknowledged the perceptual problem of listeners trying to identify the physical agency responsible for producing the sounds. He has accomplished this by making particularly abstract sonic juxtapositions. In the first movement, the 'natural' sound morphologies of real world sounds are set alongside their highly processed counterparts. These processed timbres are particularly 'electronic' sounding, and as such cannot be mistaken for sounds that have been recorded in the real world. In this case, the listener does not need to seek to identify the agency that was responsible for creating such sounds, as they know them to be a simulation.

When considering the modern outdoor soundscape, it is pertinent to ask ourselves if we still employ a perceptual mechanism dating from a distant historical point in human evolution to each new sound that we perceive? As Schafer (1977) has demonstrated, the soundscape of our society is growing in timbral diversity. However, within this soundscape the social meaning and relevance of ambient environmental sound is becoming reduced.

As Schafer describes, contemporary society has adopted standard signals for particular messages: for example, a siren sound signals danger. As interpreters of these codes, we no longer need to evaluate the specific cause of the sounds – we simply need to take action. This type of communication shares much with Barthes's definitions of mythology (Barthes, 1973, pp. 109–59), as the raw elements for communication have been worked upon to enable efficient and direct communication. Barthes argues that society has learned to trust information that others have provided without questioning its origins. This is a major social change: 'survival' strategies are less socially important now. If this linkage is followed through to a logical conclusion, perhaps the acceptance (and creation) of timbral music by the listening public has been accelerated due to the decreasing social requirements to carry out source-cause analysis in our everyday sonic world. Sophisticated timbral manipulation is no longer the single preserve of the electroacoustic composer. Today, interesting new timbres can also be found in Hollywood films and contemporary popular music and the listening public is becoming correspondingly accustomed to listening to timbre without first wondering what the source or cause of the sound actually was.

Increasing industrial noise in the soundscape has resulted in this situation of causal insignificance being amplified. For example, the noise from industrial machines is similar the world over, and we do not have to undertake too much aural enquiry to decode the physical nature of the sound. With so many similar sounds in the soundscape, it is possible that their source-causes are even becoming less relevant socially. The advancement of cheaper and more sophisticated technology, coupled with a public that is becoming increasingly media-aware, has resulted in a situation where 'new sounds' are no longer a domain solely exploited by the electroacoustic composer. In such a world the assumption that it matters what the source of a sound actually is, is possibly becoming irrelevant.

So, what does identify a sound source as belonging to reality? The work of Gibson (1966) and Windsor (1994) suggests that the surrounding sonic environment leaves a 'trace' of itself imprinted on the source. It is this trace that provides composers with powerful new compositional methods: by changing the context in which sounds exist new realities, virtual worlds and hyper-real spaces can all be produced. Thus it is now possible to reflect on, subvert, or give comment on our everyday surroundings in electroacoustic music. Ironically, it was this contextual information that Schaeffer's *reduced listening* sought to eliminate.

Models of information exchange

Schaeffer's reduced listening had one major problem: it relied on a mode of exchange that was essentially one way. Here, the audience would receive the work by direct transfer from the composer, in a way analogous to simply receiving a message over a telephone line. Extramusical associations or interpretations attached to the work by the listener have no place in reduced listening, as they are meanings that are implied by the message.

Nattiez (1990, pp. 16–19) shows that this is a rather simplistic view of musical communication. Instead, he proposes that listeners actively decode the 'message', and that the message does not simply flow from composer to listener. Using the telephone analogy, both users of the phone must negotiate so that they can share meaning in a conversation, and even then, they may possess very different individual interpretations of the message. So it is with music – the composer and listener must find a common ground for communication. That common ground can be difficult to identify in electroacoustic works, due to the wide range of sounds that electroacoustic composers can employ.

Katharine Norman's *London* (Norman, 1996) solves this problem inventively. In the opening moments, it is difficult to tell where the work is set. We hear the sounds of birds tweeting, children playing and road ambience. At this point, we could be in any city. However, as the piece progresses Norman moves us from the general to the highly specific, by means of smooth transformations between sounds that match spectrally as well as contextually. By introducing vocal fragments that are easily identifiable (such as the Cockney accents recorded from the East-End markets of London), the more general scenes such as the city ambience found earlier in the piece take on highly location-specific characteristics in retrospect. The work almost invites the listener to return to it many times.

Thus, decoding contemporary electroacoustic music is not a single reductive process as Schaeffer set out, as audiences listen to timbre and extramusical references at the same time. Because of this fact, it is probably no longer appropriate to talk of sounds as being 'sonic objects' as the objective component may not even be relevant if the sound was intended to be used for contextual or extramusical reasons. Objects, in the other sense of the word, are bounded by a frame. Sounds may elicit references to other sounds or contexts within a piece, and as such cannot be constrained within a box. Jonty Harrison illustrates this whilst writing about his work *Unsound Objects* (Harrison, 1996):

One of the main criteria in Schaeffer's definition of the 'sound object' was that through the process of 'reduced listening', one should hear sound material purely as sound, divorced from any associations with its physical origins. Despite this idea, a rich repertoire of music has been created sine the 1950s which plays precisely on the ambiguities evoked when recognition and contextualisation of sound material rub shoulders with more abstracted (and abstract) musical structures. But as these structures should themselves be organically related to the peculiarities of individual sound objects within them, the ambiguity is compounded: interconnections and multiple levels of meaning proliferate (Harrison, in Leopoldseder and Schöpf, 1997, p. 206).

Semiotics

Semiotics is a useful discipline for those concerned with electroacoustic art. Semiotics is concerned with the study of sign systems, and breaks down meanings and cultural constructs into simple elements. For the composers of and listeners to electroacoustic music, semiotics provides a clear way to conceptually separate extramusical meanings from spectromorphological (musical) structures. Unlike Schaeffer's reduced listening strategies, semiotics allows this separation of timbre and 'meaning' to be done in such a way that allows both of these aspects to coexist.

Philosophers and semioticians are constantly attempting to improve on the definition of a sign system, but the idea of how a sign is constructed is particularly useful for composers. In Saussurian semiotics, a sign has two parts, a *signifier* and a *signified* (see Nattiez, 1990, pp. 16–45 for a more extensive overview). The signifier is the object itself, and the signified concerns a possible meaning derived from that object. So in electroacoustic art, a signifier might be a recorded sound sample of a rainstorm. The signified would be the meanings generated by this sound: for example, the idea of rain, wetness, rain drops are all possible signifieds. Works which exhibit narrative qualities such as those in the radiophonic genre are mostly concerned with the signifieds of the sounds that they use.

With semiotic methods it is possible to construct ways of analysing and composing electroacoustic music that concurrently account for extramusical interpretation and musical function. Because the signifier and signified are separate entities, it is possible to think of them compositionally as working on different levels of the musical structure. For example, the underlying timbral progress of a work may use the signifier of a sound, whilst the surface structure could be concerned with communicating the signified meanings denoted by that sound.

Electroacoustic composers have the opportunity to use sounds directly from culture. Nattiez (1990, pp. 20–21) shows us that semiotics is a useful analytical tool as it demonstrates how the act of communication takes place, and how common codes and systems shape the way we decode our world. When composing with cultural material, it is necessary to understand how that material communicates, both sonically and culturally.

Aspects of reality

Contemporary society exhibits a growing trend towards the personalisation of media space.[2] Baudrillard (1981) identifies the emergence of new fly-on-the-wall television documentary styles and a demand for increasingly interactive media services. Electroacoustic tape music can miss out on this new form of media interaction. Yet electroacoustic music can make use of materials that are extremely personal in nature, ranging from recordings of children to the use of sounding materials taken from our surrounding environment. Why is it then, that such electroacoustic pieces can fail to gain an interaction with the audience on a personal level? One major factor lies in an awkward paradox: in order for others to recognise the cause of sonic materials, the composer must choose sounds that have easily comprehensible extramusical associations. But such sounds often lack the specific contextual details that are required to associate them to particular extramusical events. For example, sounds of passing cars, birdsong and environmental ambience are so common that it is difficult to assign them to particular times or places. Works featuring the noises of cities are particularly problematic. The sound of traffic, train doors closing or crowd scenes retain little location specificity. Pieces that use environmental materials that attempt to allude to a specific time or place often resort to using a few 'keynote' sounds (Schafer, 1977, p. 272) to link diverse ambiences and contexts together. Without resorting to a radiophonic style of presentation and perhaps utilising a narrative voice-over, it is difficult to introduce audience interactivity on such a direct level.

It is possible though, that the electroacoustic medium itself may be used to introduce a level of interactivity, as practised listeners will have expectations concerning the types of sounds that they are likely to hear within an electroacoustic work. As these sounds are enabled by technology, it is inevitable that the results will sound technological in some way. Electroacoustic composers search frequently for ways to subvert this situation, often by aiming to integrate a wide palette of processed, real, and synthetic sounds in their work. Processed, transformed and synthesised sounds are all in keeping with the technology used to present them to an audience. It is easy to reconcile synthetic timbres with their presentation over loudspeakers. However, a glaring gap between the sound sources and their technical presentation exists where composers have chosen to represent real-life sounds and sources. The contexts and extramusical connotations of these sounds would not have been manipulated by technology in the real world, unless the audience received them first via the media. Listeners to an electroacoustic concert where the sounds were taken from everyday life may be particularly prone to accept the presentation of recorded environments as reality itself. To integrate processed and transformed sound within such an environment is awkward, as it creates a risk that the audience will be reminded of the technological nature of the medium. This might lessen the impact of any extramusical threads presented.

The electroacoustic genre is well suited to the creation of simulated sounding-environments. Using contemporary computer technology it is possible to isolate individual sounds from complex recordings. Furthermore, it is easy to create what Wishart (1986, p. 48) terms 'surreal' environments, with sounds that have been abstracted from a variety of different contexts and spaces. Surrealism can only work if the subject matter is abstracted from real-world events. However, these events only take on a heightened significance if their real world contexts are lost. For example, in Dali's famous work *The Persistence of Memory*, objects (such as the watches) have been abstracted from reality. They are distorted and mixed with other objects that you would not normally find in close proximity to a watch. Dali's scene contains real objects (watches, trees, tables, landscapes), but is clearly not a real space.

Alternatively, a hyper-real environment exists where it is not possible for the audience to tell the difference between simulation and recorded reality itself. If such environments can be set up then many new powerful developmental techniques can be utilised to transform contexts, as well as the sounds themselves. In order to see how this might be the case, it is necessary to start by determining the differences between simulation of a real event and reality itself. This is illustrated concisely by Jean Baudrillard (1981, pp. 19–22): he invites the reader to organise a fake bank robbery as realistically as possible. Baudrillard notes that there is no existing punishment for fake hold-ups. They will be either punished as a real event or as an offence, such as wasting police time, but *never* as a simulation. From this he concludes that reality has a natural tendency to try and establish itself where possible. It is due to this fact that we are not constantly wondering if what we are perceiving is real.

Following Baudrillard's thesis, we can see that the characteristics of a good simulation include the following:

- A simulated reality must offer all the gestures and signs of the real.
- A good simulation will have the same semiotic consequences as the real.
- It is impossible to 'prove' reality.
- The longer we perceive an acoustic environment (sound landscape), the more likely it is to be accepted as real.

This last requirement provides an interesting limitation on the types of long-term structure that can be used to create realistic sonic landscapes. If a landscape takes time to establish then the structure of a work needs to be carefully considered so that the surrounding materials do not appear out of context. Conversely, composers who wish to set up the illusion of an imaginary landscape are faced with a 'reality problem'. How can they convince their audience that what they are listening to is actually a sonic landscape rather than an arbitrary collection of sounds? This is a particularly difficult task when both the sounds and the spaces that they inhabit are taken from recordings of the real world.

Wishart (1996, p. 146) shows us how abstraction can commonly occur when real world objects and spaces are combined. He suggests that the act of combining real world sounds with real spaces is closely related to surrealist art techniques. However, it is important to ask *why* abstraction occurs, as logic dictates that the result of this combination of real sounds and real spaces should be realistic in some way. The answer lies not in the sounds but in their associated contextual information. A sonic landscape can be said to exhibit 'low reality credibility' when the contextual information carried by the sounds within it is not consistent. For example, a composer could build a sonic landscape containing car sounds, sounds of people walking and sounds recorded from within a swimming pool. The landscape will probably fail to be perceived as being 'real' by the audience: the sounds of the swimming pool do not share the same extrinsic context (of a city street scene) with the car and people sounds. For maximum credibility, the contextual information exposed by all sounds within a particular sonic landscape must match. If the sounds within a simulated environment possess similar spectral types the perception of reality will be strengthened.

In such a situation, it is clear to see that if a sound possesses an unexpected timbre, even though its gestural and contextual information are consistent with spatial information, the whole soundscape might no longer be trusted to be an authentic representation of reality. This requirement can be illustrated by the following hypothetical situation. Imagine a recording of an urban traffic soundscape. With careful editing and spectral extraction, the sound of one car is removed, filtered with a simple all-pass filter and recombined with the original recording at the same time position from which it was extracted. Here, the car's spectral characteristics do not match those of others which contain similar gestural and extrinsic information and therefore lend the scene a reduced credibility. The idea of reality credibility assumes that spatial and extrinsic environmental characteristics can be perceived at the same time as the original spectral nature of the sound. This distinction avoids the concept of listeners having first to channel sounds through a perceptually restrictive reduced listening process. The spatial characteristics of the environment are an important part of reality credibility. A simple demonstration of this theory is to select any recording of an outside space and run it through a reverberation process. It will still be possible to recognise and correctly decode the sounds yet the environment itself is far from realistic.

A sonic-landscape can be identified in terms of its *landscape morphology*. There are four main categories of landscape morphology:[3]

- hyper-real
- real
- virtual
- non-real

This view of landscape morphology is potentially more useful than a sound/spaces approach as it defines the landscape in terms of the aural product of the sounds contained within it rather than being a description of the constituent parts. Abstract, imaginary landscapes will not be covered in any great detail here.[4] Real landscapes exist in recorded art as a pure re-presentation of reality (that is, no destructive sound processing has been applied.) Hyper-real, virtual and non-real landscapes can be defined as follows.

Hyper-real

Most commonly, the term *hyper-reality* refers to a situation where events appear to be 'more real than real'. Although these events are undoubtedly produced by the processes of simulation, the result has all the gestures and signs of reality. Baudrillard (1981, p. 12) cites Disneyland as the ultimate hyper-reality, as this is a place where entire towns are re-created with a saccharin cordiality.

Luc Ferrari's *Presque rien* (Ferrari, 1995) series demonstrates hyper-reality in audio-art. *Presque rien no. 1* compresses the timescale on which real events happen. Although the work is clearly the product of extensive editing processes, the end result is the aural impression of a heightened reality, where time, it seems, has no consequence.

Real

A real environment is one that has not been simulated in any way. For the purposes of this chapter, the representation of reality as recordings that have not been interfered with is also considered to be 'real'. This definition simply enables a distinction to be made between simulated virtual or hyper-real environments where the composer has changed a representation of reality and those that have not been manipulated.

Virtual

Virtual reality is pure simulation, and is ultimately intended to be perceived as such. The environments created by Wishart in *Red Bird* (Wishart, 1992) provide good examples. In this piece, humans transform into machines within large empty ambiences, animals run for shelter in windswept landscapes and the audience is invited to 'listen to reason' amidst burbling water textures. These landscapes have little to do with reality – except that they are purely surrealistic brought about by the abstraction of real events and spaces. Although the spaces that Wishart creates are highly plausible, tiny details in the sounds suggest that we might not be listening to a recording of reality. The wind sounds in the first section of the work, for example, have been processed so extensively as not to be recognisable as a simple recording. It is only the gestural contours of these sounds that retain the undulating morphologies of wind blowing.

Virtual environments can account for what is colloquially termed 'ambiguity' in electroacoustic music. Such environments are not themselves ambiguous, as they have been carefully constructed to provide the features and cues of reality, without representing reality itself. Although this may clearly leave an ambiguity in the mind of the listener, the compositional construction of these events requires careful planning.

Non-real minimal techno?

These are environments that are not surreal, nor are they identifiable as real in any way. For example, a non-real environment could consist of highly processed textural sounds that are remote surrogates of their original recordings.

Denis Smalley's *Wind Chimes* (Smalley, 1992b) includes some highly non-real environments. After the exposition of recordings and treatments based on the sporadic activation of wind chimes, the piece moves into a section where long drawn-out resonances expand to fill the spectral space. Here, there is a very definite sense of landscape, with the exception that the sounds contained within it have no discernible connection with the real world. The listener is thus directed to concentrate on the timbral evolution of the work, rather than focus on the real world sounding behaviour of the chimes.

Thus a non-real environment may possess a definite sense of space and scale, but does not contain any real world gestures or naturally occurring sounds.

The rhetoric of reality

When sounds possess contextual information, there is the possibility for that information to be used as a compositional parameter itself. 'Sonic rhetoric' is a means by which links can be made between musical processes and extrinsic contextual information. Semiotics show us that communication can result from exchange using common codes. Defined below are some basic archetypes for sonic communication. These may permit highly anecdotal materials to be used within a work without the need for an underlying narrative structure.

A 'sonic metaphor' exists where sounds with clear extramusical contexts suggest musical functions or processes. Generating a sonic metaphor is a multi-stage process. Because of the contextual and compositional manipulation that must occur before the metaphorical sound can be integrated into a simulated environment, the chance of a listener perceiving that sound as an intrusion needs to be minimised. The timescale on which a sonic metaphor operates is important, with a requirement for events within the immediate temporal context of the metaphor to possess consistent contextual information.

François Bayle's *Erosphère* (Bayle, 1990) contains many good sonic metaphors. One such instance is the sound of closing doors (Transit 1: 0'02"), followed by the sounds of a lift descending. Here, it is unlikely that Bayle was attempting to create any vision of 'reality'. The sound of the lift may be real but the use of metaphor in this way sets up what is almost a reduced listening situation for the listener. This type of listening is one where the contextual and timbral implications of the sound are ignored. Here, it is the symbolic nature of the sound that is paramount, and due to the short timescale on which this event operates, the listener's attention is directed away from both the 'liftness' of the sound, and the timbre of the lift itself. We are required to construct a new reality in our imagination and apply it to our perception of other events in the piece. Bayle does not develop further the timbral aspects of this incident. This perhaps indicates that he included the lift sounds for contextual reasons: the lift doors close off the outside reality, and we descend into a new world of subterranean sounds. How did our perception know to interpret the sound of the lift as indicating a 'descent into the work', instead of as a timbral event? This type of question is central to much acousmatic composition, where real world sounds are interjected with abstract-timbral sounds. As sonic metaphors often result from listeners expecting a perceived link between two associated contexts, they could be employed by composers wishing to steer their audience between different methods of perceiving their piece.

Metaphors can be overused easily, and when they are euphemism is frequently the result. In the English language the problem with euphemisms is that there are a small number of them, compared to other expressive phrases. In electroacoustic music, the overuse of metaphor can have the same effect. For example, we frequently observe footstep sounds as a metaphor for travelling or doors opening and closing as a metaphor for entering and leaving sections of a piece. Overuse can occur because of the unfortunate coincidence that recordings made in an outdoor environment have a high probability of containing these metaphorical sounds.

A 'sonic simile' gives a new meaning to an existing sound by juxtaposing it with new material. For example in Trevor Wishart's Vox V (Wishart, 1990) vocal sounds appear within a landscape populated by wild birds, gurgling water, horses and other natural phenomena. Yet the vocal sounds are never explicitly those of language. The simile created here gives the highly abstract vocal material a placement within a 'natural' and somewhat primordially powerful landscape. As this example demonstrates simile is a powerful compositional process that can be used to add a recognisable context to abstract material. However, it is important to recognise that simile is a process that can be applied in a linear manner and not simply as a vertical superimposition of original contexts. For a sonic simile to work, the audience must be invited to make a comparison between two contexts. This is usually effected by transforming one environment into another, typically by means of an interpolative transformation where the first is progressively replaced by the second. The most direct example of a simile used as pure rhetoric can be found within the same work in the now classic voice-bees-voice transformation (Wishart, 1990 at 2'14"). Clearly, 'ambiguity' is an important component of a linear simile. Without it, this type of transformation would not be possible.

Frequently it is necessary to overstate the case to get a message across. In electroacoustic art, hyperbole can play an important role. A 'sonic hyperbole' is a sound that possesses deliberately overstated extramusical connotations. For example, in Christian Calon's *La disparition* (Calon, 1991) the jungle scene contains not only the sound of insects and tropical birds, but a Tarzan-like vocal sample that appears to swing through some imaginary trees. For anyone exposed to Walt Disney in childhood, stereotypical jungles will probably include some kind of swinging Tarzan-like figure.

This audio hyperbole is effective in two different ways. First, as far as any listener is concerned this is a tropical jungle. This allusion is just as well, as the sounds of the surrounding wildlife are not particularly convincing in themselves. The second function of this pseudo-human utterance is to indicate that this landscape may be compositionally interfered with. Such exaggeration of a monkey's call into this Tarzan-like utterance is clearly not meant to be taken as being a 'real' event.

In sonic terms, 'personification' is where a sound has highly personal and human extramusical connotations. 'Sonic personification' can be a powerful tool for composers wishing to utilise environmental sounds as it can be used to create a point of contact with the audience. A new generation of works is emerging which employs this principle. For example, Andrew Lewis's *Scherzo* (Lewis, 1993) features sounds gathered from his children. These are subject to many radical sound treatments where the original materials are transformed into remote surrogates. However, these transformations dissolve into the sound of a child's voice playfully crying 'daddy'. The playful interplay between materials occurring earlier in the work is summarised in a readily accessible, and overtly human form. Importantly, sonic personification operates on two distinct levels. The first is where human sounds and utterances have personal connotations to the author of the work. The second is where these personal meanings take on a more general significance for a wider audience. As we do not know the author's children, *Scherzo* evokes images of children in general.

A 'sonic synecdoche' exists where only partial aural cues are given to an extramusical context. Listeners must generate their own extramusical meanings from deliberately ambiguous sonic information. If enough aural information is presented, a listener can fill in the details. Because synecdoche provokes interactivity on the part of the decoder, the scene can become personalised instantly. The idea of sonic synecdoche resolves an interesting dichotomy in electroacoustic music. Picture an audience member having read the programme notes for a piece and possibly asking the familiar question: 'Are the composer's intentions supposed to be compatible with my decoding of the work?' This difference in opinion between composer and listener is entirely acceptable. Indeed, the strength of synecdoche as a rhetorical device rests on this distinction. The composer can actively invite the audience to tease out their own individual meanings from the work. It might not matter what these meanings are – what does matter is that the audience has been stimulated to take an interactive part in the performance of the work. This interactivity is achieved as the audience is encouraged to fill in gaps in the aural information presented to them by the composer.

Because the formal nature of rhetoric is widely understood, it can be used creatively to solve the dilemma for audience members attempting to decide at a particular point in time whether to listen to a sound's timbral qualities or decode its extrinsic meanings. In summary, rhetorical codes communicate directly and can therefore be used to direct an audience's listening and perception.

Electroacoustic composers can isolate individual sounds from a recording with a high degree of precision. When these sounds are inserted into new contexts, they can be said to be 'transcontextual'.

Transcontextuality

Transcontextuality can be used as a tool to lend old or existing contexts new meanings. It is important to understand the difference between transcontextuality and neo-classicism. Although neo-classicism involved frequent borrowing and transplantation of materials from other genres, these are more usually integrated within the overall design of the work. An example from Stravinsky shows this to be the case, for example in *Pulcinella* the surface figuration is grounded firmly in the Baroque, and although Stravinsky does indeed offer a simultaneous musical critique of that era, the work as a whole broadly conforms to the stylistic design parameters for the earlier music. Hence *Pulcinella* can be termed neo-classical. Transcontextuality however does not necessarily include a historical element: the borrowing of materials may come from any genre, and that borrowing may or may not be reflected in the formal design of the work the foreign materials are inserted into. The visual artist Claes Oldenburg has created works that change the nature of the spaces they inhabit. By magnifying the details of reality, rather than abstracting or changing them, Oldenburg forms a powerful bond between his work and the context of their surroundings. His early work *The Street* is one such creation. Here, Oldenburg used materials from the streets of New York, 'processed' them and returned them to the community. He remarks:

> I take materials from the Lower East Side and transform them and give them back ... in my art I am concerned with perception of reality and composition. Which is the only way art can really be useful (Oldenburg, 1996).

In a later creation, *Lipstick (Ascending) on Caterpillar Tracks* (in Prather, 1996), Oldenburg created a giant reproduction of a lipstick tube, mounted on a base evocative of army hardware. This statue changed the context of the space it inhabited when it was positioned on the University campus at Yale in close proximity to a World War I memorial. The statue operates in a transcontextual way, being an entity in itself, yet changing the meaning of the surroundings: in this case offering social comment. I shall refer to the object which functions in a transcontextual way as the 'transcontextual agent'.

In audio art, this type of transcontextuality can be created by introducing sounds that have clearly identifiable extramusical implications into believable real world acoustic environments. In *La disparition* (Calon, 1991), Calon creates a scene where an aeroplane appears to fly over a tropical jungle. This is initially accepted by the listener, as the probability of this event occurring in reality is quite high. However, as the piece progresses, the sound of the aeroplane continues descending in pitch until it eventually forms the bass drone to the subsequent section. Whilst this occurs, the tropical scene melts away into silence. This transformation, like Oldenburg's sculptures, involves transcontextual materials. The sound of the aeroplane is the main transcontextual agent, as it performs both the function of 'aeroplane' and the musical function of a bass drone. During this transformation from aeroplane to bass drone, this sound has changed the way we perceived the context that surrounds it. This change occurs at the point where the aeroplane sound becomes too low in pitch to be identifiable as being an aeroplane. It is at that point that the contextual identity of the surrounding jungle collapses.

Transcontextual agents then, can operate in two ways. First, they can instantly change the space within which they are placed. This can be effected by building a montage of materials which include some sounds that lend the others a new meaning. Alternatively, a transcontextual agent can reveal a new meaning for a context over time. This introduces the possibility for audio artists to perform transitions between one context and another.

I have created the term 'contextual steering transformation' to describe a type of sound transformation which aims not to transform the sounds *per se*, but to transform the contexts they inhabit. Within this process, a single sound 'steers' the transformation from one context into another.

In a typical sound 'morph' or interpolative transformation, one sound appears to fade away or blend into the second. This transformation has involved two identities: the original sound and the newly created sound. In a contextual steering transformation, one sound must 'carry' the transformation and remain constant through the duration of the transformation. In the example from Calon above, this sound is the aeroplane sound. The other components of the contextual steering transformation *are* subject to change. In the Calon example, the sounds of the jungle simply fade away. However, they could just as easily have transformed into something else.

Using transcontextual materials can be problematic. Transcontextuality assumes that the audience and the composer share similar extramusical background information and experiences. For example, if the significance of a transcontextual agent is known only to the composer, the listener may fail to recognise that a transcontextual transformation has taken place. In Oldenburg's *Lipstick Ascending*, viewers will understand the significance of the sculpture if they possess knowledge of world history. As the probability of the viewer and sculptor both possessing this knowledge is high, the transcontextual element of the sculpture is easily understandable. This visual example shows that transcontextual transformations can be accomplished successfully when the contextual sources are widely known. Conversely, transcontextuality can be difficult to effect where the contexts are personal to either the listener or composer. In these situations, the composer may have to give general clues to an apparently wider context, in which the audience can fill in their own details.

Transcontextuality ultimately demands raw materials that are widely understood. To create these, composers must often drawn on pre-existing ideas, or even ready-made original materials themselves. It is this dependence on 'off-the-shelf' contexts and sounds that has directly contributed to the recycling of culture which is perhaps one of the most observable symptoms of the postmodern condition.

This transcontextual recycling of materials may eventually create problems for the audience: as more works recycle the past, the fragile network of extramusical meanings indicated by their sounds will become tangled, self-referential and eventually meaningless.

Conclusion

Postmodern thinking has called for the re-evaluation of existing models regarding the relationship between sound sources and the spaces in which they exist. I have extended traditional notions of sonic-landscapes to include hyper-real, virtual and non-real environments and have also shown that simple rhetorical codes can be used to help an audience generate their own extrinsic meanings within a planned compositional framework.

Within the remit of Schaefferian reduced listening and sonic objects none of these methods could exist. Today, electroacoustic composers thrive on the interplay between extrinsic meaning and timbral dialogue. Transcontextual methods of working are highly prevalent, yet I hope I have demonstrated that composers should use caution when applying them so as to avoid the simple recycling of older materials. The power of transcontextual techniques lies in the formation of new meanings, and not in the borrowing process for its own sake.

Although Schaeffer's original ideas did not allow for contextual manipulation of extramusical meanings, there is no reason why they should be excluded from compositional practice. The manipulation of timbre is still an important objective in electroacoustic composition, and timbral listening does require processes similar to Schaeffer's reduced listening. Today, both timbral and soundscape methods can sit alongside each other in the same work as the medium of electroacoustic music does not discriminate against any methods. Ultimately, composers are free to choose the communication methods and structural designs appropriate to their music. It is the flexibility that electroacoustic music affords composers that makes the medium truly unique.

Notes

1. See Ten Hoopen (1994) for a full discussion.
2. *Media space* exists where a communications medium is listened to, or watched by an individual member of an audience.
3. These can include both 'live' and recorded sounds.
4. See Wishart (1996) for further information.

References

Barthes, Roland (1973), *Mythologies* (tr. Lavers, Annette), London: Granada Publishing.

Baudrillard, Jean (1981), *Simulacra and Simulation* (tr. Glaser, Sheila F.), Ann Arbor: University of Michigan Press.

Gibson, James (1966), *The Senses Considered as Perceptual Systems*, Boston: Houghton Mifflin.

Leopoldseder, Hannes and Schöpf, Christine (1997), *Cyber Arts*, Vienna and New York: Springer.

Nattiez, Jean-Jacques (tr. Abbate, Carolyn) (1990), *Music and Discourse. Toward a Semiology of Music*, Princeton: Princeton University Press.

Oldenburg, Claes (1996), *An Anthology*, London: Hayward Gallery, South Bank Centre.

Prather, Marla (1996), *Claes Oldenburg* (Exhibition guide), London: Hayward Gallery, South Bank Centre.

Schaeffer, Pierre (1966), *Traité des objets musicaux*, Paris: Editions du Seuil.

Schafer, R. Murray (1977), *The Tuning of the World*, New York: Alfred A. Knopf.

Smalley, Denis (1992a), 'The listening imagination: listening in the electroacoustic era', in Paynter, John, Howell, Tim, Orton, Richard, and Seymour, Peter (eds), *Companion to Contemporary Musical Thought (Volume 1)*, pp. 514–54, London: Routledge.

Smalley, Denis (1993), 'Defining transformations', *Interface*, 22(4), pp. 279–300.

Ten Hoopen, Christiane (1994), 'Issues in timbre and perception', *Contemporary Music Review*, 10(2), pp. 61–71.

Windsor, W. Luke (1994), 'Using auditory information for events in electroacoustic music', *Contemporary Music Review*, 10(2), pp. 85–94.

Wishart, Trevor (1986), 'Sound symbols and landscapes' in Emmerson, Simon (ed.), *The Language of Electroacoustic Music*, pp. 41–60, London: Macmillan.

Wishart, Trevor (1996), *On Sonic Art*, Amsterdam: Harwood Academic Publishers (second edition).

Recordings

Bayle, François (1990), *Erosphère*, INA/GRM: INA C3002.

Calon, Christian (1991), *Ligne de vie*, Empreintes Digitales: IMED-9001-CD.

Ferrari, Luc (1995), *Presque rien*, INA/GRM: 245172.

Harrison, Jonty (1996), *Articles indéfinis*, Empreintes Digitales: IMED 9627.

Lewis, Andrew (1993), *Scherzo*. Examples available at http://www.bangor.ac.uk/music/Staff/AL/Soundclips.html.

Norman, Katharine (1996), *London*, NMC Recordings: NMC D034.

Parmegiani, Bernard (1990), *De Natura Sonorum*, INA/GRM: INA C3001.

Smalley, Denis (1992b), *Impacts intérieurs*, Empreintes Digitales: IMED-9209-CD.

Wishart, Trevor (1990), *The Vox Cycle*, Virgin Classics: VC 791108-2.

Wishart, Trevor (1992), *Red Bird*, October Music: Oct 001.

CHAPTER THREE

Beyond the acousmatic: hybrid tendencies in electroacoustic music

Simon Waters

The contemporary cultural context: from 'acousmatics' to 'sampling'

Until recently, electroacoustic composers have been less interested in the social and cultural than the acoustic construction of their music. This concern with acousmatics and the phenomenology of sound has resulted in some wonderful, if obsessively self-referential pieces of music, but it has potentially impoverished the aesthetic development of the genre and stifled some aspects of a serious investigation of the application of electronic and digital means to music. A key hypothesis in this chapter is that a change in sensibility from what I characterise as an acousmatic culture (broadly concerned with sounds as 'material', and based – in historical practice – on analogue technology) to a sampling culture (concerned with context, and based on digital technology) has occurred, and that this is intimately bound up with a broader shift in cultural perspective, sometimes characterised as a shift from the modern to the postmodern. The culture of sampling has problematised the acousmatic approach considerably, increasing the likelihood of hybrid forms which owe their existence to the collision of different musical worlds, different disciplines, different modes of thought and understanding. This chapter identifies a range of broad cultural and attitudinal shifts which may be regarded as establishing the preconditions for 'hybrid thought'. It also attempts to uncover a few of these hybridising tendencies in current electroacoustic practice and draws some connections with similar developments in other signifying practices: writing, film-making, and so forth. The function of this chapter is therefore twofold: to survey a series of issues which impact upon artistic production and new signifying practices in general, and to connect these to shifts in thought and practice relating to electroacoustic music. I have been particularly concerned to illustrate that what I have characterised as a shift in sensibility from an acousmatic[1] to a sampling culture, although linked at the material level to a technical change, is intimately bound up with issues beyond the merely technical.

Many of the cultural shifts examined share the sense of a relativisation of certain things which were perhaps previously regarded as absolutes; of boundaries which have broken down – between media, between disciplines, between knowledge-systems, between styles and genres, between so-called serious and popular arts. A process of hybridisation is at work. This inevitably leads many of our concerns to be about the nature of reuse and recontextualisation: about taking something associated with one genre, one historical time-frame, one culture and putting it in another. Sampling is a particularly powerful engine for the investigation of such phenomena.

Seven issues have been chosen as illustrative of the broad cultural shift with which I am concerned. These phenomena are interrelated and their separation therefore somewhat arbitrary, but they form a useful checklist against which to consider emergent tendencies in electroacoustic music and in the arts generally:

- New technologies: new practices and associated concepts: storage; dissemination; sampling.
- Cultural pluralism: difference; exchange; hybridisation.
- Perceptions of authority: including authorship; consensus; institution and where ownership, meaning and value might lie.
- Tradition and innovation: modern and postmodern perspectives; general/social and specialist/professional conceptions of a practice and the institutional basis of tradition.
- Representation: changes in language; coding; the learned nature of interpretation; problems in relation to verbal analysis of electroacoustic music.
- Economics: funding and the political economy of electroacoustic music.
- Environment.

New technologies

New technologies bring about the most immediately visible changes in the cultures within which the arts operate. Indeed, a consideration of the impact and influence of new technologies cuts across all of the other areas of conceptual shift listed above and many issues emerging here will be elaborated further under these later headings.

The change from analogue to digital technology is resulting in a wholesale reconfiguring of our experience of music, at levels from the global to the personal, from the economic to the aesthetic. As an issue directly affecting composers using electronic technology it has been most intelligently addressed in terms of a problematics of human-machine interface by Mike Vaughan (Vaughan, 1994, pp. 119–21). The essential changes lie in the nature of the data itself which, being in digital systems non-linear, symbolic, and therefore formally arbitrary in relation to the information it represents, allows new modes of control and addressing. Such changes are exemplified in the notions of storage and 'instant recall'. As the relationship between data and information is a constructed mapping rather than a physical analogue, interfaces can be designed which are familiar from other practices or which are customised to particular requirements. As working environments across disciplines become more similar, common concerns emerge, as does a common critical language, and such disciplines may hybridise. As the technology becomes cheaper and its availability broadens it is consolidated in society in ways which potentially radically restructure activities like composing and listening.

Storage and 'instant recall'

The vast increase in data storage, and the speed with which that data can be recalled, is paradigmatic of the intimate interrelation of technical and aesthetic change. Whereas analogue storage allowed only linear access, digital storage allows virtually instantaneous addressing of data at any point. Scanning vast amounts of material in order to locate an appropriate selection therefore becomes a much more efficient and realistic proposition. However, the inexpensive nature of digital storage (compared with, for example, analogue tape) also tends to lead to the archiving of much greater amounts of material and to the putting into abeyance of much decision making. An inability to keep an adequate mental grasp of the vast amounts of potential musical material available for a given compositional decision has a crucial impact on composing practice, in the sense that what is technically possible often transmutes into what is aesthetically desirable. It is thus possible to read polystylism and musical eclecticism not only as a rejection of modernist predilections for formal coherence but as simple mechanical adaptation to the inadequacy of human memory.

Viewed from a broader perspective the issue of memory at the cultural rather than the personal level is equally problematic. The collective memory or cultural data bank can be represented (metaphorically) as a bathtub from which, historically, as much flowed out as in, but which has long since become plugged and overflowed. As a result of the increasingly efficient 'plugging effect' of new media storage (photography, film and video, all forms of sound recording, in fact any form of data retention), cultural activity has ceased to be a strictly historical phenomenon, in which artefacts and ideas are constantly being lost and forgotten, and has become instead an accumulative phenomenon in which artefacts and ideas from all historical periods and cultures exist simultaneously in the present. This releases such a confusion of meaning-generating contexts from different times and places that the common cultural experience which enabled critical assessment has all but disappeared. This lack of consensus affects compositional judgement at the public and private levels. How can one decide what is current if there is no sense of historical flow and how can one judge the intentions of others from what they produce? Is this quotation a cynical appropriation or a parody? Is its political agenda conservatism or radicalism?

Evaluation is particularly problematic for a generation of composers convinced of the benefits of investigation, integrity and personal work. It is far more difficult to distinguish between postmodern ironic juxtaposition and pure laziness or incompetence than it was to see value in the earnest searchings of modernism.

The quest for ever more reliable storage and rapid access may have led us to overlook two preconditions for creativity which are not aided by such an archival, potentially museal approach – inefficiency and forgetting. I propose these quite seriously as threatened species in the creative ecology. Information overload is not only a characteristic of a given instant, but is an ongoing process in which current activity is always potentially invaded or impinged upon by vast banks of previous data which need to be taken into consideration. Storage therefore occupies a paradoxical position for the composer. The aesthetic plurality that results from the lack of a consensual critical frame, and which itself stems from the simultaneous existence of all histories and places that recording/storage allows (the overflowing bathtub metaphor), is exciting. Suddenly there is unprecedented scope for aesthetic experiment, and this results from technology's transformation of the cultural context as much as from its instrumentality in specific goal-oriented musical tasks. But there is a sense of loss in the knowledge that filtering processes must now be consciously constructed, or the result of human inadequacy, rather than the result of real technical constraint or of the 'resistance' of the material.

Interfaces, hybridisation, vocabulary

The increasingly similar interfaces presented to us for the control of computers make the previously very different tasks of organising and transforming text, static and moving visual images and sound into experientially ever more similar processes. The new electronic technologies therefore form a seductive potential meeting point for many previously separate arts practices. Such interfaces make use of identical concepts – frame, freeze, copy, paste, loop – as controlling strategies, and this is already resulting in a commonality of language between practitioners who were previously unaware of conceptual connections between their fields of activity.

Of course the conceptual connections themselves are not new, as a browse through Paul Klee's notebooks (Spiller, 1961) or other documents associated with the Bauhaus will attest, but the extent of conscious acknowledgement of such a connection is now far greater. This interconnection reaches its zenith in the concept of hypermedia, in which complete control over and navigation through the presentation and transformation of all media is available from a single computer platform. Technological determinists are fond of arguing that such possibilities render obsolete previously functional technologies such as painting and the book. A more rational view would be that painting and books are likely to continue to occupy a lively place in our culture, but that those who choose to continue to work in such 'old technologies' will in future inevitably have to consider their work and its 'meaning' in the light of the existence of new technologies (and their associated conceptual baggage) because these are likely to become very widespread.

Technology and social practice

The paradox for composers presented by mass storage and 'instant recall' is reflected in a similarly paradoxical relation between music technologies and public use. One of the most significant ways in which storage technologies have become consolidated in society is exemplified by the Walkman; something (music) which was until relatively recently an explicitly social phenomenon, a shared process in which people participated inevitably, not just as listeners but as makers and doers, has the potential to exist primarily as a commodity. The argument follows that 'walkpeople', isolated in their personal portable acoustic space, are indicative of a practice which has become primarily non-participative, desocialised, and exists predominantly to placate its audience, rather than to excite, challenge or stimulate them. But of course the counterbalancing factor is that mass-production techniques have driven down the cost of new technologies to the point of widespread accessibility and that the sampler, as the fundamental tool of musical reuse, points the way to a resurgence of composition, rather than consumption, as a model for the future political economy of music.[2]

Institutional and economic pressures towards the first of the two models mentioned (passive consumption) are powerful, the operation of our education in music currently seeming to make it different from other fields of activity like the visual arts, or the written and spoken word. This is because, whereas we all see and therefore inevitably develop some sense of a visual language, and we all speak, read and (mostly) write to some extent and therefore also have a sense of the way words work, our musical sense is developed primarily as non-expert recipients: we participate primarily by listening. But of course listening is not merely passive consumption, and sampling may yet prove crucial in restructuring and stimulating broader public expectations of listening.

The culture of sampling is by no means restricted to the sonic arts. Parallel developments in other media include Woody Allen's film *What's up Tiger Lily*, which began life as a fairly vicious Japanese film but which Allen, treating it as a 'found object', recut and dubbed,[3] turning it into a comedy – an instructive example of the power of the acoustic domain to modulate the meaning of image. A quotation from a recent conference on new media gives a sense of the literary world's engagement with the same processes:[4]

> The books written by Paul Valéry, Walter Benjamin, Ludwig Wittgenstein, Marshall McLuhan, Gilles Deleuze, Douglas Hofstadter, and Niklas Luhmann can be understood as attempts to do justice to the New Media world at a level of technical depiction. And what is more: these books are no longer books in the strict sense of the word, but mosaics consisting of quotations and fragments of thought. They perform an art of writing which might be called cinematic – composing books as if they were movies. These books try to burst through the limits of the book form. Of course, most of these attempts have failed. But even this failure is instructive. The information processing system 'book' is clearly no longer up to the complexity of our social systems. For this reason, authors who are aware of this and yet want to remain authors, organise their books according to structures and patterns taken from non-linear information processing systems (Bolz, 1994, p. 2).

Cost

In addition to the fact that mass-production techniques have driven down the cost of new technologies to the point of widespread accessibility, the cost of travel has also reduced to a point which stimulates a radical restructuring of our mental geography. This increased mobility happens also at increased speed, so that it is not only our geography, but our sense of time, which is being altered. Both economic and temporal issues are considered at greater length below.

Five principles

Roy Ascott[5] has identified five principles which may be regarded as particularly enhanced by digital technologies: *connectivity, immersion, interaction, transformation* and *emergence*. Connectivity and interaction have been discussed above in relation to interfaces and hypermedia, although the connectivity which is enhanced is not only between disciplines but between individuals, institutions and locations. Immersion relates to the scientific insight that the observer is always an implicit participant in the observation being made which translates in compositional terms into a concern with the sensory immersion of the subject (listener) in the work. In electroacoustic music the technique of multi-loudspeaker diffusion emerged relatively early as a solution to this problem, but it is only more recently that the visual world has addressed similar concerns in experiments which project visual data directly onto the retina, removing any sense of a separate external 'represented' world. (Even this has its precedent in J.M.W. Turner's experiments with the retinal afterimage of the sun in the 1840s (Crary, 1990, pp. 138–43)). The term transformation reflects a prioritising of time, rather than space, as the concern of those in digitally-based arts practice. A 'time-base' is frequently identified by those artists who eschew conventional categorisation as the essential factor in their work, and is obviously crucial to any analysis of common ground in interdisciplinary arts practices. Emergence signifies a conscious utilisation of the changing boundaries between the subject (listener, interpreter) and the composer (artist, maker). This is particularly clear in situations where the former interacts with what the latter has made, and the work can be said to emerge in its completion by the user, rather than having been designed in its entirety by the artist and then 'presented'.

Cultural plurality and hybridity

We are increasingly aware of, and participatory in, a plurality of cultures – cultures associated with disciplines and working patterns, with social expectations, with gender roles or with nation states – each of which has many voices, multiple stories of how the world is, each with its own dynamic validity. Identities, allegiances and constituting contexts can be individually chosen to an extent not possible within the

consensus-based socially determining epistemological structures characteristic of more geographically constrained, self-contained societies.
Cultural identity has thus become mutable and open to choice. The
complex and polymorphous nature of societies is evident not only in an
increased awareness of oversimple ethnic/racial and sexuality/gender
separations, but also in an awareness of the inadequacy of analysing
cultural phenomena on the basis of unwieldy monolithic concepts such
as 'mass culture', 'high art', 'popular culture' and in the complex notion
of consensus itself.

Cultural plurality provides a striking social rationale for an increasingly interdisciplinary approach to theory and practice in that it draws
attention to the cultural and historical specificity of separations between 'disciplines' and of the idea of 'arts' as a phenomenon separable
from social/utilitarian or social/ritual function.

An awareness that there are many cultures which shape us and which
we sustain and transform through our participation in them has two
fundamental effects on a composer. One is empowerment, because it
acknowledges the possibility that an individual can help to shape a
culture. The other is to provide a continuously critical context in which
the (often dominant) culture to which the artist or composer belongs is
always juxtaposed with cultures which construct or describe the world
differently.

The increased ease with which we can travel, by air and other means,
has reconstituted our imaginary map of the world. Geographical proximity is ceasing to be a fundamental issue of connection as electronic
communications technology allows broadcasters, writers and designers
to work from home via modem, and surgeons in the USA to operate on
patients in London via remote satellite link. This is exciting but also
causes problems, as proximity, previously a major determinant in cultural identity and commonality (and therefore in possible meanings for
any given experience) becomes less relevant. Its relevance for
electroacoustic composition is that judgements of value or comprehensibility are likely to be shared by composers and support structures
(international festivals and conferences) between whom there is frequent contact but that potential audiences are unlikely to share this
same specialised network of connections. The security of this 'international acclaim' from their peers has insulated composers from the need
to address more local social and economic issues.

Cultural pluralism has surfaced musically in many ways and has
resulted both in an immensely broadened field of different (and distinct)
musical possibilities and in an incredible hybridisation of concern and
language. Pluralism (which implies difference and therefore some degree

of separateness) and hybridity, although ideologically distinct, often coexist in musical practice. An obvious manifestation is 'World Music', which in Britain was initially very dependent on organisations like WOMAD[6] and figures like Peter Gabriel and DJ Andy Kershaw for its success, and which embraces a number of culturally separatist tendencies but which has also produced intriguing hybrid musical activity. Even in an isolated regional town it is now possible to find a cross-section of music from Venezuela or Zaire in a record store. And there has also been a hybridising of genres – Bristol 'trip-hop' group Massive Attack have worked with classical Indian musicians; Frank Zappa's three 'final' CDs make use of the *Ensemble Modern* both as improvisers and 'conventional' contemporary performers; Irish folk band Moving Hearts use soprano sax as a melody instrument as idiomatic as a tin whistle or uillean pipes, and in a similar manner Indian musicians have confounded the technical limitations of the violin and clarinet to incorporate them idiomatically within a sophisticated non-western classical tradition. Contemporary pirate radio stations (such as Pulse FM, which operates semi-legally from Harringay in North London) use a rapid montage sampling technique which deliberately incorporates as many genres as possible – perhaps a reggae beat, with chords from a film soundtrack, fragments of jazz saxophone and operatic vocals – and naturally enough such developments are reflected in electroacoustic music.

Sampling, in addition to functioning as a tool of time manipulation and repetition, encourages this type of recontextualisation, allowing the easy manipulation, transformation and juxtaposition of genre or culture. As 'morphing' techniques become more widespread, collisions of culture and genre increasingly result in complex hybridisation.

One particular tendency which is illustrative both of the instinct to hybridisation and of juxtaposition of different 'realities' (of genre, technique, etc.) has been theorised by Alejandro Viñao (1988), among others, as relating to the literary movement of *realismo fantastico*, exemplified by Jorge Luis Borges, Gabriel Garcia Marquez and others, in which everyday objects and situations can imperceptibly mutate into magical or impossible ones. *Realismo fantastico* has been internationally influential[7] and in Britain there is a considerable group of electroacoustic composers, some with Latin American connections, who might be regarded as working within a sort of 'magical realism', being particularly interested in the morphological changing of one sound object or environment into another. This is a concern shared at a technical level by Trevor Wishart whose *Vox 5* is frequently cited as an investigation of morphological shift between indexically significant

sounds (Wishart, 1994). Viñao's *Chant d'ailleurs* (Viñao, 1994) provides another sophisticated musical example of this type of hybridisation,
as the transformation takes place on at least two distinct musical levels.
At the level of pure acoustic fact, digital interpolation is used to transform the sound of a Turkish shawm into the sound of a female human
voice; and at the 'higher' level of genre, expressive elements and semantic strategies from Mongolian folk musics transform into and interact
with western extended vocal techniques and an acousmatic sensibility
without any apparent conflict.[8]

Perceptions of authority

The multiple narratives which emerge in a pluralistic society – the
multiple stories of how the world is – serve to draw attention to those
meta-narratives which seem to be invested with a particular authority,
perhaps the most notable of these in the late twentieth century being the
narrative of scientific knowledge. Jean-François Lyotard has characterised the increasing scepticism about the status of such 'objective truths'
as an 'incredulity toward meta-narratives' (Lyotard, 1986, p. xxiv).
Such healthy scepticism towards authorities is not without its problems,
as we tend to construct our own ways of being in the world, of making
our experience mean something, against the legitimating authority of
narratives which are consensual or in some way 'bigger than us'. When
such consensus disappears and all authority and power structures become open to critique, the nature of the relation between the individual
and the social is fundamentally changed. The individual is invested with
massively increased levels of potential power and responsibility, and
overloaded by the need for constant conscious decision making.

In relation to composition such seemingly abstruse considerations are
most significant in that they concern a shifting of the balance between
composer and listener, investing the latter with an authority to decide
something's value or meaning which until recently was the preserve of
the composer. Authorship (compositional autonomy) can be de-
constructed as another kind of institutionalised power. Comfortable
ideas about a 'canon' of objectively 'Great Art' or 'Great Music' which
is timeless and international are also undermined, as attention is drawn
to the historically contingent, ideological nature of the way in which
such a 'consensus' emerges. But without these comfortable certainties it
becomes increasingly difficult to find general criteria for criticism, evaluation or legitimation of the arts (or anything else, for these upheavals
are as prevalent in scientific as in artistic thought). Perhaps one of the

few remaining legitimate criteria for a composer may be the need to discover or verify something through activity.

Authority resides to a great extent in language. Foucault and others have demonstrated the extent to which the concepts which are in place to explain a phenomenon can become self-perpetuating, and 'music' and 'electroacoustic composition' are no exception. Of course, at one level terms such as 'visual art', 'music', 'drama', 'dance', and their subdivisions into genres or styles – 'electroacoustic music', 'free jazz', 'microtonality', 'jungle' – have an obvious currency and utility. On another level they act as constraints, which need constant testing and reformulating and against which new types of activity are constantly working. Boundaries between disciplines and genres are given immense authority by their enshrinement in the institutions which mediate our artistic experience: colleges, universities, museums, galleries, concert halls, theatres, funding agencies, television programmes; yet it is clearly the interaction of choice and historical accident rather than some innate order which has resulted in our world being parcelled experientially as it is. Paradoxically, the scientific disciplines have been quicker to hybridise and reconstitute themselves than the arts. It seems possible, however, that as music is at almost every point mediated by electronic technology, and as aesthetic distinctions become increasingly problematic, the notion of 'electroacoustic music' as a definable area of activity may become redundant. It is increasingly characteristic for young electroacoustic composers to be involved in other musical or artistic activity, and many successful musicians and artists are increasingly unhappy about labelling themselves too narrowly as, for example, 'choreographer' or 'composer', resorting instead to more general terms such as 'maker', or just 'artist', in an attempt not to delimit their field of possible creativity.

Access, replication, distribution, ownership

Through their ability to manipulate any data by means of symbolic languages, computers have opened access to many people previously disenfranchised from the compositional process either through lack of technical skill or by the mystique and protective languages involved. The means of production and dissemination have become widespread and accessible. The flexible nature of the interface between user and data allows the development of tools which look familiar but which are mapped onto unfamiliar skills or processes. This allows the rapid production of phenomena which seem to exhibit the characteristics previously associated with skill, intelligence and 'professionalism'. 'It is now relatively simple, for example, for someone with little conventional musical knowledge to produce a printed score and a digitally recorded 'performance' of considerable sophistication' (Strange, 1987, p. 19). This is a threat to those power élites who have relied on such characteristics to justify their privileged status. It has resulted in rapid shifts of 'aesthetic' criteria, as specialists attempt to keep distance between their own production and that of non-specialists. In general, it has led to a situation identified by many authors (for example, Born, 1995), in which the criteria of aesthetic success have become synonymous with those of technical innovation. This concern with innovation for its own sake can be criticised for reflecting the interest of a small group at a particular historical moment at the expense of acknowledging the more complex relation between innovation and tradition that exists in other cultures.

If the criteria of 'successful' composition have not always equated precisely with those of technical innovation, they have nevertheless been sufficiently confused with pure technical skill for Mike Vaughan to be able to write, without fear of rebuke:

> With respect to the poietic dimension, it is generally thought that it is appropriate for those processes of construction associated with the studio environment to remain hidden in performance (Vaughan, 1994, p. 116).

Increasingly however, composers have been prepared to challenge this aesthetic norm. Those who do so with a critical agenda tend to react against the smooth surface which is now easy to produce in any medium using digital technology. In the digital composition studio the urge to polish and clarify – to smooth out – is very strong, as a result of which certain types of filtered resonance have now become as much of a cliché[9] as obviously reversed sounds, or as loops with glitches in them used to be. The work of Tom Wallace, for example, marks a deliberate refusal of this aesthetic position, this being most evident in abrupt cuts to silence and in fades which draw attention to themselves by their use of unusual or uneven envelopes.[10] While clearly a composer with plenty of conventional technical skill, Wallace reacts against the 'smooth surface', which he sees as falsely indicative of such skill, and therefore associated with spurious notions of professionalism.

Another refusal of surface smoothness takes the form of the deliberate introduction of 'surface noise' associated with vinyl recordings, evident in the work *Tautology* by David Prior.[11] This establishes an additional discursive dimension to the work which is analogous to the spatial (left/right or distant/present continua), but which establishes an additional continuum of 'resolution' (of clear/unclear or 'hi-fi'/'lo-fi' sound). It is significant for the current state of electroacoustic music that such tendencies were preceded by similarly interesting work in the 'pop' music world. Portishead, a band which emerged from the Bristol club scene,[12] use turntables and samplers and have established their own distinctive studio production aesthetic which not only makes use of explicit quotes from many other records but attempts to reproduce, and make play with, different characteristic historic production techniques. These have included the 'sonic signatures' of 1960s spy films, Miles Davis/early Blue Note jazz, Isaac Hayes, and many others, often by using only a short explicit sample of the original which they always credit. A typical track, *Strangers*,[13] begins with a fragment of a Wayne Shorter sax solo before juxtaposing various different genres and degrees of presence and clarity in a manner which is simultaneously archaeological and hybridising in instinct. The extent to which they are prepared to experiment to achieve their particular aesthetic predilections – privately pressing LPs of some of their own material in order to re-record it 'off-vinyl' for remixing into the publicly-released CD; utilising elaborately unconventional recording situations and equipment – is indicative of the level of 'electroacoustic' subtlety and complexity achieved in more inventive pop music.[14]

Authorship and ownership

The nature of digital information allows every duplicate to be an identical clone of its original, making replication simple. Digital networks have dissolved the distinction between replication and mass dissemination. Indeed the 'clonability' of digital data makes concepts of copy and original extremely problematic. As material of all sorts (especially music, text and images) is freely copied between users and as collaborative work via networks becomes increasingly prevalent, the identification of 'authorship' also becomes more difficult, and new conceptions of intellectual property emerge. One of the musicians who was very early to recognise the limits of existing laws (and the limits of current debate) in dealing with the authorship and ownership problems opened up by sampling technology was the Canadian, John Oswald. Oswald coined the unfortunate term 'plunderphonics' to refer to his music which is constructed totally from samples of pre-existing work. He gave this title to his first CD but, predictably, the links between the word 'plunder' and the concept of piracy made his claims – that the work was about the appropriation and changing of meaning – difficult to support in court and most of the 1000 copies of the CD were destroyed. A typically provocative example of Oswald's work, Z, is 18 seconds long and consists entirely of samples between 200 milliseconds and 1 second in length taken from a CD by New York saxophonist John Zorn. (There are 35 samples and 47 events.) As the Zorn CD is itself a series of highly condensed versions of Ornette Coleman jazz compositions, one can regard the work as consisting of nested levels of reinterpretation.

The issue of ownership, of territory, of intellectual property has been intimately bound up with the technologies of representation and repetition available. Until the advent of electronic means of reproduction, timbre had remained an unencodable (unnotatable) area of music and remained therefore in some way outside the constraints on ownership and reuse which applied to pitch and rhythm. When notation allowed the reproduction, storage and dissemination of pitch and rhythm, composers and others were quick to impose legal restrictions so that the concept of authorship might be protected. As sampling provides a means of reproducing, storing and disseminating timbre, ethical as well as aesthetic questions come into play. Is it *theft* to use sound from another person, time, society, genre? Does the ease with which material can be 'lifted' from one context, and reused elsewhere in either transformed or identical state, and the general currency of this practice, make it socially – rather than legally – right to do so? What happens to notions of intellectual property in such a situation? Is it *authentic* to use sound from another person, time, society or genre? What about questions of artistic integrity? Should the same constraints apply to reuse of a timbre as when reusing a melody or a rhythm? It is just as possible to reuse material from one's own, as from another's work. Is this a different issue? When does the work become public property or common culture? What are the limits of 'the work' in a culture of transformation?

Naturally these are issues which are particularly pertinent to (but by no means limited to) music, as sampling culture – the culture of recontextualisation – is equally evident in other art forms.

Tradition and innovation

Any discussion of tradition and innovation clearly relates closely to the problematising of authority and to the notions of culture discussed above. Such considerations have a particular poignancy for those currently involved in composing. The ethos of modernism was one of perpetual innovation, of reinventing the whole history of the practice of composition in every work. Paradoxically one of the results of this was a profound respect for history, the artefacts of which were regarded with awkward reverence. Despite modernism's rejection of the past – its positivistic language and ideology, its faith in progress and perfectibility – much of its associated ideology remained unchanged from the romantic era. This was evident in the role and status of the artist (especially the composer) who was invested with an almost divine right to determine the meaning and importance of his own output. Electroacoustic composition, by confining the composer to the studio and concerning itself essentially with material and formal innovation, can be seen as an archetypal modernist pursuit. This impression is heightened by aspects of the early history of the medium, where the legitimating strategy was clearly that of scientific enquiry, with the laboratory providing the model for the studio and a compositional methodology based on 'the experiment' in which technicians perform operations on the composer's behalf.

Postmodernism, if it has any unambiguously identifiable character, is marked by a rejection of innovation as its guiding principle and by the substitution of recontextualisation. As critics from McLuhan (1964) to Kittler (1990) have pointed out, changes in the nature and structure of our communications technologies fundamentally alter the meanings of what is transmitted by, for example, determining the context of reception or by selecting certain material as significant and thus preventing 'viewing outside the frame'. It is no longer innovation in material but the context in which that material is used or experienced that determines what it might mean. In linguistic terms this is a shift in focus from the signified to the signifier. As a result, the artefacts of the past reappear in new permutations and all historical periods are regarded as potential contemporary material. New methods of dissemination – CD, video, DAT, television, the Internet – tend to stress this simultaneous availability of times and cultures while also drawing attention to the principle of recontextualisation: Madonna in a Cathedral, William Byrd on an aeroplane, Sarajevo in your sitting room.

The modern tendency to regard tradition as a series of historical objects and as the antithesis of innovation is a predominantly eurocentric phenomenon, which fails to acknowledge that traditions, to have continuing social currency, tend to change constantly. A contrasting Japanese attitude towards history and tradition is best exemplified by the case of a national shrine – a fourteenth century Buddhist temple – which is completely rebuilt from new materials every two years, and in which the tradition is regarded as residing not in the object itself but in the continuing knowledge of appropriate materials and building techniques. This more complex relationship between tradition and innovation, evident in many cultures, is beginning to reinform western mainstream practices.

The constructed nature of memory – the manner in which traditions are constructed after the event – has also become more evident within a culture increasingly in thrall to spurious notions of 'heritage'. Investigations into the relationship between tradition and innovation are paralleled by those into the relationship between history and fiction. Here the insight from poststructuralist critical theory – that history and fiction are not as different, not as mutually exclusive as we might have imagined – is useful. It encourages acknowledgement that history is constructed from a series of individual accounts, partial viewpoints, each with its own quota of elaboration or untruth, and that our access to it is always mediated through such narratives and texts. The (paradoxically) historical nature of fiction which, being written at a particular historical and cultural point, inevitably encodes whatever collective thought processes are current within that context and grows from the concerns and language of that moment, is also evident.

Sampling as a technique is paradigmatic of the uneasy relation between tradition and innovation, incorporating the archival instinct of the former and the speculative and exploratory impulse of the latter. Sampling can be regarded as the ultimate time-manipulation tool, the ultimate musical tool of repetition and therefore of recontextualisation. It allows the manipulation of temporally specific sound data or musical information at every level from the micro-sonic to the historical. Although this might also be regarded as true for earlier recording technologies, it is the immediacy with which specific data can be addressed or manipulated in the digital domain and the flexibility of controlling strategies and transformational procedures available which make the shift from analogue recording to digital sampling culturally and musically significant. Sampling allows, in Attali's terms, 'an extremely effective exploration of the past, at a time when the present no longer answers to everyone's needs' (Attali, 1985, p. 100).

Some of the ethical issues relating to sampling and reuse of material can be addressed in relation to this insight. One of the arguments against sampling or reusing historical (even recent historical) material is that it is in some way inevitably inauthentic to do so. Such arguments are usually predicated on the primacy of the composer's original intention and are intent upon the disclosure of the original experience. This is an argument which also surfaces within the performance of instrumental music, most notably with regard to authentic performance practices which purport to recreate the experience of, for example, an eighteenth century concerto. A reasoned response is that such attempts both do and do not recreate an 'authentic' experience. There is an analogy here between the early music debate and the acousmatic/

sampling debate. In acousmatic (purely acoustic) terms it is quite clear that using harpsichords, gut-strung violins and baroque flutes in an appropriate acoustic will generate a sound which is closer to that of the eighteenth-century than modern instruments are capable of doing. But other variables such as social context (the context in which the work is heard and understood), the imagination, knowledge and cultural associations of the audience are as pervasive as the purely acoustic. However authentic the spectral quality of the performance, listening to Vivaldi on a walkman in an aeroplane is an experience which speaks primarily of the late twentieth century, and impulses to 'authenticity' in performance can thus be read as much as aspects of late twentieth-century tendencies to professional specialisation in music as of sensitivity to original historical context. To continue the analogy in terms of a 'sampling culture': as audience control over listening context becomes so great that it effectively establishes an interaction with the compositional process, there is no reason why the varied experiences, interests and capacities for imagining new meaning should any longer be the privilege of the composer. As the audience is now, by definition, almost completely unpredictable in its experience, perhaps those who continue to compose as specialists are justified in leaving traces of other genres, other pieces, other meaning systems within their work in order to allow the audience a broader imaginative scope.

Arguments about regard for tradition and chronological continuity are particularly difficult to sustain when it is realised that even those recordings which seem most obviously to be accurate and continuous documents of a single performance, such as major orchestral recordings, are constructed from multiple short fragments; and that the famous 'three tenors' recording, which accompanied the 1994 World Cup in Italy, is believed to have been assembled from tapes made by the three men at different times in different countries.

Other concepts of tradition and authenticity sidestep the notion of authorial intention and substitute a notion of public property in which particularly well-known or well-loved musical production is regarded as subject to common cultural ownership and therefore proscribed from alteration or reuse. Such arguments are by no means restricted to 'art' musics and heated debate about the ethics of re-mastering classic jazz tracks for CD, re-mixing Rolling Stones and Frank Zappa recordings and reusing the voices of Dolly Parton and Michael Jackson occupies many pages of recent fringe-academic publications (Colli, 1994; Cutler, 1994; Gans, 1995; Oswald, 1987).

Finally, the notion of authorial intention is in itself difficult to pin down. Theoretical separations between 'poietic' and 'esthesic' interpretation (Nattiez, 1990) are not verified by experience in the altogether messier world of practice. Composition is always a play between intention and chance, the final form of a work often contingent upon a series of not essentially music-related pressures. As Chris Cutler observes: 'All "originals" are already palimpsests, reworkings and revisions – it is only that the "works-in-progress", sketches and versions under revision don't usually see the light of day, and so "don't exist" for the consuming public' (Cutler, 1994, p. 49).

Whatever an individual composer's position on artistic integrity, one has to accept as an artist that an audience will always construct hundreds of different possible readings from even the most simple piece of electroacoustic music. Different aspects will be regarded as prominent or significant by different people. So the composer, too, should retain the right to rework, to reinterpret his or her own material, to remix or recompose it.[15]

Signs and representation

Much can be extrapolated from the above remarks about how something – a word, a sound, a picture, a sign of any kind – can be said to mean something. Meaning obviously has something to do with tradition, consensus or some other external legitimating authority, forming a set of guidelines against which individually varying interpretations can align. But these external authorities can be increasingly open to challenge (Lyotard, 1986; Rorty, 1989). What results is an increasingly slippery relation between words (or other signs) and things; an increasing acknowledgement that we *choose* to make things significant, rather than uncovering some inherent meaning. Our familiarity with the symbolic languages used in computing, in which the relation between the symbol and the 'meaning' is wholly arbitrary, has enhanced this sense of the contingent nature of languages. As a result of such insights *mapping* has emerged as a crucial skill, indicative of an epistemological shift from serial to non-linear modes of thought and as a concept worthy of serious study (Wood and Taylor, 1993). As computers allow any input data to be interpreted as a control function, a signal, a series of parametric values, software has emerged which begins to address the notion of such universal interconnection. Symbolic Composer[16] was developed as an engine to allow certain types of mathematical description (Brownian motion, Lorenz attractors, Mandelbrot fractals, etc.) to be easily utilised in musical applications, and has subsequently broadened in scope to allow the interpretation of data in almost any form.

Max[17] allows the construction of individually tailored interfaces from graphic objects which represent blocks of machine code. On a more metaphoric level, the concept of mapping has become an essential aspect of recent compositional practice. As the concept becomes more widespread, however, the significance of merely being able to map one set of information onto another, as in some early stochastic works by Xenakis or more recent American 'computer music', becomes reduced and transfers instead to the skill or appropriateness of the mapping.

As an example of ingenuity in mapping, Ron Kuivila's *Der Schnueffelstaat* (composed in 1991) is a characterful instance which also serves to indicate how a work can investigate a particular structuring principle – in this case the Foucauldian notion of surveillance. Based on the image of a swarm of bees, the work's title translates as 'noisy state' and is taken from the name of a protest committee formed in Switzerland in response to government surveillance of the artistic community:

> A video camera is suspended over the [performance] area to provide a bird's eye view. The image is sent to a computer where it is digitised and analysed. The computer also redisplays the image as a moderate resolution ... video projection. Superimposed on this video are 'bees' represented by little Swiss flags. These ... sense and follow movement. They also notice one another and exhibit a kind of 'swarming' behaviour. In the absence of any movement, the flags fly around randomly in ever increasing patterns looking for change. If they cannot find anything moving they will eventually fall dormant. Each 'bee' generates a sound via a MIDI controlled synthesiser.[18]

In addition to involvement with systems of coding and signifying, composers are constantly involved in semiotic research at the interpretative level too,[19] investigating the unpredictable and undetermined way in which the meaning of something is decided partly by its 'author' and partly by its 'readers'.[20]

Composers are increasingly aware that even the most acousmatic of works is at some level mediated by language. Our tendency to analyse in linguistic terms foregrounds language-mediated aspects of a work for the listener. When some of the sounds are indexical or even documentary the link with verbal coding systems is nearer the surface. Åke Parmerud's *Les Objets Obscurs* (Parmerud, 1994), realised in the studios of the GRM in 1991, focuses on the question of whether or not the sounds in an acousmatic work are intended to be indexical (in other words to refer to a specific identifiable activity or object) by turning the whole process into a sophisticated game which is explicitly tied to the linguistic. The piece takes the form of four riddles – poetic conceits spoken in French – which refer obscurely to particular objec... identity of which the audience is invited to guess. Each spoken riddle leads into its sonic equivalent in which the disguised sound object forms the answer to both the spoken and the musical riddle. The final riddle is the subject in which the audience has been engaged and is revealed at the end to be music itself.

This conscious multi-level play with music's ability to refer to specifics, to relate to spoken language and other meaning-making codes and simultaneously to be pure acoustic fact, seems to be one of the richer directions in which electroacoustic music is currently moving.

Economics

Underpinning all of the above shifts is the reality of new economic constraint, which for the arts (and arts education) has primarily meant a move away from subsidy towards mixed economy. Academic electroacoustic music is just beginning to adapt to the culture of the market. Increased competition between institutions for students and resources with funding structured around student numbers, research profiles, spurious 'quality assessments' and performance indicators, could potentially lead to aesthetic constraint, as electroacoustic music is particularly resource and time intensive and therefore 'inefficient'. Outside universities, changes in state subsidy for the arts have aggravated the sense that certain practices are legitimate and valued (because they are funded), whereas others are culturally valueless, and electroacoustic music is beginning to lose out here.[21] Because commercial backing is generally only available for the uncontentious, a preoccupation with 'tradition' and 'heritage' has been reinforced at the expense of 'risk' and 'innovation'.

Many electroacoustic artists function either in an economic subculture or through loose ties with the education system, beyond the reach of conventional arts funding structures. In the UK, government policy has substantially undermined this subculture by increasing the level of income required for subsistence and simultaneously closing loopholes which enabled non-earning artists to survive. This is less true in many mainland European countries, which protect such activity on the basis that it would be counterproductive to polarise a motivated, intelligent and articulate faction.

An additional, more positive, factor is that mass-production techniques have driven down the cost of new technologies to the point of widespread accessibility. This promotes a radical reconfiguring of the political economy of electroacoustic music and of electronics in music making. A consideration of this shift in terms of the emergence of a 'sampling culture' follows below. An example of this phenomenon in the visual arts which parallels the 'street' use of samplers is the Pixelvision craze in the USA, in which film and video makers have begun to make work using a low definition Fisher-Price 'toy' video camera because of the surreal qualities of image transformation produced.

A political economy of electroacoustic music and of electronics in music making

The shift from acousmatic electroacoustic music to what I have referred to as 'sampling culture' can be read as a shift in the position of the central locus of electroacoustic activity – from a specialised economy in which production took place in the music academy, the university studio, the research establishment, to a mixed economy in which the above are a productive subset but which now includes the thousands of bedrooms and converted garages equipped with samplers and DAT machines, as well as the clubland DJs and independent radio producers with their 'scratch' aesthetic and openness to the reuse of *any* material. This shift in no way invalidates the more rarefied work which continues to be produced, but it does fundamentally alter its potential meaning. In a situation where techniques and technologies appear on the street simultaneously with their arrival in the research studio, academic electroacoustic music will no longer be able to trade on novelty or mere technical innovation.

Such a shift from specialised to general use is an historical commonplace for human tools. The point here is that the specialised/non-specialised distinction has become effectively blurred, as has the distinction between 'creative' and 'disseminative' technologies. The sampler is paradigmatic here but the CD player, too, can now be a powerful instrument of performance and of context shift, as well as a high quality source of sampled 'material'. Technologies of mass dissemination have begun to blur in function with technologies of conventional instrumentality, the sampler having long replaced other keyboards as the instrument of choice alongside the electric guitar. Sampling can be regarded, then, as representing an important step in the re-empowerment of 'listeners' as composers, both in the sense that new configurations of familiar sounds encourage 'listening again' and in the more profound sense that sampling blurs the distinction between technologies of production and reproduction and therefore between composer and listener.

Those composers newly enfranchised by the profusion of inexpensive digital tools have reacted to the broadened technical scope offered by increased dynamic range and spectral clarity not by embracing whole-sale the aesthetic values of the acousmatic specialist (although these have also clearly not been completely rejected), but by bringing into play *additional* aesthetic criteria, such as the continuum of available resolution from distorted to clear reproduction, from (deliberately) re-duced dynamic or spectral range to 'professional' clarity. These can be regarded as introducing additional potential expressivity into music involving electronic technology. The inspiration for this is not meekly aesthetic but is often expressly political in motivation – a critique of the technological determinism which is seen as associated with some as-pects of academic electroacoustic music. A recurrent conviction is that old and 'restrictive' technologies need not inhibit expressive possibility – that the most significant aesthetic constraints are those of imagination rather than technology, which is the ideology informing for example Philip Jeck's performances with multiple *Dansette* record players.[22] Equally significant is the notion that 'cutting-edge' music does not need to rely on the practical resources and powerful legitimating logic of the institution.

This latter point is taken up by Gregory Whitehead, in a critique of radio as an art form in which he addresses the functioning of electroacoustic music within the social domain and specifically within the domain of the listener:

> the investigation of radio has disappeared into the investigation of *sound*, the wireless body stripped and redressed to provide a broad-cast identity for the nebulous permutations of diverse *ars acustica*.

and adds, more pertinently:

> These are *musique concrète*, noise art, sound poetry, soundscapes, and the like. The equation of radio art with the simple act of broadcasting such diverse audio productions has been particularly true in Europe, where many state broadcasting systems have estab-lished experimental units from time to time. Since these units operate without any pressure to establish a vital relationship to an audi-ence, it is not surprising that thinking through the *problem* of the listener has for the most part remained well outside the province of such experiments (Whitehead, 1992, p. 253 and footnote, pp. 262–3).

This seems to strike at the core of acousmatic music's development as a practice, identifying privileged institutional position, insulation from market forces, and scant regard for audiences (with the exception of the composer and *coterie*) as key constitutive elements.

Environment

Finally, a broad contextual shift which may ultimately emerge as the most urgent is seen in the gradually increasing awareness of environmental imperatives. Composers from otherwise quite different ideological perspectives are seen to be showing interest in what might be regarded as sustainable or environmentally ethical practice. A broad shift in attitude towards ecological sensitivity is evident among the young, particularly among schoolchildren, and this shared ground between artists and young people may yet prove a significant factor in revitalising aesthetic education and research.

Responses to environmental and ecological contexts have brought together artists with shared concerns in a manner likely to enhance the communication between different practices. One practical response among electroacoustic composers has been to immerse themselves and their work within the landscape, rather than framing it within a contrived display or performance context such as a gallery, concert hall or theatre. (Was it Cage who said that Western art lost its way when it moved indoors?) This has been one of many radical approaches taken by R. Murray Schafer and his followers, who have developed the concept of 'acoustic ecology' and the related notions of 'soundscape', 'sound pollution' and 'the hi-fi environment' which reflect this concern to increase the dynamic range of acoustic experience (Schafer, 1977). Some of Murray Schafer's work seems to parallel that of contemporary environmental installations by British visual artists Andy Goldsworthy and Richard Long, one particular composition making use of the different coefficients of sound transmission of damp and dry air above a lake in Canada to effect real-time treatment of a trombone ensemble. Perhaps uncoincidentally, Canada has produced a considerable number of electroacoustic composers whose work has drawn attention to landscape and the environment through a relatively untreated documentary style recording, in which the presence of the composer as sound gatherer is quite explicit.[23] Artists working with installation have become much more concerned to investigate the relationship between sonic and social space.[24] In some cases, this has embraced a specific political agenda involving sound and recording being used to enable a particular community to reflect upon itself and its relationship with its environment.[25] Other trends encourage spectacle and theatricality as an explicit strategy, linking new 'precise' digital technology to old 'imprecise' mechanical systems.[26] A further, more spurious, ecological argument has been that it is more responsible to reuse old sounds than to generate new ones, and several sampling composers use this notion of 'recycling' as a justification for their use of other people's material.[27]

Summary

The complex changes described above impact on individuals, communities and the relationship between the two in a manner that is not totally predictable. What is clear is that electroacoustic music as a practice is dependent upon contexts beyond the merely acoustic, and that as these contexts change it is likely to respond. As with other arts practices this response may vary from a protective reifying of certain activities as 'core', to an inclusive and speculative tendency intent on formulating new types of practice. This multiplicity is likely to be more aesthetically healthy and to provide a greater argument for continuing support for such music than if only one of these possibilities were to be pursued. Activity involving other media is likely to become less peripheral and certainly to become more compelling, but the idea that it will become dominant and somehow undermine acousmatic music seems irrational. Such activity is far more likely to become one of many equal 'others', of at least equal accessibility, and with different concerns.

The extremes of the two tendencies characterised above are inherently problematic. The protectionist (acousmatic) tendency fails to acknowledge that changes of context, even if 'outside' the discipline, reconstitute the way things within it are generally understood or interpreted (as did the photograph for the visual culture in which painting operates). The 'new practices' faction fail to acknowledge the gradual and evolutionary nature of human responses, even to stimuli which have themselves changed quite rapidly, and the amount of acquaintance time necessary for communities to develop new strategies for interpreting and finding significance in such stimuli. The middle ground – those caught within the discipline of electroacoustic music but struggling to escape its confines and those whose strategy has been to force a collision between new possibilities and acknowledged skills – has so far provided most of the evidence for aesthetic optimism.

Innovations at the edge of a practice are often the result of enthusiastic inclusiveness resulting in a creative misunderstanding or reinterpretation of aspects of an unfamiliar discipline or technique, but the gradual nature of the movement towards new practice which results is often conspicuously more successful than more radical attempts to integrate work across or between disciplines. The immense broadening of activity under the umbrella of composition during the late twentieth century probably justifies its description, in imitation of a similar consideration of sculpture (Krauss, 1985), as operating within an 'expanded field'. As a result, perhaps electroacoustic music is simply becoming less distinct as an activity from other forms of musical activity, whether these be instrumental music which shares acousmatic principles (such as much of Helmut Lachenmann's work which is referred to in Germany as *musique concrète instrumentale*, or some of the works of Boulez, for example *Répons* and *Mémoriale: explosante-fixe*); an increased concern with microtonal construction and the harmonic series (evident in the work of an instrumental composer like James Dillon, but also in electroacoustic music); or the blurring of distinctions between the 'serious' and the 'popular' in many areas – the fact that some ambient music sounds like an impoverished form of electroacoustic music.

Much current electroacoustic music can be read as an attempt to come to terms with the new contexts outlined in this chapter, but the practice of composition changes not only in response to 'external' criteria but also in response to pressures from within the activity itself. It is characteristic of many artists that they are driven by the need to test the limits of their medium, to break out of the conceptual constraints which they perceive as characterising the field in which they work, and electroacoustic composers are no exception. Of course, not all of the attempts are good. But even the failures are instructive. Perhaps, to paraphrase Norbert Bolz's (1994) observations about the book, cited earlier, purely acousmatic electroacoustic music is simply no longer up to the complexity of our contemporary social realities.

Notes

1. The concept of acousmatic culture is understood as revolving around Pierre Schaeffer's notions (Schaeffer, 1966), elaborated by Michel Chion (Chion, 1983; 1991), of *l'écoute reduite* (*reduced listening*) and *l'objet sonore* (*the sound object*).
2. Much in the manner predicted by Attali (1985).
3. 'We took a Japanese film and took away the soundtrack, then we made it into a comedy, so there were people running round killing people, and it was a comedy.' (Woody Allen in an unidentified radio interview.)
4. Netherlands Design Institute/*Mediamatic* 'Doors of Perception' Conference, Amsterdam, 30–31 October 1993.
5. Speaking at South West Arts/Bath College of Higher Education 'Symposium on Interdisciplinarity in the Arts', Corsham Court, 12–13 March 1993.
6. 'World of Music and Dance'.
7. A movement of *fantastischer Realismus* emerged for example in Vienna.

8. 'I developed an imaginary singing style, with its own melisma, its own ornamental identity, the identity of a chanting "tradition" that I invented. The computer is also part of this imaginary style. The vocal sounds it manipulates and the new timbres it creates are articulated and "performed" in a way that is consistent with the chanting style of the singer.' (from the composer's CD note (Viñao, 1994).)

9. Of course the notion of cliché is itself indicative of the prevalence of the notion of *avoidance* of traces of technical construction, and of the inadequately thought-through relationship between electroacoustic 'tradition' (such as it is) and innovation.

10. Tom Wallace: *andRain* (electroacoustic music, University of East Anglia, 1994, unpublished).

11. Produced at Bangor University, Wales 1994.

12. Other examples include Tricky and the more mainstream Massive Attack.

13. Portishead: 'Strangers', from the CD *Dummy* (Portishead, 1994).

14. Paradoxically, Laurie Anderson, one of the most self-consciously experimental artists in the 'popular' domain, has been less interested in the potential of production techniques, concentrating on experiment in performance, which has resulted in rather conventional documentation of her work.

15. This is an issue that has particularly preoccupied me in my own work; for example *Drift* (1991), *Unearthing* (1993), *AfterImage* (1993) (unpublished).

16. Symbolic Composer is a Lisp-based algorithmic composing environment produced by Tonality Systems of Amsterdam.

17. Max is an object-oriented programming language developed at IRCAM by Miller Puckette and produced by Opcode Systems Inc.

18. Composer's programme note, STEIM, Amsterdam, 1993.

19. At what Nattiez (1990) would call the 'esthesic' level.

20. In relation to my own work this investigation can be regarded as an increasing concern to make polysemic works: works which allow or even encourage differences in reading.

21. In Britain the Arts Council's Electroacoustic Music Bursary scheme was discontinued in 1994 and, despite numerous rumoured capital projects funded from National Lottery or Millenium Fund sources, there is now no UK state support for independent electroacoustic composers beyond (infrequent) commissions of single works.

22. Philip Jeck, who trained as a visual artist, has been working with turntables in live performance and installation since the early 1980s. His 1993 audio-visual collaboration, *Vinyl Requiem*, made use of 180 Dansettes stacked and whitewashed to form a huge projection screen, and was premièred in London and Ghent.

23. For example Claude Schryer's *Les oiseaux de Bullion* and Christian Calon's *Temps incertains*. The composer is also present in an explicit, if less 'environmental', manner in Hildegard Westerkamp's *Breathing Room* and Dan Lander's *I'm Looking at My Hand*. All four works feature on the CD *Électro clips: 25 three minute electroacoustic snapshots* (Montréal, 1990).

24. For example Miroslav Rogala (Poland), Mathias Fuchs (Austria).

25. For example Gregg Wagstaff (Scotland).

26. For example Matt Heckert (USA).

27. Suzi Gablik's *The Reenchantment of Art* (Gablik, 1991) is one attempt to identify recent increased interest in the relationship between arts and environment as a coherent tendency. This looks, among other things, at Joseph Beuys whose performance stressed the shamanistic and obsessive aspects of arts making, irrespective of the constraints of concepts of 'the discipline'. Similar concerns were evident in the *Arte Povera* movement in the 1960s, notably in the work of Jannis Kounellis, and in the 'Poor Theatre' or 'Third Theatre' (by analogy with 'Third World') of Grotowski (Grotowski, 1968) and Eugenio Barba (Barba, 1979).

References

Attali, Jacques (1985), *Noise: The Political Economy of Music*, Manchester: Manchester University Press.

Barba, Eugenio (1979), *The Floating Islands: Reflections with Odin Teatret*, Holstebro: Drama Books.

Bolz, Norbert (1994), 'The deluge of sense', *Mediamatic*, vol. 8, Amsterdam: Mediamatic (CD-ROM, transcription of speech at 'Doors of Perception' Conference, Amsterdam 1993).

Born, Georgina (1995), *Rationalising Culture: IRCAM, Boulez and the Institutionalisation of the Musical Avant-Garde*, Berkeley: University of California Press.

Chion, Michel (1983), *Guide des objets sonores*, Paris: INA/Buchet/ Chastel.

Chion, Michel (1991), *L'art des sons fixés, ou la musique concrètement*, Fontaine: Editions Métamkine/Nota Bene/Sono-Concept.

Colli, Guiseppe (1994), 'AAD-ADD-DDD: Remixes: cosmetics or fraud?', *unfiled: Music Under New Technology* (ReR/Recommended Sourcebook 0401), pp. 46–8.

Cutler, Chris (1994), 'Remix Notes', *unfiled: Music Under New Technology* (ReR/Recommended Sourcebook 0401), pp. 49–50.

Crary, Jonathan (1990), *Techniques of the Observer: On Vision and Modernity in the Nineteenth Century*, Cambridge, Mass.: October/ MIT Press.

Gablik, Suzi (1991), *The Reenchantment of Art*, New York/London: Thames and Hudson.

Gans, David (1995), 'The man who stole Michael Jackson's face', *Wired*, vol.3.02, pp. 136–8 (US edition).

Grotowski, Jerzy (1968), *Towards a Poor Theatre*, Holstebro: Odin Teatrets Forlag.

Kittler, Friedrich (1990), *Discourse Networks 1800/1900*, Stanford: Stanford University Press.

Krauss, Rosalind (1985), 'Sculpture in the expanded field', in Foster, Hal (ed.), *Postmodern Culture*, pp. 31–42, London: Pluto Press.

Lyotard, Jean-François (1986), *The Postmodern Condition: a Report on Knowledge*, Manchester: Manchester University Press.

McLuhan, Marshall (1964), *Understanding Media: the Extensions of Man*, London: Routledge and Kegan Paul.

McLuhan, Marshall and Fiore, Quentin (1967), *The Medium is the Massage*, Harmondsworth: Penguin.

Nattiez, Jean-Jacques (1990), *Music and Discourse, Toward a Semiology of Music*, Princeton: Princeton University Press.

Oswald, John (1987), 'Plunderphonics, or audio piracy as a compositional prerogative', *ReR Quarterly*, 2(1), pp. 24–9.

Rorty, Richard (1989), *Contingency, Irony and Solidarity*, Cambridge: Cambridge University Press.

Schaeffer, Pierre (1966), *Traité des objets musicaux*, Paris: Editions du Seuil.

Schafer, R. Murray (1977), *The Tuning of the World*, New York: Knopf.

Spiller, Jürg (ed.) (1961), *Paul Klee Notebooks Volume 1: The Thinking Eye*, London: Lund Humphries.

Strange, Allen (1987), 'Guest editorial: creativity vs. mechanics', *Keyboard*, 13(7), p. 19.

Vaughan, Mike (1994), 'The human-machine interface in electroacoustic music composition', *Contemporary Music Review*, 10(2), pp. 111–27.

Viñao, Alejandro (1988), 'Magic Realism in Music: Four Electroacoustic Compositions', PhD Thesis, City University, London.

Whitehead, Gregory (1992), 'Out of the dark: notes on the nobodies of radio art', in Whitehead, Gregory and Kahn, Douglas (eds), *Wireless Imagination: Sound, Radio, and the Avant-garde*, pp. 253–63, Cambridge, Mass.: MIT Press.

Wishart, Trevor (1994), *Audible Design*, York: Orpheus the Pantomime.

Wood, John and Taylor, Paul (1994), 'Mapping the mapper', *Arachnet Electronic Journal on Virtual Culture*, ftp://ftp.lib.ncsu.edu/pub/stacks/aejvc/aejvc-v2n02-wood-mapping.

Recordings

Montréal (1990), *Électro clips*, Empreintes Digitales, IMED-9004-CD.

Parmerud, Åke (1994), *Les objets obscurs*, Phono Suecia PSCD 72.

Portishead (1994), *Dummy*, Go! Discs Limited, Go!Beat 828 522-2.

Viñao, Alejandro (1994), *Hildegard's Dream*, INA/GRM: INA C 1015.

PART TWO
Cultural noise

CHAPTER FOUR

Plunderphonics

Chris Cutler

New art and music do not communicate an individual's conceptions in ordered structures, but they implement processes which
are, as are our daily lives, opportunities for perception (observation and listening) (John Cage on the influence of Marshall McLuhan
on his music (Kostelanetz, 1971, p. 170)).

Introduction

*Sounds like a dive downwards as a sped up tape slows rapidly to settle
into a recognisable, slightly high-pitched Dolly Parton. It continues to
slow down, but more gradually now. The instruments thicken and their
timbres stretch and grow richer. Details unheard at the right speed
suddenly cut across the sound. Dolly is changing sex, she's a man
already; the backing has become hallucinatory and strange. The grain
of the song is opened up and the ear, seduced by detail, lets a throng of
surprising associations and ideas fall in behind it. The same thing is
suddenly very different. Who would have expected this extraordinary
composition to have been buried in a generic country song, one thousand times heard already and one thousand times copied and forgotten?*

So I hear John Oswald's version of Dolly Parton's version of *The Great
Pretender*, effectively a recording of Oswald playing Parton's single once
through, transformed via varispeed media (first a high speed cassette
duplicator, then an infinitely variable speed turntable, finally a hand-
controlled reel-to-reel tape – all edited seamlessly together). Apart from
the economy of this single procedure of controlled deceleration, which is,
as it were, played by Oswald, no modifications have been made to the
original recording. However, although the source is plainly fixed and
given, the choice, treatment and reading of this source are all highly
conscious products of Oswald's own intention and skill. So much so that
it is easy to argue that the piece, although 'only' Parton's record, undoubtedly forms, in Oswald's version, a self-standing composition with

its own structure and logic – both of which are profoundly different from those of the original. Oswald's *Pretender* would still work for a listener who had never heard the Parton version, and in a way the Parton version never could. Though the Parton version is, of course, *given* – along with and against the plundered version. What Oswald has created – because the result of his work is something startlingly new – is a powerful, aesthetic, significant, polysemic but highly focused and enjoyable sound artefact; both a source of direct listening pleasure and (for our purposes) a persuasive case for the validity and eloquence of its means.

John Oswald's *Pretender* and other pieces (all originating from existing copyright recordings but employing radically different techniques) were included on an EP and later a CD, *Plunderphonic* (Oswald, 1988/1998). Both were given away free to radio stations and the press. None was sold. The liner note reads: 'This disc may be reproduced but neither it, nor any reproductions of it are to be bought or sold. Copies are available only to public access and broadcast organisations, including libraries, radio or periodicals.' The 12 inch EP, consisting of four pieces – *Pretender* (Parton), *Don't* (Presley), *Spring* (Stravinsky), *Pocket* (Basie) – was made between 1979 and 1988 and released in May 1988, with some support from the Arts Council of Canada. The CD, containing these and twenty other pieces was realised between 1979–89 and released on 31 October 1989 and was financed entirely by Oswald himself. Between Christmas Eve 1989 and the end of January 1990 all distribution ceased and all extant copies were destroyed. Of all the plundered artists it was Michael Jackson who pursued the CD to destruction. Curiously Jackson's own plundering, for instance, the one minute and six seconds of The Cleveland Symphony Orchestra's recording of Beethoven's Ninth which opens Jackson's *Will you be there?* on the CD *Dangerous*, for which Jackson claims no less than six credits, including composer copyright (adding plagiarism to sound piracy), seems to have escaped his notice.

Necessity and choice (continued)

In 1980 I wrote that 'From the moment of the first recording, the actual performances of musicians on the one hand, and all possible sound on the other, had become the proper matter of music creation.' (Cutler, 1991, p. 33). I failed, however, to underline the consequence that 'all sound' has to include other people's already recorded work; and that when all sound is just raw material, then recorded sound is always raw – even when it is cooked. This omission I wish now in part to redress.

Although recording offered all audible sound as material for musical organisation, art music composers were slow to exploit it, and remain so today. One reason is that the inherited paradigms through which art music continues to identify itself have not escaped their roots in notation, a system of mediation which determines both what musical material is available and what possible forms of organisation can be applied to it. The determination of material and organisation follows from the character of notation as a discontinuous system of instructions developed to model visually what we know as melody, harmony and rhythm represented by, and limited to, arrangements of fixed tones (quantised, mostly twelve to an octave) and fixed durations (of notes and silences). Notation does not merely quantise the material, reducing it to simple units but, constrained by writability, readability and playability, is able to encompass only a very limited degree of complexity within those units. In fact the whole edifice of western art music can be said, after a fashion, to be constructed upon and through notation[1] which, amongst other things, creates 'the composer' who is thus constitutionally bound to it.

No wonder then that recording technology continues to cause such consternation. On the one hand it offers control of musical parameters beyond even the wildest dreams of the most radical mid-twentieth century composer; on the other it terminally threatens the deepest roots of the inherited art music paradigm, replacing notation with the direct transcription of performances and rendering the clear distinction between performance and composition null.

Perhaps this accounts for the curious relationship between the art music world and the new technology which has, from the start, been equivocal or at least highly qualified (Edgard Varese notably excepted). And it is why the story I shall have to tell is so full of tentative high art experiments that seem to die without issue and why, although many creative innovations in the new medium were indeed made on the fringes of high art, their adoption and subsequent extension has come typically through other, less ideologically intimidated (or less paradigmatically confused?) musical genres. Old art music paradigms and new technology are simply not *able* to fit together.[2]

For art music then, recording is inherently problematic – and surely plunderphonics is recording's most troublesome child, breaking taboos that art music had not even imagined. For instance, while plagiarism was already strictly off limits (flaunting non-negotiable rules concerning originality, individuality and property rights), plunderphonics was proposing routinely to appropriate as its raw material not merely other people's tunes or styles but finished recordings of them! It offered a medium in which, far from art music's essential creation *ex nihilo*, the origination, guidance and confirmation of a sound object may be carried through by *listening* alone.

The new medium proposes, the old paradigms recoil. Yet I want to argue that it is precisely in this forbidden zone that much of what is genuinely new in the creative potential of new technology resides. In other words, the moral and legal boundaries which currently constitute important determinants in claims for musical legitimacy, impede and restrain some of the most exciting possibilities in the changed circumstances of the age of recording. History to date is clear on such conflicts: the old paradigms will give way. The question is – *to what*?

One of the conditions of a new art form is that it produce a metalanguage, a theory through which it can adequately be described. A new musical form will need such a theory. My sense is that Oswald's *Plunderphonic* has brought at last into sharp relief many of the critical questions around which such a theory can be raised. For by coining the name, Oswald has identified and consolidated a musical practice which until now has been without focus. And like all such namings, it seems naturally to apply retrospectively, creating its own archaeology, precursors and origins.

Originality

Of all the processes and productions which have emerged from the new medium of recording, plunderphonics is the most consciously self-reflexive; it begins and ends only with recordings, with the already played. Thus, as I have remarked above, it cannot help but challenge our current understanding of originality, individuality and property rights. To the extent that sound recording as a medium negates that of notation and echoes in a transformed form that of biological memory, this should not be so surprising.[3] In ritual and folk musics, for instance, originality as we understand it would be a misunderstanding – or a transgression – since proper performance is repetition. Where personal contributions are made or expected, these must remain within clearly prescribed limits and iterate sanctioned and traditional forms.

Such musics have no place for genius, individuality or originality as we know them nor for the institution of intellectual property. Yet these were precisely the concepts and values central to the formation of the discourse that identified the musical, intellectual and political revolution that formed the basis for what we now know as the classical tradition. Indeed, they were held as marks of its superiority over earlier forms. Thus, far from describing hubris or transgression, originality and the individual voice became central criteria of value for a music whose future was to be marked by the restless and challenging pursuit of progress and innovation. Writing became essential, and not only for transmission. A score was an individual's signature on a work. It also made unequivocal the author's claim to the legal ownership of a sound blueprint – 'blueprint' because a score is mute and others have to give it body, sound, and meaning. Moreover, notation established the difference and immortality of a work in the abstract, irrespective of its performance.

Copyright

The arrival of recording, however, made each performance of a score as permanent and fixed as the score itself. Copyright was no longer so simple.[4] When John Coltrane records *My Favourite Things* (Coltrane, 1961), a great percentage of which contains no sequence of notes found in the written score, the assigning of the composing rights to Rogers and Hammerstein hardly recognises the compositional work of Coltrane, Garrison, Tyner and Jones. A percentage can now be granted for an 'arrangement' but this does not satisfy the creative input of such performers either. Likewise, when a collective improvisation is registered under the name, as often still occurs, of a bandleader, nothing is expressed by this except the power relations pertaining in the group. Only if it is registered in the names of all the participants, are collective creative energies honoured – and historically, it took decades to get copyright bodies to recognise such 'unscored' works, and their status is still anomalous and poorly rated.[5] Still, this is an improvement: until the mid 1970s, in order to claim a composer's copyright for an improvised or studio originated work, one had to produce some kind of score constructed from the record – a topsy-turvy practice in which the music created the composer. Moreover, to earn a royalty on a piece which started and ended with a copyright tune but had fifteen minutes of free improvising in the middle, a title or titles had to be given for the improvised parts or all the money would go to the author of the bookending melody. In other words, the response of copyright authorities to the new realities of recording was to cobble together piecemeal compromises in the hope that, between the copyrights held in the composition and the patent rights granted over a specific recording, most questions of assignment could be adjudicated, and violations identified and punished. No one wanted to address the fact that recording technology had called into question not merely the mechanics but the adequacy of the prevailing concept of copyright. It was Oswald, with the release of his not-for-sale EP and then CD who, by naming, theorising and defending the use of 'macrosamples' and 'electroquotes', finally forced the issue. It was not so much that the principles and processes involved were without precedent but rather that through Oswald they were at last brought together in a focused and fully conscious form.

The immediate result was disproportionate industry pressure, threats and the forcible withdrawal from circulation and destruction of all extant copies. This despite the fact that the CD in question was arguably an original work (in the old paradigmatic sense), was not for sale (thereby not exploiting other people's copyrights for gain) and was released precisely to raise the very questions which its suppression underlined but immediately stifled. Nevertheless, the genie was out of the bottle.

The fact is that, considered as raw material, a recorded sound is *technically indiscriminate of source*. All recorded sound, as recorded sound, is information of the same quality. A recording of a recording is just a recording. No more, no less. We have to start here. Only then can we begin to examine, as with photomontage (which takes as its strength of meaning the fact that a photograph of a photograph is – a photograph) how the message of the medium is qualified by a communicative intent that distorts its limits. Judgements about what is plagiarism and what is quotation, what is legitimate use and what, in fact if not law, is public domain material, cannot be answered by recourse to legislation derived from technologies that are unable even to comprehend such questions. When 'the same thing' is so different that it constitutes a *new* thing, it is not 'the same thing' anymore – even if, like Oswald's hearing of the Dolly Parton record, it manifestly is the 'same thing' and no other. The key to this apparent paradox lies in the protean self-reflexivity of recording technology, allied with its elision of the acts of production and reproduction, both of which characteristics are incompatible with the old models, centred on notation, from which our current thinking derives, and which commercial copyright laws continue to reflect.

Thus plunderphonics as a practice radically undermines three of the central pillars of the art music paradigm: originality – it deals only with copies; individuality – it speaks only with the voice of others; and copyright – the breaching of which is a condition of its very existence.

Recording history: the gramophone

As an attribute unique to recording, the history of plunderphonics is in part the history of the self-realisation of the recording process; its coming, so to speak, to consciousness.[6] Sound recording began with experiments in acoustics and the discovery that different pitches and timbres of sound could be rendered visible, most notably in 1856 by Leon Scott de Martinville attaching a stylus to a membrane, causing the membrane to vibrate with a sound and allowing it to engrave its track on a glass cylinder coated with lampblack moving at a fixed speed. Such experiments were conducted only to convert otherwise invisible, transient sound into a 'writing' (*phono-graph* means 'voice-writer'), a fixed visible form that would allow it to be seen and studied. It was some ten years before it occurred to anyone that by simply reversing the process, the sound thus written might be recovered. And it was not until the late 1870s that the first, purely mechanical phonograph was constructed, without clear purpose, speculatively appearing as a novelty item, talking doll mechanism and 'dictaphone'. The music gramophone really started to take hold after the electrification of the whole process in 1926, but the breakthrough for the record as a producing (as opposed to reproducing) medium, came only in 1948 in the studios of French Radio with the birth of *musique concrète*. There were no technological advances to explain this breakthrough, only a thinking advance; the chance interpenetrations of time, place and problematic.

The first *concrète* pieces, performed at the *Concert de Bruits* in Paris by engineer/composer Pierre Schaeffer (Schaeffer, 1990), were made by manipulating gramophone records in real time, employing techniques embedded in their physical form: varying the speed, reversing the direction of spin, making 'closed grooves' to create repeated ostinati etc. Within two years the radio station, in the face of resistance from Schaeffer, had re-equipped the studio with tape recorders; and Schaeffer, now head of the *Groupe de musique concrète*, continued to develop the same aesthetic of sound organisation, and to extend the transformational procedures learned through turntable manipulations with the vastly more flexible resources of magnetic tape. Other composers began to experiment with disc manipulation around the same time, including Tristram Cary in London and Mauricio Kagel in Buenos Aires. Tape had completely displaced direct-to-disc recording by 1950 and the studio that was to become an instrument was the tape studio. Disc experiments seemed merely to have become a primitive forerunner to tape work. It is curious that, in spite of the intimacy of record and recording, the first commercially available *musique concrète* on disc was not released until 1956.

Tape

Where the gramophone was an acoustic instrument, the magnetic recorder, also invented at the end of the nineteenth century, was always electrical. The gramophone, however, had numerous initial advantages: it was easier to amplify (the energy of the recoverable signal was greater to start with), and as soon as Emile Berliner replaced the cylinder with the disc and developed a process to press copies from a single master (1895), records were easy to mass produce. Wire, and then tape, were both much more difficult. For these and other reasons, tape was not regularly employed in music until after the Second World War, when German improvements in recording and playback quality and in stable magnetic tape technology were generally adopted throughout the world. Within five years tape had become standard in all professional recording applications.

The vinyl disc meanwhile held its place as the principal commercial playback medium and thus the ubiquitous public source of recorded sound. This division between the professionally productive and socially reproductive media was to have important consequences, since it was on the gramophone record that music appeared in its public, most evocative form; and when resonant cultural fragments began to be taken into living sound art, it was naturally from records, from the 'real' artefacts that bricoleurs would draw. But before we get to this part of the story, I want to take a quick look at plundering precedents in some other fields.

History/plunder

From early in the twentieth century conditions existed that one would expect to have encouraged sound plundering experiments as a matter of course. First, the fact of sound recording itself, its existence, its provision of a medium which offers the sonic simulacrum of an actual sound event in a permanent and alienable form. Moreover, in principle, a sound recording, like a photograph, is merely surface. It has no depths, reveals no process and is no palimpsest. It is just there; always the first, always a copy. It has no aura, nor any connection to a present source. And with its special claims toward objectivity and transparency, the tongue of a recording is always eloquently forked and thus already placed firmly in the realm of art.[7]

Second, montage, collage, borrowing, bricolage have been endemic in the visual arts since at least the turn of the century. The importation of ready-made fragments into original works was a staple of cubism (newspaper, label samples, advertising and so on), futurism and early soviet art. Dada took this much further (Kurt Schwitters above all and the photomontagists) and as early as 1914 Marcel Duchamp had exhibited his bottle rack, a work in which, for the first time, a complete unmodified object was simply imported whole into an 'art space'. Yet strangely it was 25 years before John Cage in his *Imaginary Landscape No. 1* (1939) brought a gramophone record into a public performance as an instrument – and he still only used test tones and the effect of speed changes.

Having said this, I recently learned that at a Dada event in 1920 Stefan Wolpe used eight gramophones to play records at widely different speeds simultaneously – a true precedent, but without consequences; and of course Ottorino Respighi did call for a gramophone recording of a nightingale in his 1924 *Pini di Roma* – a technicality this, but imaginative nonetheless (though a bird call would have sufficed). Moreover, Darius Milhaud (from 1922), Laszlo Moholy-Nagy at the Bauhaus (1923) and Edgard Varese (1936) had all experimented with disc manipulation, but none eventually employed them in a final work. Paul Hindemith and Ernst Toch did produce three recorded 'studies' (*Grammophonmusik*, 1929–30), but these have been lost, so it is difficult to say much about them except that, judging from the absence of offspring, their influence was clearly small.[8] More prescient, because the medium was more flexible, were sound constructions made by filmmakers in the late 1920s and 1930s, using techniques developed for film, such as splicing and montaging, and working directly onto optical film soundtrack (for instance, in Germany, Walter Ruttman's *Weekend* and Fritz Walter Bischoff's lost sound symphony, *Hallo! Hier Welle Erdball*; and, in Russia, constructivist experiments including G.V. Alexandrov's *A Sentimental Romance* and Dziga Vertov's *Enthusiasm*). There had also been some pieces of film music which featured 'various treatments of sounds' – probably created with discs before being transferred to celluloid – by such composers as Yves Baudrier, Arthur Honnegger and Maurice Jaubert (Davies, 1994).

The ideas were around, but isolated in special project applications. And strangely, optical recording techniques developed for film in the 1920s, although endowed with many of the attributes of magnetic tape, simply never crossed over into the purely musical domain – despite

Edgard Varese's visionary proposal in 1940 for an optical sound studio in Hollywood – a proposal which, needless to say, was ignored.

With so many precedents in the world of the visual arts and the long availability of the means of direct importation and plunder, it does seem surprising that it took so long for there to be similar developments in the world of music. And when, at last, the first clear intimations of the two principal elements crucial to plunderphonic practice did arrive, they arrived in two very different spheres, each surrounded by its own quite separate publicity and theory. The key works were Pierre Schaeffer's early experiments with radio sound archive discs (for example *Etude aux tourniquets*, 1948 in Schaeffer, 1990) and John Cage's unequivocal importation of ready-made material into his *Imaginary Landscape No. 4* (1951) for twelve radios; where all the sounds, voices and music were plundered whole, and at random, from the ionosphere. In 1952, *Imaginary Landscape No. 5* specified as sound material forty-two gramophone records. Thus, although Schaeffer used pre-recorded materials, these were 'concrete' sounds, not already recorded compositions; while Cage made his construction out of 'copyright' works, although this fact was purely incidental to the intention of the piece.

It was not until 1961 that an unequivocal exposition of plunderphonic techniques arrived in James Tenney's celebrated *Collage No. 1 (Blue Suede)* (Tenney, 1992), a manipulation of Elvis Presley's hit record *Blue Suede Shoes*. The gauntlet was down; Tenney had picked up a 'non art', lowbrow work and turned it into 'art'; not as with scored music by writing variations on a popular air, but simply by subjecting a gramophone record to various physical and electrical procedures. Still no copyright difficulties.

To refer or not to refer

Now, it can easily be argued that performances with – and recordings which comprise – ready-made sounds, including other people's completed works, reflect a concern endemic in twentieth-century art with art media in and of themselves, apart from all representational attributes. This can take the form, for instance, of an insistence that all that is imitation can be stripped away, leaving only sensual and essential forms with no external referents; or a belief that all semiotic systems consist of *nothing but* referentiality – signalled by the addition, as it were, of imaginary inverted commas to everything. But it is only a loss of faith, or illusion, or nerve, that stands between this century's younger belief in 'pure' languages and today's acceptance of the 'endless play of signification'. Moreover, plunderphonics can be linked, historically and theoretically, to both perceptions. Thus a recording may be considered as no more than the anonymous carrier of a 'pure' – which is to say a non-referential – sound; or it may be an instance of a text that cannot exist without reference. In the first way, as Michel Chion's 'ten commandments for an art of fixed sounds' makes clear, the composer 'distinguishes completely sounds from their sonic source ... he has done with mourning the presence of the cause' (Chion, 1991, p. 22). Here the goal is to 'purify' the sound, to strip it of its origin and memories (though it may well be that that same erased origin remains still to haunt it). In the second way, the recording, for instance a sample, may be no more than a fragment, a knowing self-reference; a version, and may be used to point at this very quality in itself.

As a found (or stolen) object, a sound is no more than available – for articulation, fragmentation, reorigination; it may be given the form of pure 'acousmatics' or made an instance of the availability and interchangeability – the flatness – of a recording, its origin not so much erased as rendered infinitely relative. These applications, of course, do not exhaust it: as a pirated cultural artefact, a found object, as debris from the sonic environment, a plundered sound also holds out an invitation to be used *because* of its cause and because of all the associations and cultural apparatus that surround it. And surely, what has been done with 'captured' visual images (Warhol, Rauschenberg, Lichtenstein), or with directly imported objects (Duchamp, the mutilated poster works of Harris, Rotella, De la Villegle and others) – all of which depend upon their actuality and provenance (as ready-mades) – can equally be done with captured 'images' of sound.

Plundered sound carries, above all, the unique ability not just *to refer* but *to be*, it offers not just a new means but a new meaning. It is this dual character that confuses the debates about originality which so vex it.

High and low

Popular musics got off to a slow start with sound piracy. Nevertheless, they soon proved far more able to explore its inherent possibilities than art musics, which even after fifty years of sporadic experiment remained unable rigorously so to do. It is interesting perhaps that Tenney, who made the most radical essay into unashamed plunder, chose popular music as his primary source. In a later piece, *Viet Flakes*, from 1967 (Tenney, 1993), he mixed pop, classical and Asian traditional musics together and in so doing drew attention to another significant facet of the life of music on gramophone records, namely that, in the same way that they conceal and level their sources, records as objects make no distinction between 'high' and 'low' culture, 'art' and 'pop'.[9] A record makes all musics equally accessible – in every sense. No special clothes are needed, no expensive tickets need be bought, no travel is necessary, one need belong to no special interest or social group, nor be in a special place at a special time. Indeed, from the moment recordings existed, a new kind of 'past' and 'present' were born – both immediately available on demand. Time and space are homogenised in the home loudspeaker or the headphone and the pop CD costs the same as the classical CD and probably comes from the same shop. All commodities are equal.

For young musicians growing up in the electric recording age, immersed in this shoreless sea of available sound, electronics, Maltese folk music, bebop, rhythm-and-blues, show tunes, film soundtracks and the latest top ten hit were all equally on tap. Tastes, interests, studies could be nourished at the pace and following the desire of the listener. Sounds, techniques and styles could flit across genres as fast as you could change a record, tune a dial or analyse and imitate what you heard. A kind of sound intoxication arose. Certainly it was the ideas and applications encountered in recorded music of all types which led a significant fringe of the teenage generation of the late 1960s into experiments with sound, stylistic bricolage, importations, the use of noise, electronics, 'inappropriate' instruments and – crucially – recording techniques.[10] The influence of art music and especially the work of Varese, Schaeffer, Stockhausen and others cannot be overestimated in this context and, more than anything, it would be the crossplay between high and low art that would feature increasingly as a vital factor in the development of much innovative music. In plunderphonics too, the leakages – or maybe simply synchronicities – between productions in what were once easily demarcated as belonging in high or low art discourses, are blatant. Indeed, in more and more applications, the distinction is meaningless and impossible to draw.

But there are simpler reasons for the special affinity between low art and plundering. For instance, although the first plunder pieces (viz. the early *concrète* and the Cage works mentioned) belonged firmly in the art camp, blatant plundering nevertheless remained fairly off limits there, precluded essentially by the non-negotiable concern with originality and peer status – and also with the craft aspect of creating from scratch: originating out of a 'creative centre' rather than 'just messing about with other people's work'. The world of low art had few such scruples: indeed, in a profound sense plundering was endemic to it – in the 'folk' practices of copying and covering for instance (few people played original compositions), or in the use of public domain forms and genres as vessels for expressive variation (the blues form, sets of stand-ard chord progressions and so on). The twentieth-century art kind of originality and novelty simply was not an issue here. Moreover, in the 'hands on', low expectation, *terra nova* world of rock, musicians were happy to make fools of themselves 'rediscovering America' the hard way.

What I find especially instructive was how, in a sound world princi-pally mediated by recording, high and low art worlds increasingly appropriated from one another. Also, how problems that were glossed over when art was art and there was no genre confusion (like Tenney's appropriation of copyright, but lowbrow, recordings) suddenly threat-ened to become dangerously problematic when genres blurred and both plunder and original began to operate in the same disputed (art/com-mercial) space.

Low art takes a hand

Rock precedents for pure studio tapework come from Frank Zappa, with his decidedly Varese-esque concrete pieces on the albums *Abso-lutely Free*, *Lumpy Gravy* and *Only In It For The Money*, all made in 1967. *Only In It For The Money* also contains an unequivocally plun-dered Surf music extract, and The Beatles's pure tapework on *Tomorrow Never Knows* from the 1966 album *Revolver*. *Revolution No 9* on *The White Album* is also full of plundered radio material. In the early 1960s radios were ubiquitous in the high art world and in some intermediary groups such as AMM and Faust (in the latter, on their second UK tour, guest member Uli Trepte played 'Space Box' – a short-wave radio and effects – as his main instrument).

Such examples – taken in combination with, first, the increasing independence, confidence and self-consciousness of some rock musi-cians; second, a generation of musicians coming out of art schools; third, the mass availability of ever cheaper home recording equipment; and, finally, a climate of experiment and plenitude – made straight-forward plunder inevitable. This promise was first substantially filled by The Residents (1974/1987). Their second released album, *Third Reich and Roll* (1975), a highly self-reflexive commentary on rock culture and hit records, curiously employed a technique analogous to that used by Stockhausen (1970) for his Beethoven Anniversary recording, *Opus 1970*, which had nothing to do with influence and everything to do with the medium. What Stockhausen had done was to prepare tapes of fragments of Beethoven's music which ran continuously throughout the performance of the piece. Each player could open and shut his own loudspeaker at will and was instantaneously to 'develop' what he heard instrumentally (condense, extend, transpose, modulate, synchronise, imitate, distort). To different ends The Residents followed a similar procedure: instead of Beethoven, they copied well known pop songs to one track of a four-track tape to which they then played along (transposed, modulated, distorted, commented on, intensified), thus building up tracks. Though they subsequently erased most of the source material, you can often, as with *Opus 1970*, still hear the plundered originals breaking through.

In 1977 it was The Residents again who produced the first unequivocal 100 per cent plunder to come out of pop, following in the high art footsteps of James Tenney's Presley-based *Collage No. 1*, and the later, more successful work *Omaggio a Jerry Lee Lewis* by American composer Richard Trythall (Trythall, 1977) (plundered from various recordings of Lewis's *Whole Lotta Shakin' Goin' On*). Trythall comments: 'Like the table or newspaper in a cubist painting, the familiar musical object served the listener as an orientation point within a maze of new material, ... the studio manipulations ... carried the source material into new, unexpected areas, while maintaining its past associations' (programme note on ReR CMCD (Trythall, 1977)). The Residents's work was a 7-inch single titled *Beyond The Valley Of A Day In The Life* and subtitled 'The Residents Play The Beatles/The Beatles Play The Residents'. It came packaged as an art object in a numbered, limited edition and hand-silkscreened cover, but was sold to – and known by – a rock public. One side of this single was a cover version of The Beatles song *Flying*. The other was pure plunderphonics. This whole side was assembled from extracts dubbed off Beatles records, looped, multitracked, composed with razor blades and tape. It is an ingenious construction, and remains a landmark.

Sampling and scratching

Although there were some notable experiments and a few successful productions, tape and disc technologies made plundering difficult and time-consuming and thus suitable only for specific applications. What brought plundering to the centre of mass consumption low art music was a new technology that made sound piracy so easy that it did not make sense not to do it. This development was digital sampling, launched affordably by Ensoniq in the mid-1980s. Digital sampling is a purely electronic digital recording system which takes samples or 'vertical slices' of sound and converts them into binary information, into data, which tells a sound producing system how to reconstruct, rather than reproduce it – instantly.

At a fast enough sampling rate the detailed contours of a sound can be so minutely traced that playback quality is comparable with any analogue recording system. The revolutionary power associated with a digital system is that the sound when stored consists of information in a form that can be transformed, edited or rewritten electronically, without 'doing' anything to any actual analogue recording but only to a code. This really is a kind of a writing. When it is stored, modified or reproduced, no grooves, magnetised traces or any other contiguous imprint link the sound to its means of storage (by imprint I mean as when an object is pressed into soft wax and leaves its analogue trace). It is stored rather as discrete data, which act as instructions for the eventual reconstruction of a sound (as a visual object when electronically scanned is translated only into a binary code). Digital sampling allows any recorded sound to be linked to a keyboard or to a Midi trigger and, using electronic tools (computer software), to be stretched, visualised on screen as waveforms and rewritten or edited with keys or a light pencil. All and any parameters can be modified and any existing electronic processing applied. Only at the end of all these processes will an audible sound be recreated. This may then be listened to and, if it is not what is wanted, reworked until it is, and only then saved. It means that a work like Cage's four-minute long *Williams Mix* (the first tape collage made in America), which took a year to cut together, could now be programmed and executed quite quickly using only a domestic computer.

The mass application is even more basic. It simply puts any sound it records – or which has been recorded and stored as software – on a normal keyboard, pitched according to the key touched. The user can record, model and assign to the keys any sounds at all. At last here is a musical instrument which is a recording device and a performing instrument, whose voice is simply the control and modulation of recordings. How could this technology not give the green light to plundering? It was so simple. No expertise was needed, just a user-friendly keyboard, some stuff to sample (records and CDs are easy – and right there at home), and plenty of time to try things out. Producing could be no more than critical consuming; an empirical activity of 'Pick 'n' Mix'. Nor was that all. Sampling was introduced into a musical climate where in low art plundering was already deeply established in the form of 'scratching', which in its turn echoed in a radically sophisticated form the disc manipulation techniques innovated in high culture by Hindemith and Koch, Milhaud, Varese, Honegger, Kagel, Cary, Schaeffer et al., but now guided by a wholly different aesthetic.

From scratch

The term 'scratching' was coined to describe the practice of the realtime manipulation of 12-inch discs on highly adapted turntables. It grew up in US discos where DJs began to programme the records they played, running them together, cutting one into another on beat and in key, superimposing, crossfading and so on. Soon this developed to the point where a good DJ could play records as an accompanying or soloing instrument, along with a rhythm box, other tracks or singing. New and extended techniques emerged: for instance the rhythmic slipping of a disc to and fro rapidly by hand on a low friction mat to create rhythms and cross rhythms, alongside old *concrète* techniques: controlled speed alterations and *sillons fermés* riffs.

> Two manual decks and a rhythm box is all you need. Get a bunch of good rhythm records, choose your favourite parts and groove along with the rhythm machine. Using your hands, scratch the record by repeating the grooves you dig so much. Fade one record into the other and keep that rhythm box going. Now start talking and singing over the record with your own microphone. Now you're making your own music out of other people's records. That's what scratching is (McLaren, 1982).

It was only after scratching had become fashionable in the mid-1970s in radical black disco music that it moved back toward art applications, adopted quite brilliantly by Christian Marclay (Marclay, 1988). Marclay used all the above techniques and more, and also incorporated an idea of Milan Knizac's, who had been experimenting since 1963 with deliberately mutilated discs, particularly composite discs comprising segments of different records glued together. Of course, everything Marclay does (like Knizac) is 100 per cent plundered, but on some recordings he too, like John Oswald on his seminal *Plunderphonic* recordings, creates works which, echoing Tenney and Trythall, concentrate on a single artist, thus producing a work which is about an artist and made only from that artist's sonic simulacrum. Listen, for instance, to the *Maria Callas* and *Jimi Hendrix* tracks on the 10-inch EP *More Encores* (subtitled 'Christian Marclay plays with the records of Louis Armstrong, Jane Birkin & Serge Gainsbourg, John Cage, Maria Callas, Frederic Chopin,

Martin Denney, Arthur Ferrante & Louis Teicher, Fred Frith, Jimi Hendrix, Christian Marclay, Johann Strauss, John Zorn'). Marclay rose to prominence as a member of the early 1980s New York scene, on the experimental fringe of what was still thought of unequivocally as low art. He emerged from the context of disco and scratching, not *concrète* or other artworld experiments, with discs (though they were part of his personal history). His cultural status (like the status of certain other alumni of the New York school such as John Zorn) slowly shifted, from low to high, via gallery installations and visual works and through the release of records such as *Record Without A Cover* (1985), which has only one playable side (the other has titles and text pressed into it) and comes unwrapped with the instruction: 'Do not store in a protective package'. Then there was the 1987 grooveless LP, packaged in a black suede pouch and released in a limited and signed edition of 50 by Ecart Editions. Marclay's work appears as a late flowering of an attenuated and, even at its height, marginal high art form, reinvented and reinvigorated by low art creativity. It traces the radical inter-penetrations of low and high art in the levelling age of sound recording; the swing between high art experiment, low art creativity and high art reappropriation, as the two approach one another until, at their fringes, they become indistinguishable. This aesthetic levelling is a property of the medium and this indistinguishability signals not a collapse but the coming into being of a new aesthetic form.

Oswald plays records

Curiously, the apotheosis of the record as an instrument – as the raw material of a new creation – occurred just as the gramophone record itself was becoming obsolete and when a new technology that would surpass the wildest ambitions of any scratcher, acousmaticist, tape composer or sound organiser was sweeping all earlier record/playback production systems before it. Far from destroying disc manipulation, sampling seems to have breathed new life into it. Turntable techniques live on in live House and Techno. Marclay goes from strength to strength, more credits for 'turntables' appear on many different CDs and younger players like Otomo Yoshihide are emerging with an even more organic and intimate relation to the record/player as an expressive instrument.[11]

It is almost as if sampling had recreated the gramophone record as a craft instrument, an analogue, expressive voice, made authentic by nostalgia. Obsolescence empowers a new mythology for the old phonograph, completing the circle from passive repeater to creative producer, from dead mechanism to expressive voice, from the death of performance to its guarantee. It is precisely the authenticity of the 12-inch disc that keeps it in manufacture; it has become anachronistically indispensable.

Disc-tape-disc

Applications of a new technology to art are often first inspired by existing art paradigms, frequently simplifying or developing existing procedures. Then new ideas emerge that more directly engage the technology for itself. These arise as a product of use, accident, experiment or cross fertilisation – but always through hands-on interaction. New applications then feed back again into new uses of the old technologies and so on. For a long time such dynamic inter-penetrations can drive aspects of both. Painting and film, for instance, have just such a productive history. A similar process could be traced in the tension between recording and performance. A particularly obvious example of this is the way that hard cuts and edits made with tape for musical effect inspire played 'edits' – brilliantly exemplified in the work of John Zorn. This process can be traced more broadly, and more profoundly, in the growth and refinement of the new sound aesthetic itself, which from its origins in the crisis in art music at the turn of the century through to contemporary practices in many fields, is characterised by the dynamic interactions between fluid and fixed media. New instrumental techniques inform, and are informed by, new recording techniques. Each refines a shared sonic language, sets problems, makes propositions. Each takes a certain measure of itself from the other, both living and dead: 'Records are ... dead' as Christian Marclay carefully points out.[12]

More dead than quick

What is essential, and new, is that by far the largest part of the music that we hear is recorded music, live music making up only a small percentage of our total listening. Moreover, recording is now the primary medium through which musical ideas and inspiration spread (this says nothing about quality, it is merely a quantitative fact). For example, one of the gravitational centres of improvisation, which is in every respect the antithesis of fixed sound or notated music, is its relation to recorded sound, including recordings of itself or of other improvisations.

This performance-recording loop winds through the rise of jazz as a mass culture music, through rock experiments and on to the most abstract noise productions of today. Whatever living music does, chances are that the results will be recorded – and this will be their immortality. In the new situation, it is only what is not recorded that belongs to its participants while what is recorded is placed inevitably in the public domain.

Moreover, as noted earlier, recorded music leaves its genre community and enters the universe of recordings. As such the mutual interactions between composers, performers and recordings refer back to sound and structure and not to particular music communities. Leakage, seepage, adoption, osmosis, abstraction, contagion: these describe the life of sound work today. They account for the general aesthetic convergence at the fringes of genres once mutually exclusive, and across the gulf of high and low art. There is a whole range of sound work now, about which it simply makes no sense to speak in terms of high or low, art or popular, indeed where the two interpenetrate so deeply that to attempt to discriminate between them is to fail to understand the sound revolution which has been effected through the medium of sound recording.

Plunderphonics addresses precisely this realm of the recorded. It treats of the point where both public domain and contemporary sound world meet the transformational and organisational aspects of recording technology; where listening and production, criticism and creation elide. It is also where copyright law from another age cannot follow, where – as Oswald himself remarked – 'If creativity is a field, copyright is the fence'.[13]

Pop eats itself

I want to look now at some of the many applications of plundering beyond those of directly referential or self-reflexive intent like those of Tenney, Trythall, The Residents, Oswald and Marclay.

First, and most obvious, is the widespread plundering of records for samples that are recycled on Hip Hop, House and Techno records in particular, but increasingly on pop records in general. This means that drum parts, bass parts (often loops of a particular bar), horn parts, all manner of details (James Brown whoops etc.) will be dubbed off records and built up layer by layer into a new piece. This is essentially the same procedure as that adopted by The Residents in their Beatles piece, except that nowadays the range and power of electronic treatments is far greater than before and the results achieved are of far greater technical complexity. Rhythms and tempi can be adjusted and synchronised, pitches altered, dynamic shape rewritten, and so on. Selections sampled may be traceable or untraceable, it need not matter. Reference is not the aim so much as a kind of creative consumerism, a bricolage assembly from parts. Rather than start with instruments or a score, you start with a large record and CD collection and then copy, manipulate and laminate.

Moral and copyright arguments rage around this. Following several copyright infringement cases, bigger studios employ someone to note all samples and to register and credit all composers, artists and original recording owners. 'Sampling licences' are negotiated and paid for. This is hugely time consuming and slightly ridiculous and really not an option for amateurs and small fish. Oswald's *Plexure*, for instance, has so many tiny cuts and samples on it that, not only are their identities impossible to register by listening, but compiling credit data would be like assembling a telephone directory for a medium sized town. Finding, applying, accounting and paying the 4000-plus copyright and patent holders would likewise be a full-time occupation, effectively impossible. Therefore such works simply could not exist. We have to address the question whether this is what we really want.

For now, I am more interested in the way pop really starts to eat itself. Here together are cannibalism, laziness and the feeling that everything has already been originated, so that it is enough endlessly to reinterpret and rearrange it all. The old idea of originality in production gives way to another (if to one at all) of originality in consumption, in hearing.

Cassiber

Other applications use plundered parts principally as sound elements, which relate in a constitutive or alienated way to the syntax of a piece. They may or may not carry referential weight, this being only one optional attribute which the user may choose to employ. The Anglo-German group Cassiber (comprising Chris Cutler, Heiner Goebbels and Christoph Anders (Cassiber, 1990)) uses just such techniques in which samples act both as structure and as fragments of cultural debris. Cassiber creates complexities; no piece is reducible to a score, a set of instructions, a formula. Simultaneity and superimposed viewpoints are characteristic of much of the work – as is the tension between invention and passion on the one hand and 'dead' materials on the other.

When the group was formed, singer Christoph Anders worked with a table stacked with prepared cassettes, each containing loops or raw extracts taken from all manner of musics (on one Cassiber piece, there might be fragments of Schubert, Schoenberg, The Shangri-La's, Maria Callas and Them). The invention of the sampler put in his hands a similar facility, except with more material and infinitely greater transformational power, all accessible immediately on a normal keyboard. It means that, in a way impossible – though desired – before, they can be *played*. They can be as unstable as any performed musical part – and as discontinuous. Cassiber's use of familiar fragments, though these are often recognisable – and thus clearly referential – does not depend on this quality, which is accepted merely as a possible aspect, but rather on their musical role within the piece. Where House and Rap use samples to reinforce what is familiar, Goebbels and Anders use them to make the familiar strange, dislocated, more like debris – but (and this is the key) as structural rather than decorative debris. It is an effect only plundered materials can deliver.[14]

The issue

What is the issue? Is it whether sound can be copyrighted, or snatches of a performance? If so, where do we draw the line: at length or recognisability? Or does mass produced, mass disseminated music have a kind of folk status? Is it so ubiquitous and so involuntary (you are obliged to be immersed in it much of your waking time) that it falls legitimately into the category of 'public domain'? Since violent action (destruction of works, legal prohibition, litigation and distraint) have been applied by one side of the argument, these are questions we cannot avoid.

Review of applications

There it is

There are cases such as that of Cage, in *Imaginary Landscape nos 2* and *4*, where materials are all derived directly from records or radio and subjected to various manipulations. Though there are copyright implications, the practice implies that music picked randomly 'out of the air' is simply there. Most of Cage's work is more a kind of listening than a kind of producing.

Partial importations

An example of partial importation is *My Life in the Bush of Ghosts* (Eno and Byrne, 1994) and the work of Italians Roberto Musci and Giovanni Venosta (1990). In both cases recordings of ethnic music are used as important voices and the rest of the material is constructed around them. The same might be done with whale songs, sound effects records and so on; I detect political implications in the absence of copyright problems on such recordings. At least, it is far from obvious to me why an appeal to public domain status should be any more or less valid for 'ethnic' music than it is for most pop – or any other recorded music.

Total importation

This might rather be thought of as interpretation or re-hearing of existing recordings. Here we are in the territory of Tenney, Trythall, The Residents, Marclay and quintessentially, of plunderphonic pioneer John Oswald. Existing recordings are not randomly or instrumentally incorporated so much as they become the simultaneous subject and object of a creative work. Current copyright law is unable to distinguish between a plagiarised and a new work in such cases, since its concerns are still drawn from old pen and paper paradigms. In the visual arts Duchamp with ready-mades, Warhol with soupcans and brillo boxes, Lichtenstein with cartoons and Sherry Levine with re-photographed 'famous' photographs are only some of the many who have, one way or another, broached the primary artistic question of 'originality', which Oswald too cannot help but raise.

Sources irrelevant

This is where recognition of parts plundered is not necessary or important. There is no self-reflexivity involved; sound may be drawn as if 'out of nothing', bent to new purposes or simply used as raw material. Also within this category falls the whole mundane universe of sampling or stealing 'sounds': drum sounds (not parts), guitar chords, riffs, vocal interjections and so on, sometimes creatively used but more often simply a way of saving time and money. Why spend hours creating or copying a sound when you can snatch it straight off a CD and get it into your own sampler-sequencer?

Sources untraceable

These are manipulations which take the sounds plundered and stretch and treat them so radically that it is impossible to divine their source at all. Techniques like these are used in electronic, concrete, acousmatic, radiophonic, film and other abstract sound productions. Within these lies a whole universe of viewpoints. For instance, the positive exploration of new worlds of sound and new possibilities of aestheticisation – or the idea that there is no need to originate any more, since what is already there offers such endless possibilities – or the expression of an implied helplessness in the face of contemporary conditions: namely, everything that can be done has been done and we can only rearrange the pieces. This is a field where what may seem to be quite similar procedures may nevertheless express such wildly different understandings as a hopeless tinkering amidst the ruins or a celebration of the infinitude of the infinitesimal.

Final comments

Several currents run together here. There is the technological aspect: plundering is impossible in the absence of sound recording. There is the cultural aspect: since the turn of the century the importation of ready-made materials into artworks has been a common practice, and one which has accumulated eloquence and significance. The re-seeing or re-hearing of familiar material is a well established practice and, in high art at least, accusations of plagiarism are seldom raised. More to the point, the two-way traffic between high and low art (each borrowing and quoting from the other) has proceeded apace. Today it is often impossible to draw a clear line between them – witness certain advertisements, Philip Glass, Jeff Koons, New York subway graffiti.

It seems inevitable that in such a climate the applications of a recording technology that gives instant playback, transposition and processing facilities will not be intimidated by the old proscriptions of plagiarism or the ideal of originality. What is lacking now is a discourse under which the new practices can be discussed and adjudicated. The old values and paradigms of property and copyright, skill, originality, harmonic logic, design and so forth are simply not adequate to the task. Until we are able to give a good account of what is being done, how to think and speak about it, it will remain impossible to adjudicate between legitimate and illegitimate works and applications. Meanwhile outrages such as those perpetrated on John Oswald will continue unchecked.

A final note: on proportion

Current copyright law differs from country to country, but in general follows international accords. It certainly allows 'fair use' which would include parody, quotation and reference, though these may need to be argued and defended. This is a minefield in which only lawyers profit. So where The Beatles had to pay up for quoting *In The Mood* at the end of *All You Need Is Love*, and Oswald had his work destroyed, Two Live Crew's parody of Roy Orbison's *Pretty Woman* got off free as 'fair use'. Or take Negativland's parody of U2's *I Still Haven't Found What I'm Looking For* (1991). This was also recalled and destroyed after Island Records sued the group and its record company, identifying illegally stolen samples as one of the main causes. But Negativland are famous precisely for their tapework and cut-up techniques, as well as their sharp fragmenting and commenting on the media debris by which we are all, like it or not, daily assaulted. This piece was funny, as well as telling and not commercial – in all these respects unlike the record by Two Live Crew. It and the group and the record company all got hammered (all copies recalled and destroyed, $25,000 fine and other financial penalties, assignation of Negativland's rights to Island records). Now compare the case of disco mixers DNA who made a techno manipulation of Suzanne Vega's song *Tom's Diner*, released it on an independent label, sold a few thousand copies and then, when Vega's record company heard it, were offered not a crippling lawsuit but a deal for an 'official' release. Questions of works unstarted, or only circulating privately, or of a climate where ideas and opportunities are simply abandoned – all for fear of copyright difficulties – are not even broached here. There is no proportion because there is no clarity. The rethinking of copyright law is long overdue. Recording has been with us now for more than 100 years.

Postcript: everyday sample and plunder

I have restricted myself above to artworld precedents and applications of plunderphones but, of course, sampling and 'electroquotation' have long been endemic to the production of rap and other popular musics. In 1994 I interviewed freelance studio engineer Bob Drake about his work with Ice T. and other rap artists. He described what was then standard practice. Since then, the technology has been radically updated and is even easier to use; indeed composing with other people's work has now been thoroughly integrated into instrument design and studio practice.

A typical group's producer has a machine like a Linn/Akai MPC60, which has 12 pads like a drum machine, lots of memory for sequencing, and most important, it's a huge sampler too. This person spends time at home with their huge record collection finding suitable bits to build a new song with. Usually they'll start with a drum loop, perhaps from a James Brown record – 1, 2 maybe 4 bars. Then a loop with a bass line (maybe with drums on too) say from the Zapp band – 1 or 2 bars. Horn section from an Earth, Wind and Fire album, electric piano from some incredibly obscure funk album, add a few more drum loops to fatten it up and give it a rolling, driving feel. Some percussion, tambourine, hi-hat samples. A lot of producers have their own 'signature' hi-hat and tambourines which they use on all their stuff and won't tell anyone where they sampled them from; if you recognise it you're a true fanatic scholar of all the old records. The 808 kick drum is a major part of the sound, the 'boom'. It comes from the Roland TR 808 drum machine if you turn the decay on the bass drum all the way up. Very few people actually own an 808, but there are plenty of samples around. You can also make a good boom by sampling an oscillator, somewhere between 60–100 Hertz and adding a regular kick drum sample to it. The sound is so deep it can be way up in the mix like it's supposed to be and not get in the way of anything else.

So all these loops and sounds are put on different pads on the MPC60 and sequenced into a song form. Before it's actually a song, with breaks, choruses and so on, the whole big rolling piles of samples and loops is called a 'beat'. But to arrive at this, getting all the loops and samples – most of which were originally in different tempi – to play in perfect synch with one another, is a whole job in itself. They all have to be synched up with the metronome in the sequencer. Drummers speeding up and slowing down with the four bars of a sample, horn sections slightly behind or ahead of the beat – all the natural human 'imperfections' – sometimes make it necessary to break a loop into two or four separate segments, shortening or lengthening each to get it 'in time'. All these loops have little idiosyncrasies, people talking, band/audience members shouting, stuff going on in the background, scratches and pops from the old vinyl, all of which add up and contribute to the overall end sound.

When it's been shaped into a song, it's all printed on the multitrack, each sample and loop on its own track and the 'live' parts are added: maybe a bass guitar, wah-wah guitar, sax. Then the vocals and scratches. The scratches are added by the DJ, the guy with the turntable and crates full of old records. The DJ is almost like a soloist and spaces are left in the song structure for scratching, the same way a rock band leaves a space for a guitar solo and for fills and flavouring throughout the song. They're really good at knowing just where to get the right little phrases and sounds which somehow relate to the lyrics of the song, often rearranging the words of an old song, or piecing lines from several songs together to make them say what they want for the new song. A really great DJ is unbelievable and fun to watch and listen to: real performers (Cutler, 1994, p. 13).

Notes

1. As I have argued in 'Necessity and choice in musical forms', section II (i), in Cutler (1991).
2. There were sporadic experiments, as we shall see, and notably Varese grasped the nettle early. Pierre Schaeffer made the radical proposal, but precisely from his work as an engineer, and not emerging out of the art music tradition. A few followed – Stockhausen, Berio, Nono and others – and new schools formed which in part or whole abandoned mediating notation (concrete, electronic, acousmatic, electroacoustic musics, for example), but these too tried to retain, so far as was possible, the old status and values for their creators, merely replacing the score with direct personal manipulation, and continuing to make the same claims to originality, personal ownership, creation *ex nihilo*, etc. John Cage was an interesting exception: his originality and individuality were claimed precisely in their negation.
3. For the full argument of this claim see 'Necessity and choice in musical forms', section III (ii), in Cutler (1991).
4. The first Copyright Act in England was passed in 1709. The current Act dates from 1988 and includes rights of the author to remuneration for all public performances (including broadcasts, jukeboxes, muzak, fairground rides, concerts, discotheques, film, TV and so on) as well as for recordings of all kinds. The recording is copyrighted separately from the composition, so that every individual recording of a composition also has an owner.
5. Most copyright bodies still discriminate between works which earn a lot by the minute ('serious' composed works) and those which earn a little (pop music, for instance and improvised compositions). Criteria for making such decisions vary, reflecting the prejudices of the day.
6. Which is to say, where it raises questions that reflect upon its own identity.
7. And through its documentary authenticity also in the realm of the political, as the purity of the retouched photograph and doctored tape attest.
8. Hugh Davies recently brought to my attention a report from a 1993 conference in Berlin where it was reported that in the mid-1980s Hindemith's discs had been offered to the director of a German musicological institute. He refused them after which they were almost certainly destroyed.
9. I shall treat the quotation marks as read from here on.
10. See Cutler (1991) chapters on The Residents, Necessity and Choice, Progressive Music in the UK.
11. Hear, for instance, his 'Ground Zero' recording *Revolutionary Pekinese Opera* (Yoshihide, 1986).
12. From an interview with J. Dean Kuipers *Ear* magazine (1993).

13. From the Plunderphonic CD booklet.
14. For example *Start the show* from the CD *A face we all know* (Cassiber, 1990).

References

Chion, Michel (1991), *L'Art des sons fixés*, Fontaine: Editions Metamkine/Nota Bene/Sono-Concept.
Cutler, Chris (1991), 'Necessity and choice in musical forms', III(i), *File Under Popular*, London: ReR Megacorp (revised edition).
Cutler, Chris (1994), 'Sampling notes: in the studio', *unfiled: Music Under New Technology* (ReR/Recommended Sourcebook 0401) pp. 13–14.
Davies, Hugh (1994), 'A history of sampling', *unfiled: Music Under New Technology* (ReR/Recommended Sourcebook 0401) pp. 5–12.
Kostelanetz, Richard (ed.) (1971), *John Cage*, London: Allen Lane/ Penguin.
McLaren, Malcolm (1982), *B-Bu-Buffalo Gals* (sleeve note), Charisma: MALC12.

Recordings

Cassiber (1990), *A Face We All Know*, ReR: CCD 1989.
Coltrane, John (1961), *My Favourite Things*, Atlantic: 7567-81346-2.
Eno, Brian and Byrne, David (1994), *My Life in the Bush of Ghosts*, EG: EGCD 48.
Marclay, Christian (1988), *More Encores.* (EP) No Man's Land: NML 8816.
Musci, Roberto and Venosta, Giovanni (1990), *Messages and Portraits*, ReR: MVCD1.
Negativland (1991) *U2*, SST CD 272 (destroyed).
Oswald, John (1988/1998), *Plunderphonics* (EP), released by John Oswald; *Plunderphonic* (CD) (1989), as previous (destroyed); *Discosphere* (CD) (1991), ReR: JOCD; *Plexure* (CD) (1993), Avant: AVAN 16.
The Residents (1974/1987), *The Beatles Play The Residents/The Residents Play The Beatles*, (7-inch single), Ralph Records (1974); (CD reissue *Third Reich and Roll* bonus track), (1987) East Side Digital: ESD 80032.
Schaeffer, Pierre (1990), *L'oeuvre musicale intégrale*, INA/GRM: C1006-1009.

Stockhausen, Karlheinz (1970), *Opus 1970*, Deutsche Grammophon (LP): 139 461.

Tenney, James (1992), *Collage No. 1 (Blue Suede)*, 'Selected Works' (CD), Artifact: FP001.

Tenney, James (1993), *Viet Flakes*, MusicWorks: MW56.

Trythall, Richard (1977), *Ommagio a Jerry Lee Lewis*, CRI (LP) (1977): SD 302; ReR (CD): CMCD 1980.

Yoshihide, Otomo [Ground Zero] (1986), *Revolutionary Pekinese Opera*, ReR: GZ1.

Acknowledgements

This chapter, published in two parts in *Resonance*, 3(2) and 4(1), was commissioned and originally published in *MusicWorks*, 60 (Fall 1994).

CHAPTER FIVE

Crossing cultural boundaries through technology?

Simon Emmerson

Introduction

In recent years there has been an increasing interest in the use of instruments (and their performance traditions) from other, usually non-western, cultures in contemporary western art music in general and electroacoustic music in particular. Many such instruments come from highly developed traditions which may be little understood by the western composer; many performance practices, attitudes and aesthetics may likewise be misunderstood in both directions. The problems and opportunities afforded by technology becomes a major issue.

This chapter examines the possible bases for such intercultural interactions from the composer's perspective. But the relationship of academic writer to composer is complex. The academic claims some degree of 'objectivity' – a more reflective approach might be to take back this difficult word and at least claim 'reason' as being a touchstone. But as for the composer we are faced with an immediate paradox: within the western (Euro-American) tradition *composers are never wrong*! They may be good, bad or misguided, but never 'right' or 'wrong'.[1]

But what extraordinary hubris is this? Upon what pedestal has the composer been placed? (A dangerous and unstable place to be at the best of times.) One reason for this increasing isolation (though not the elevation) is quite simple: within this tradition the composer's influences and output have become increasingly dislocated. The encouragement to 'be original' (which we shall return to) leads increasingly to a concealment of overt models from the past. The origins of a work must appear to lie as much as possible within the composer's sphere and the job of 'teasing out' the lineage of the ideas falls to the analytical historian. The larger pattern emerges only afterwards.

Composers have also been 'magpies' in their voracious appetites for finding fuel for their inspiration; but never so much as in the twentieth century has this appetite been so explicitly declared, from the sciences, philosophy, other arts and humanities – and increasingly these have come from other cultures. The composer, however, has often appropriated these ideas through strongly filtered sources. So-called 'Great Art' has often been created from complete misunderstanding. Composers have frequently been allowed to get away with cultural murder.[2]

I am concerned in this chapter, therefore, with the meta-level of the composition. I will attempt to examine the complex tensions and interactions in relating two traditions within one composition; no attempt will be made to hide contradictions, delusions (including self-delusions) on the part of composer and performers. The question will be addressed as to what forms successful acculturation between two highly developed traditions might take.

I will attempt the impossible: to combine my role as academic and composer and to try to confront these issues with two case studies, two works combining eastern and western resources. My work *Pathways* is for flute, cello, sitar, tablas, keyboard (controlling sampler) and live electronics, written in 1989. It was written for the ensemble Shiva Nova whose policy was at the time to combine classical Indian and western instruments and performance traditions, using electronic resources if demanded. Second, *Points of Return* a work for kayagum (Korean zither) and electronics provisionally completed in 1998.[3]

'Tradition': description or definition?

Traditions have fuzzy edges, both in space and time. Even to define a tradition at all may be to fall into the trap of reifying the notion after the event, yet we use the term for want of a better. We must beware that empiricism does not give way to dogmatism. For example, as 'classical sonata form' was observed, codified and hence frozen within the pedagogical frameworks of mid-nineteenth century Europe, so we must be careful to *describe* rather than to *define* our traditions. Traditions contain a varying balance of change and continuity; enough of one to adapt to changing circumstances, enough of the other to maintain a sense of identity and continuity.

There is inevitably a problem of language and translation. In cases such as these, I may not be comparing like with like at any level: terms translated as 'melody', 'tonality' and 'rhythm' may, of course, carry quite different meanings and connotations between different traditions.[4] Practice, however, will not wait upon linguistic niceties. In the past, migrations (voluntary or forced) have caused more than usually severe discontinuities and juxtapositions.[5] In setting about an intercultural exchange without such immediate pressures – as in work, religion, relaxation or other practical needs – we inevitably establish more 'aesthetic' expectations and elevate the enterprise from artisan to 'art'. This is a millstone we must attempt to throw off.

The first problem we encounter is that we must overcome the generalisations of common speech and, for that matter, of academic writing. Do I represent any tradition at all? If so, to what extent? The progressive fragmentation of western art music into a multiplicity of approaches during the twentieth century gives me *a priori* an identity crisis, or more properly an identification crisis.

Someone else may try to pigeonhole me into an identifiable school or tradition; I might accept, but I may more likely resist. The same holds true for the European-trained members of Shiva Nova who may be called upon to interpret a wide range of styles and approaches as professional musicians. They, too, cannot be pigeonholed into a single tradition.

But let us look at that again: am I not now generalising at a different level, namely that of style? To say that western art music has no single identifiable style is to say very little – nor have the many musics of Africa and Asia. But for a brief moment since the Renaissance the ideal was assumed to be a unity and universality of values, transcending the 'local', finally emerging in ideas for 'absolute music' in Europe in the nineteenth century. If the style convergence of this tradition (always somewhat fuzzy at its French and Russian fringes) was brief and limited, the ghosts of this universal and catholic thinking survive into the relationships I want to examine. My value systems are certainly determined:

1. by a view of notation;
2. by assumptions on the relation of composer and performer;
3. by assumptions on the fixity of the work.

Such meta-structures of western art music are more impervious to change than their contemporary manifestation in a variety of styles leads us to believe. Indeed, these have even emphasised if we consider that the footprints of the well intentioned revolutions of the 1960s have all but been washed away.[6]

But this particular view of history – in terms of 'movements' and 'meta-structures' – gives me little credit for self-awareness and appears to remove my responsibility for my own destiny.[7] These definitions of 'my' tradition are not 'natural' but 'cultural' variables. But are they infinitely variable by me at will? I cannot believe so. The nature and behaviour of the physical world defines the absolutes of the field in which I operate, culture its 'accepted' areas of use and their 'value' – different for different groups, places and times. I operate within these constraints – a bounded free will.

Western art music evolved not only low-level composition rules but also a higher order set of assumptions about its own evolution (which encompasses occasionally a revolution) at the same time:

1. 'My' tradition since the Renaissance has given me increasing encouragement to believe I can do anything, indeed that I should not replicate what has been done before. Yet -

2. This rests on an assumption that there are rules to break in the first place which have some sort of 'natural basis'. This only the 'true artist' can understand, thus creating new models – at its most extreme 'the music of the future' – from the old. This, it is agreed, is the antidote to a conservative and academic approach to 'passing on the tradition' (the 'Beckmesser tradition', we might say)[8] and is the basis of the romantic ideal of 'musical progress'.[9]

Such centrifugal and fragmentary forces lie deep in the nature of the ideology relating individual and group in post-renaissance European art and science. We should not forget that the phrase *avant-garde* was first used by Henri de Saint-Simon in France (1825) at almost exactly the same time as Mendelssohn's inauguration of the museum culture in western concert music with the revival of Bach's Matthew Passion (1829) – the past and the future at once, western civilisation's triumphal claim to conquest over all time, let alone all space.[10]

But these generalisations may be made both ways. Do I label the Indian-trained members of Shiva Nova as representative of 'their' tradition? The schools of vocal or instrumental performance (*gharanas*) are as varied and rival each other as do the performance traditions of western Europe (Neuman, 1990, ch.5).

A generation of performers retaining their direct pedagogic links to the Indian subcontinent is giving way to the first generation taught largely outside of India. The same tensions exist between some eastern art music and popular and vernacular forms as have existed increasingly in the west between 'pop' and 'art' musics. The problem facing us is how to present an alternative to great traditions joining the club of alienated art forms within the museum culture of the West while avoiding the pitfalls of the commercialisation of the worst of 'world music' marketing.[11]

Beyond the crude exchange

Following on from our examination of generalisations, we can easily eliminate some of the cruder examples of stylistic exchange that composers may wish to carry out. 'Improvisation' is an inadequate word to describe the intricate through-composition of the *raga*. To transplant it to musicians untrained in the necessary listening and performance processes through long days of practice would be a crass mistake which would not be corrected by giving composers courses in Indian music (even, I stress, in its practice) if these did not reflect a living musical need.

Common ground may be found in the notion of 'interpretation', perhaps also of 'mediation'. All the musicians of Shiva Nova (western or Indian) interpret something. This 'something' combines a wide variety of data types and codes in varying proportions: written, memorised, internalised to be interpreted ('revealed') according to a similarly wide variety of skills: personal and interpersonal. The fact that the relation of these various parts is so divergent across different music cultures does not mean that we should give up any attempt to find the necessary points of engagement.

All the three assumptions given above on the nature of western music may be challenged by this engagement. The following is a case study contribution intended neither to be definitive nor comprehensive.

Notation: its uses and limits; the relation with an oral tradition

The history and development of western art music notation needs to be rethought in terms which allow its advantages and disadvantages to be seen clearly. The function of western notation was to act to unify, standardise and simplify for universal application.

It started off as an aid to memory. Performance practice – 'interpretation' or 'expression' – remained part of the ongoing oral tradition. But western notation absorbed and rationalised increasing swathes of performance practice, possibly at first due to standardisation (of liturgy) but later due to the (emerging) composer's increasing desire to determine the result.[12] This forced the performer to concentrate interpretation on an ever more constrained group of variables. Indeed, in western art music, notation increasingly became a self-supporting vehicle of expression with its own laws increasingly independent of a supporting performance practice (Small, 1977, pp. 30–32).

But as with writing in general the effects were to be wider. In the west we have lost the ability to memorise whole Homeric epics, preferring to preserve and freeze their evolution at a point in time and to make sacred such a fixed text.

In the nineteenth century a second major function of western notation came to the fore: its use for transcription of oral music. At first the domain of 'folk song collectors' (and of composers such as Chopin, Liszt and others who had rarely heard any such music in its original setting), this was to emerge as the serious endeavour of the youngest musicology, ethnomusicology. The double 'sieves'[13] of pitch (scale) and time (metre) were evidently barely adequate for much of this work – especially as recording was now available to allow repeated listening to material. From the detailed transcriptions made by Bartok in the villages of Hungary (and elsewhere) the clash of the prescriptive notation and the descriptive score he sought to make of a rich oral culture was obvious (for example, Bartok, 1976, p. 184). As a 'set of instructions' the western notation system was plainly inadequate to *describe* such a unique event. It could never hope to provide sufficient information for an adequate performance. We are free to abstract those elements which the notation has allowed us to preserve – this includes no timbral information, for example.

The influence of western notation is pervasive but not complete. Different musics have different balances between the mnemonic and definitive roles of notation. Even in such a recent development as jazz we see the advent of notation, possession and copyright take over from a predominantly common holding of the oral traditions from which it sprang. Yet spontaneity and deviation from the given 'text', whether a notated 'new work' or a 'standard', remain the hallmark of innovation in jazz.

In Korea the relationship is more complex. Traditional *sanjo* pieces were until recently unnotated and learnt in strict master/pupil relationships.

> In the oral tradition of *sanjo*, the student has to rely completely on the guidance of his teacher, who transmits everything individually and directly. The student gradually learns to play his teacher's basic patterns in a strictly imitative way ... After the student has achieved a fair degree of proficiency as a *sanjo* performer, he will handle various flexible and spontaneous techniques and finally shape his own musical personality (Song, 1982, p. 112).

However, *sanjo* is now notated in detail in western notation (with annotation in Korean), but this is not treated in the same way as a western work. There is much supplementary detailed annotation for ornamentation, and tempo, though notated, is still a matter of interpretative freedom. The student still learns the work with a teacher until it appears to conform to the model and only at that point does the real work of interpretation begin when ornamentation and extension can be added or at least become more original.[14] A 'perfect' performance of the written text is not a performance.

Song goes on to remark that this introduction of western notation has had profound effects both negative and (possibly) positive.

> As a result, a line of demarcation between performer and composer has firmly emerged among younger musicians, gradually restricting the creative ability in the improvisational *sanjo* style. University-educated students of this generation have not developed the improvisational art of the great *sanjo* masters of the past ... However the younger musicians may be able to create new styles of composition for instrumental solo music based upon some of the traditional values of a bygone generation (Song, 1982, p. 114).

For a solo tradition[15] this might work well, but it is often not fully understood the ways in which in most cases notation changes relationships within an *ensemble*. Of course, most ensembles – from oral or written traditions – need coordination; from the 'absent' time lines of African music to the drum kits of jazz and rock music. The increasing dependence on notation changes the focus, however, away from fellow performers towards the text. Thus a group reading a score often needs a common time to be imposed from outside; it relinquishes responsibility to a conductor/coordinator – a key freedom is surrendered.

But we have one new invention which may hinder and help our endeavour: the computer. Its power was rapidly applied to western music in all the forms we have discussed. Composition, analysis, transcription, sound production, processing, storage and distribution are all now in one way or another within its domain.

Given the origins of the computer within western industrial society, it is not surprising that programs which have been developed have mirrored powerfully the preoccupations of western music. The dominance of composing software packages which slavishly embody the worst excesses of the definitive and prescriptive aspects of notation within the western tradition could be the most destructive force unless leavened by a flexibility to the oral traditions with which it comes into contact.[16]

We have seen its acceptance and increasing use within ethnomusicology at the analytical stage, based originally on Seeger's melogram but now able to transcribe oral music to a wide variety of notations. The descriptive is well established, but is still not well enough known by our 'typical' western composer. In addition, the ever stronger relationship with psychology of music research is opening up work on the possible 'generative grammars' of the music of oral cultures.

However, an unaddressed need remains: the development of more flexible notation systems; these may also be stimulated by the development of a new generation of music interfaces. The keyboard and the digital clock being the ultimate 'sieves'.

This is not philosophical speculation: within the repertoire created for Shiva Nova were several works created using computer sequencers, which resulted in a quite stunning impoverishment of rhythmic language through a paradoxical desire to come to terms with new rhythmic modes (some derived from Indian *tala*, literally transcribed). The problem lay simply in the use of notation to effect this investigation. A further paradox was that these simplified rhythmic and melodic compositions were very difficult to play! Notation may be a very inefficient way indeed of communicating a highly structured thought. We should dream of a technology which bypasses some of these constraints: a combination of ear and eye – a new 'superscore'.

Problems of notation and performance practice in this exchange cannot be separated and must be solved at the same time. Gone is the composer who has what she/he believes is a one-to-one relationship of notated symbol to acoustic result. Notations may work at other levels than at the individual event level – at the gesture level or the phrase structure level, for example.

Mnemonic notations at all these levels could make a fundamental comeback. In western music the relation to performance practice of graphic and other non-standard notations developed in the 1960s was weak. This was usually deliberate, in line with the encouragement of 'multiple readings' and 'open work' of that period. But in practice, without a widespread oral tradition developing, the individualism inherent in European post-renaissance art was (paradoxically) reinforced rather than undermined. Such innovative notations often became in practice the private domain of the groups 'specialising' in their decoding.[17] Notwithstanding the explicit aims of some educational innovations of that era these freer notations soon fell out of regular use, usually when the groups themselves disbanded or moved onto other interests.

But the immediacy of computer graphics has been slow to be applied to sound and music notation. Furthermore, the extension of the idea of 'score' to include recordings of example material allows the virtually instant creation of an aural[18] tradition (discussed below). This means that mnemonic and graphic notation codes could create a whole new set of tools for the live musician as well as the studio composer.[19]

The identity of the work: score, performance or process?

But if the score ceases to be the 'object' of our work, what is the aim? Of course, first the process. Bartok believed we might rebuild art music from the bottom up: a true alternative to Schoenberg within the first wave of modernism and one which (ironically) hints at a truly postmodern condition.

> The excesses of the Romanticists began to be unbearable for many. There were composers who felt: "this road does not lead us anywhere; there is no other solution but a complete break with the nineteenth century."
>
> Invaluable help was given to this change (or let us rather call it rejuvenation) by a kind of peasant music unknown till then.
>
> It is the ideal starting point for a musical renaissance, and a composer in search of new ways cannot be led by a better master (Bartok, 1976, pp. 340–41).

The process is one of education and understanding. But how do we distinguish this from, at best, tourism, at worst, plundering? Of course plundering is more common. Music has been stolen for thousands of years without acknowledgement; but we live in a more global light. We want to preserve the variety of our planet; plundering today might be of the last Dodo egg, the last stages of an oral tradition as it westernises or 'modernises'; we have to take the sometimes agonising decision as to whether artificial preservation is 'better' than assimilation.[20]

For many composers (myself included) a performance is always the aim – in its widest and most humanist sense. I wish to establish the conditions for a meaningful interaction of western/non-western – call them what you will – in the arena of live musical discourse. In this sense computer 'interaction' (the subject of another chapter in this book) is not applicable here. I maintain a belief in the 'touch of the now' as an essential ingredient in intercultural interaction. Using the Internet for such interaction will once again demand filtering through whatever notation (in its broadest sense) is used to convey musical material.

But just as one of western art music's increasing obsessions has been that of the 'fixity of the work', so we have a mirror problem in any musical tradition which relies not on notes written but on notes performed in an interactive ensemble. If you like we can call it the 'fixity of the personnel': of course this is true of jazz and most popular and vernacular musical genres. The western concert score usually fixes the personnel and minimises the individual 'personalities' of the performers.[21] The many waves of 'cross-over' musics which have appeared in western concert halls throughout the twentieth century have suffered from this conflict: was the collaboration with a 'genre' or with a specific artist or group?[22] Usually in practice, the latter. The work thus has the life span of the group not the orchestra.

There are questions of short-term and long-term continuity within ensembles such as Shiva Nova. In a western ensemble with an orientation towards notation performers may more easily be replaced. Sitar players cannot simply 'slot in' to an ensemble that should ideally be functioning as a single organism. In the longer term the ensemble has now changed instrumental personnel completely and the work I composed for them could not be performed. Recording saves such cases from historical annihilation – as with any oral tradition.

The notion of the author: the collaboration between composer and performer

In western music the idea of the 'original' work is at odds with the idea of 'model' at the root of both other traditions in our present discussion.

> In both Korean *sanjo* and Indian *raga*, the arts of performance and creation merge into one, that is, improvisation ... [which] cannot be regarded as a concept separate from composition ... (Song, 1982, p. 111).

In an interesting discussion comparing these two traditions[23] Song Bang-song (Song, 1982) highlights the emphasis that both have on the elaboration of a given model handed down orally; he is forced to use the term 'improvisation' while acknowledging its complete inadequacy. In the *sanjo* tradition he separates three factors in the establishment of a personal style: preservation, elaboration and creation. Each may be attempted only after complete understanding of the previous.[24] The same may basically be said for the traditional methods of teaching the Indian tradition (Sorrell and Narayan, 1980). The performer in these two traditions is no less credited with interpretative skill than any in the West (although criteria for judging this may be different) but crucially the 'work' has no author. Furthermore, as remarked in the introduction, the western composer – while possibly taught through traditional models of compositions 'from the past' (a significant phrase) – quickly learns that innovation and originality both value change over preservation. This may sound superficially attractive but can (and in many cases has) degenerated into a tower of Babel of private utterances.

Our western world is obsessed with ownership; copyright and royalties are a central plank of the system of remuneration for composers. This was made easy through notation (the score – an object) and, later, recording (initially an object but now, problematically, simply 'a stream of binary information'). Performances were more important as purveyors of these objects, than they were valued uniquely in themselves.

We know the possible dangers when such a system confronts an oral (or even notated traditional) music. From a commonly held pool of resources there emerges a fragmented and impoverished list held by the performing rights societies. A well-known 'protest' singer of the 1960s magically becomes the composer of an older vernacular song. Even in emerging traditions we have great problems of ownership claims. We know of many cases from jazz where the band leader has taken the credit (and royalties) for something essentially composed collectively by the group.

This conflict can only be resolved if we shift the emphasis from supporting composers to manufacture a product to supporting them to develop new processes of working and performing. However the record of such work is important[25] as it is needed to develop a new working tradition – one mediated and aided by the new technology, thus enabling the critical development of new ideas and musical forms. But the record is not the aim, it is the trace of a process, helping a later generation in their search for expression and not necessarily intended as a model for re-creation.

The sounding result: what is important for the listener?

Ethnomusicology discriminates between so-called 'etic' and 'emic' qualities of musical discourse. Based on linguistics – the two terms 'phonetic' and 'phonemic' – the former refers to an agreed measurable 'acoustic' event, clearly described and differentiated from its neighbours and other similar events; this may or may not be a significant event within the language. The concept 'emic' is more complicated and involves a cluster of etic events which, in the language concerned, have the same function. For an emic analysis, some differences will not be significant. For example, an English speaker learns how the two most common forms of the liquid vowel 'l' in the word 'little' are best pronounced, yet it does not matter if they are reversed as the meaning is not changed – an etic difference. In the Russian language the two forms of the letter 'l' often result in different meanings of otherwise identical words[26] – an emic difference.

What at first hearing we perceive as significant will be based on our previous experience and an expectation based on circumstance. But this creation of 'new measures of significance' is precisely the task of any such intercultural enterprise. We may have to acknowledge that our new expressiveness cannot be defined 'within' the culture we observe. We have no automatic right to an emic interpretation in this case. We are in a truly experimental situation. If our western composer invokes the 'right to be wrong' at this stage and declares emic intentions for the work – possibly based on complete misreadings and misunderstandings – he/she strongly reinforces the purely western basis for the evaluation of such projects[27] thus defeating much of their object.

Even within western art music timbre has played an ambiguous role. The very fact that 'composition' was often taught separately from 'orchestration' and that piano reductions of new works were the first to be published so that the public could (before recording) get to know 'the work' indicates clearly the primacy of pitch. In this sense timbre in much music of this tradition had an etic role. Changing the instrument had little impact on the 'meaning' of a melody.[28] Increasingly in the twentieth century timbre took on emic qualities – it could not be reduced or altered without 'change of meaning'. This is self-evident for our electroacoustic composer.

An electroacoustic composer may first and foremost be fascinated by the timbre of the new instruments. As the basis for an acousmatic composition this may be an excellent start. The sounds are often rich in ways unheard in western instrumentation – although once again the emic raises its significance if we do not appreciate, for example, the deliberate buzzes (often bottle tops and the like) added to the Zimbabwean *zanza* or the slight distortion provoked by the correct placing of a piece of thread on the bridge of a *tambura* – both of which might be heard as 'unclean' to the over-zealous composer recording engineer.

But within a live instrumental piece, to go beyond the attraction of the timbre to something which engages our attention and directs it to the virtuosity and expressiveness of another performance tradition is something that marks out the move from an etic to an emic reading. How might the composer allow that to happen?

Responses

I cannot become an Indian-trained musician overnight. But my own existing faculties must not be applied in ways which lose what I myself observe excites me in the music. To state such an obvious point needs explanation: There are plenty of examples of composers killing stone dead the spontaneity and vitality which they themselves admire in non-western music through insensitive appropriation of surface technique (usually, once again, through an inadequate notation system and inadequate formalised 'rules'). Too simple an understanding of acculturation may hinder the very process we aim to foster. I would be wrong to *assume* that Shiva Nova's (Indian trained) sitar player would lose some of his spontaneity through his desire to use western notation, and I would also be patronising to think that the western-trained musicians are *a priori* hopeless improvisers.

But this is simply the stuff of any personal – let alone musical – exchange, the origins of any relationship in the process of being worked out. So why is it special? I think such exchanges are fundamental, providing they are indeed real exchanges. This is not a superfluous remark: Shiva Nova had several works written for them following a cursory meeting with the composer, who would then be locked away for months until the work (I mean the *score*) arrived through the post. This is why often the most interpenetrating multi-cultural exchanges are produced within performing ensembles without a 'composer' in sight.

Western art music is in an advanced state of disintegration (which is absolutely not the same as decay!). A series of increasingly pronounced anomalies has resulted from efforts to strengthen the tradition. The retreat to purely personal expression, the cult of the personality and the idea of the masterwork are still very much with us, reinforced through a complex superstructure of copyright, publishing and promotion. The composer is both producer and product within this system.

The intervention of technology, the opportunities: the recording as supplement to the score and enhancement of the oral/aural tradition

I shall argue that while we might once have seen the recording as quite antithetical to the oral tradition; it has become a potential new tool in its development. Recordings have in many cases supplemented scores as the 'trace' of the work, encouraging further performances and developing performance practice. Young rock guitarists may now learn the classic 'licks' from recordings of their heroes. Of course the danger is that, just as the traditional score became sacred text, so too the composer's sanctioned recording becomes 'the word'.[29]

The western tradition encourages composers to change media quickly within the tradition, for example, a string quartet this year, a chamber opera next, a song cycle to follow, and so on. Sadly, this has sometimes been extended to include 'an experimental work with ethnic instruments' tucked in between two of these items. The ever increasing pressures of work usually give insufficient time to come to terms with the performance or wider aesthetic implications of this new adventure. Recordings allow an immersion in the etic aspects of the new tradition under study but only practical application and repeated working contact can ever begin to break into the emic signifiers and then only to a limited degree. I recorded all the sessions I had with Dharambir Singh and Inok Paek. These usually consisted of a combination of playing and verbal commentary, an invaluable archive which I could replay, try to understand, raise questions concerning, or memorise and transcribe. The recording opens up the opportunity for this dynamic interactive personal learning curve to be enhanced.

Yet the assumption only comes completely to fruition if we consider that such material be re-presented as part of the score. To communicate the ideas of the work the notation is clearly not sufficient – and there is no immediate 'tradition' to fill in the interpretative layers between text and performance and between performance and audience.[30] Given that the works from which I have drawn this experience also involved electroacoustic resources we might suggest that the technology available has for some years been capable of redefining the idea of 'score'. Let us (temporarily) call this new object the 'super-score'.

Technology and the 'super-score'

The super-score of the future could be a multimedia object bringing together in various combinations:

- *Traditional notation* While the western tradition's notation may be dominant at present, its own variety (including tablatures) may be enhanced by traditional notations from other cultures and sources.
- *Extended notation* The short-term nature of many innovations of the 'avant garde' within western music in the period since 1950 has been remarked upon above. But specific and illustrated new notations may prove more robust.
- *Recording of example material for the live performer* This could illustrate new techniques and their representation in notation, or their use in less defined discourse. It could also deal with proposed 'expressive' questions of interpretation.
- *Electroacoustic materials* While 'mixed' works of electroacoustic music have most commonly been 'for tape' and in Michel Chion's phrase (Chion, 1991) a genre of *sons fixés*, this need not be the case as more flexible and interactive instrument-electroacoustic sound

relationships emerge. These might be files prepared for the following entry.

- *Software for performance*   For the emerging interactive performance genres – from simple triggering of soundfiles to fully-fledged interactive material interpreted in real time.
- *Patches for live electronic treatment*   Related to the above, although possibly in library form for loading into specific electronic processors.
- *Examples of live electronic treatment*   As specific electronic processors fade into museums of technology, one way of allowing an update to take place is through giving very specific sound models of the desired transformations which future systems could imitate.[31]
- *An example recorded performance*   The danger of such a recording being seen as definitive – a model to be imitated – might be overcome if varying interpretations were included.[32]
- *Commentary (written and recorded spoken texts)*   This could extend the traditional programme note into a hypertext (which could refer to any of the elements above and below), including background information, interviews with composer, performers, pedagogical material.
- *Video performance material*   For multimedia presentations.
- *Video example material*   Much of the above explanatory material could be with video: demonstrations of fingerings, special techniques and performance practices.
- *Graphic material*   For example, photographs of suggested staging, lighting arrangements, composer; circuit diagrams, equipment interconnections.

Some illustrations

I want to make some detailed illustrations by way of a closing section to this chapter, examining each non-western instrument in turn and the function of the electronics. It might be better to say 'each instrumentalist'; this would be more accurate as we have stressed the individual and personal skills of these traditions and how the composer must engage these to have any hope of a meaningful exchange. In fact, with respect to Shiva Nova there were changes in personnel over the four years the work was in their repertoire, although the core group remained unchanged.

The decision had been made to base the core of the composition on *raga Hori Kafi*;[33] developing instrumental material for the western instruments from *kafi that*. I then invited the Indian instrument musicians to use materials from this *raga* in any other circumstances in the piece which felt to them to be appropriate.

With respect to the sitar part, I consulted extensively with its first interpreter Dharambir Singh. He read western notation well and had interpreted some detailed scores for Shiva Nova. His versatility in *raga* performance, especially with respect to duration, was prodigious. In the third movement of the piece the sitar and tablas performed a 'short' (unnotated) version of *raga Hori Kafi* accompanied by the western instruments having the function of a more complex *tambura* (drone), while in the other movements we agreed, after consultation and experimentation, to a 'skeleton' notation which gave 'central pitches' (not specifically tonical, but all members of the *kafi that*) which plotted a shape throughout the movement around which melodic fragments could be composed ('improvised').

This contrasted strongly with the method of working with the tabla player Sarwar Sabri. After much listening and discussion I had similarly constructed a skeleton notation, indicating downbeats, *jawal* and *sawab* phrase lengths, occasional suggestions for 'accent colours' using the indications 'ti', 'ga' and so forth, from the traditional mnemonic system for tablas performance. Even during the evolution of the score the director of the ensemble (Priti Paintal) had agreed to teach Sabri (who did not like to read any notation during performance) the part by rote, or at least in short ideas based on a series of signals. It is at this stage in the process that the interaction took its own momentum free from the constraints of the written score. Over the course of the first few rehearsals and performances Sabri progressively freed his interpretation from that which had been laid down (and only, in truth, partly realised at the first read-through). The coordination with other instruments was exactly as intended although the material took on a life of its own; the spirit of the indications remained, but little else. This is not to say that the performance was different on each occasion – comparison of recordings over quite a considerable period show an extraordinary consistency – just that he appeared successfully to have integrated into 'my' piece the 'model-variation' tradition from which he came.

The western composer can become anxious at this stage: what exactly *is* the work. The idea that it might be the score is progressively undermined; Dharambir's interpretation of a skeleton pitch sequence is containable within western traditions of 'filling out' limited indications in a score (common in much baroque practice), but Sabri had effectively left the notation behind. He had internalised its intentions, respected its coordination with others (which was in any case second nature within his 'normal' performance practice) and realised a truly musical result.

Perhaps 'the work' is then the resulting performance or a recording? Possibly. This might suggest that the composer should go back and 'rewrite' the score with this interpretation in mind. But that defeats the object of the valuable process that has taken place. I would suggest that that process itself becomes the object of communication to another ensemble in another place. In this respect technology can be used to assist this essentially aural and experiential exchange. It has the power to free the 'score' from such absurd definitive limitations.

Electronics as mediation

I had recorded all the instruments extensively but in the end used only four sounds: a sitar sound without the initial attack; a cello harmonic (held single pitch); a flute fluttertongue (usually slowed down); a cello 'seagull' sound (harmonic glissando). These were used melodically (albeit in a generally slow motion) via a standard sampler of that era.[34] At the time I was surprised I did not want to use any tabla sounds on the sampler. But the results of its electronic transposition are extremely poor. Like the voice, it cannot easily be transposed; we tend to hold on to its recognition and hence it sounds poor ('mickey mouse') if not treated with care. In any case its articulation is so much better live and trying to avoid this impoverishment through sampling whole phrases gives an artificial quality due to the literal repetition.

The samples chosen were transposed in such a way as to reveal their complex inner life. One can contrast two pairs: the sitar sample (transposed down) growls and slowly opens up its beautiful aura of shimmering metallic harmonics; this relates nicely to the so-called 'seagull' harmonics produced as the cellist runs a finger lightly down a string. Then two very contrasting sustained unchanging sounds: a cello harmonic, pure and clear; and a flute fluttertongue, used slowed down to reveal its pulsating, almost noisy, breathy sound that underpins the final movement. This can be linked directly to the tabla rhythms, although it is more regular. Thus we have a web of interconnecting timbres mediated and linked through the electronics.

Live electronic modulation[35] had two functions, to enhance presence and landscape – the two are related. There were four processes: a stereophonic feedback delay of such very short duration that a pitched 'reverberation aura' is added to sounds (the pitches being derived from the *kafi that*), this was used in the first movement to create a pitched resonance from the unpitched tabla sounds, thus linking it to the world of the other instruments; a ninety-nine-second reverberation process to 'freeze' certain sounds, this was used to create harmonic pedal points 'behind' melodic foreground; stereo echoes of delay times deliberately chosen to create complex harmonic textures, for example, exact phrase repetitions create heterophonic layers of material; finally flange and small transposition ('detune') transformations were used to 'liven up' the presence of both instruments and sampled sounds. All of these had been chosen with an ear to 'linkages' between the timbral types, also enhanced through amplification, sound balance and projection.

In working with the Korean kayagum player Inok Paek who has a doctorate in ethnomusicology from Queen's University, Belfast, I was collaborating with a musician who was already grappling with problems of 'translation' between cultures. Since her earliest years in the UK she had commissioned composers to write new works for her (usually with electronics). I would like to address two issues in this instance. As explained above, she comes from a 'modernised' *sanjo* tradition which had learnt from both (western) score and teacher. My relief at realising her ease at reading notation quickly disappeared when I attempted to relate an existing *sanjo* score to its recording. Tempi, timbral ornamentation and nuance did not merely add to what was written but generated the (for me) musical interest. To attempt to drive this into reverse – to create a work which was 'scored' was a prodigious task of immensely greater difficulty than presupposed. In fact, it could only be done with the regular advice of the performer. As with the earlier collaboration it became apparent that increasingly detailed notation would become suffocating and I opted for a simplified form, using a time-space method of defining tempo. Even here the performer may fluctuate tempo at will to an even greater extent than with a traditional performance.

Over the months of regular consultation and discussion, working notions of melody and interpretation (ornamentation) emerged. Any relation to *sanjo* was quickly lost. The problems thrown up by this being a solo work are substantially different from those for an ensemble. There is no immediate 'other' tradition in instrumental terms as in the mixing of European and Indian in Shiva Nova. In this work the western ideas are found in aspects of the musical material. The kayagum is a fretless instrument usually tuned to a pentatonic scale repeated over three octaves; scordatura is possible (but unheard in the traditional repertoire). Thus normally, as notes may be bent by up to a minor third, the other pitches of the western scale system are found as part of the embellishments[36] in Korean music. Hidden in the material is an 'ironic' use of totally chromatic pitch fields that 'collapse' – due to the physical nature of the instrument – into their pentatonic *ur-form*. The eastern organology 'wins'. The electronics, however, have a function of 'extending' the tradition. True polyphony does not occur in traditional Korean music, but the contemporary works which Inok Paek had commissioned all had the added dimension of foreground/background contrast.[37] As I had planned this work to be with live electronics – leaving the performer absolutely free in matters of tempo and interpretation – I had to consider building into the work material which would be suitable for 'capturing and electroacoustic processing'. While there were many variants on the processes finally designed, they had two basic functions. One was the freezing and further projection of textures which would form a backdrop to melodic working. The material played live was itself different from the traditional melodic types, namely trills and tremolos. Some of these 'rustle' sounds have been worked out with the performer to have quite specific timbral trajectories.

A second set of transformations (as in the other work discussed) places the instrument in a landscape, enhancing its 'presence' – almost to an intentionally surreal degree.[38] Each performance of the work has resulted in changes and new ideas, even to the extent that the studio recording resulted in significant refinement of the electroacoustic treatments; these, in turn, will reflect back into future live performances. It is quite possible that no definitive version will emerge.

Postscript: on time

The enemy of intercultural projects for composers is that the entire infrastructure of education, support and production is partitioned into phases. Learning skills and education are assumed to have been concluded by sometime in a composer's early twenties. The composer is then deemed 'ready' to produce. Many do so with relatively little further input, generating their own 're-education' when needed.

But the need for more structured and continuous access to resources for experiencing and learning new skills has only scantily been recognised in recent years. Both areas discussed in this chapter are cases in point; composers who wish to learn new skills in electronic music or intercultural projects have extraordinarily little access to the necessary learning tools after the end of formal education. When they do it is rarely for sufficient time to allow the real development of nuance (in performance or composition) in the chosen field.

I have advocated above a move to supporting process rather than product, but the shift may need to be much deeper. Musicians (composers and performers, but for that matter listeners and promoters) have need of longer term access to facilities – but not just production facilities. From the 1950s to the 1980s composers had to uproot to centres of excellence for access to computer music facilities, often for months at a time – disrupting to social life, yet still a frustratingly short time to learn the new systems; this is now progressively giving way to home studios as the technology becomes cheaper. A welcome change, but the need for communities of experience and exchange remains. The Internet holds out such a hope for the distribution medium although Ivan Illich predicted thirty years ago the need for human interchange and exchange to result from such networks, in addition to access to technical tools (Illich, 1971). This is crucial; if the Internet becomes just another (more efficient) medium of exchange for objects then it will not have fulfilled its potential. I could send my finished western art music score anywhere in the world in a fraction of a second but that would be little better than 'pigeon post' at changing the musical relationships we have discussed here.

For intercultural projects such as these, much longer-term strategies are needed both within education and throughout a working life. The models of western art music are inapplicable in most such contexts; for creative new forms to emerge there is need to understand that current roles may irreversibly change.

A quote from Pierre Schaeffer written originally in 1953 unites these two areas in this concern. In his 'postulates and rules' for the 'understanding of the 'concrète' attitude' we read:

> *Fifth rule – Work and time*, indispensable to all true assimilation (Schaeffer, 1973, p. 30).

Within the disintegration and confusion of western art music at the end of the millennium there can be excitement rather than despair and the ever-present possibility of renewal, both personal and cultural.

Notes

1. Adorno, of course, came closest to arguing a 'right' path in the sense of 'historically authentic' in his discussion of Schoenberg and Stravinsky (Adorno, 1967; 1973).
2. As have practitioners of the other arts. Nattiez (1990) has called this appropriately 'misreading'.
3. Though still an ongoing project at the time of writing (1999).
4. Nettl (1983), Chapter 7 has an excellent discussion of these problems and how ethnomusicologists have tackled them. See also Farrell (1997).

5. The study of ethnomusicology is more often than not the study of hybrid and juxtaposed cultures even where (as with Austro-German musical culture) they later claim a degree of 'purity' or 'authenticity'.

6. Radical attempts to change the institutional arrangements of composer, performer, publisher and promoter within the concert hall tradition may seem less obvious thirty years later but the successors to these movements may be found on the Internet (see chapter 8 and other contributions to this volume).

7. The least I can do is claim once again a composer's prerogative for self-delusion! It may be as deluding to believe an individual can change the system as that they are 'inevitably' part of a historical infrastructure.

8. It is significant that Wagner's opera *Die Meistersinger von Nürnberg* is set precisely at the time when a tradition – derived from a wandering minstrel (oral) tradition of model/elaboration – had been formalised into the laws he ridicules in the opera.

9. The absurd extent to which this was taken might best be typified in the early works of Stockhausen none of which has the same instrumentation or compositional 'method' (though we may, as always, see continuity at a higher level). This was explicitly stated as an aim by the composer (Stockhausen, 1963).

10. Finally brought to fruition in music in the theoretically infinite archives available over the Internet.

11. This is by no means a blanket condemnation of world music marketing but of those aspects which adulterate the original material without sufficient information to the consumer. There is an exact parallel with current debates on food production and distribution, here.

12. Corresponding, as well, to a shift from the glorification of God to that of the individual composer.

13. See Xenakis (1992) and Wishart (1996) for different ways of seeing western music notation as consisting of 'sieves' from a continuum of possibilities.

14. Inok Paek (personal communication). This description superficially resembles the learning of any western piece but the notation ceases to have such a predominant role in the final performance.

15. The present writer, on a visit to Korea in 1997, witnessed a group class of *kayagum* (and other instruments); clearly, this aspect of westernisation ('modernisation') has also developed.

16. At the time of writing not many composing packages facilitate a flexible non-metric graphic notation for pitched material or detailed designation of timbre, for example.

17. Karkoschka (1972) is a classic inventory of many of these developments.

18. 'Oral' and 'aural' are terms that can become ambiguous. Ethnomusicologists use the term 'oral' (pertaining to 'mouth') to include vocal and instrumental traditions passed on through practice and the ear (usually not written down); electroacoustic composers – with less or no dependence on performers – stress the ear and hence 'aural' aspect of their work. The ear as a major tool of learning remains at the focus of both uses of the term.

19. The words *research* and *experiment* have been denigrated in their latterday associations with an over-literate musical culture and an over-reliance on

technological 'solutions' to musical problems. Composition and performance practice research can make a fundamental contribution to this process if freed from this constraint.

20. And it is possible that problematising it in this way is also not helpful!

21. Or at least regulates them in placing them subservient to the 'sound' of the orchestra as heard through the interpretation of the conductor!

22. Works by Gunther Schuller and Duke Ellington come to mind.

23. The present writer – as composer – had not seen this text at the time of writing either of his compositions using similar resources.

24. Within the pre-notated (oral) tradition he suggests that this process could take 'at least ten years of constant work and practice' (Song, 1982, p. 112) – this is only superficially a long time if one compares it with a western concert soloist.

25. The record of all stages of a collaborative process, not just the performance result.

26. Anecdotally, the present writer gave a talk in Seoul (Korea) in 1997; the translator found his (standard southern English) pronunciation 'extremely difficult' to follow as she had learnt American English. Differences in vowel shade are extremely important in Korean and she (almost) heard the differences as emic in the first instance.

27. Doing no more than continuing a very long tradition of appropriation of 'other musics' by the western tradition since the middle ages (at least).

28. This is a generalisation: for any competent composer the sound was important, the melody and harmony suggested their orchestration.

29. cf. the Stockhausen complete edition recordings (Stockhausen Verlag). The shortcomings of the 'Stravinsky conducts Stravinsky' recordings are well known and have limited this process.

30. There may be reference to such traditions, of course, but here I refer to works which have tried to mediate between traditions rather than their wholesale importation.

31. Many of the live electronic works of the 1960s and 1970s which use now barely available analogue processors are in great need of this kind of description.

32. Some kinds of composition would benefit from multiple readings being included while for others the composer may disagree with any reading being fixed in this way.

33. While in principle other *ragas* could be used, the predominance of the *kafi* scale in the notated aspects of all the instrumental parts has effectively fixed this *raga* as the ideal one. I was introduced to it (and the subtle variations in pitch allowed) by Dharambir Singh.

34. A Yamaha TX16W which compared with other types had excellent control over sound quality and envelope.

35. Produced using a Yamaha DMP7 (which was also the mixer) but equivalents may be used.

36. But it must be stressed that the language here does not imply 'secondary' or less important.

37. Works by Bennett Hogg (*The Savage Curtain*) and Javier Alvarez (*Mannam*), both with electroacoustic tape, most notably.

38. It would not be too fanciful to 'see' the instrument in a Korean woodcut

with water-sounds as backdrop and the reflective surface of a cliff face close by.

References

Adorno, Theodor W. (1967), *Prisms*, London: Neville Spearman.
Adorno, Theodor W. (1973), *Philosophy of Modern Music*, London: The Seabury Press.
Bartok, Bela (1976), *Bela Bartok Essays* (Suchoff, Benjamin (ed.)), London: Faber and Faber.
Chion, Michel (1991), *L'art des sons fixés, ou la musique concrètement*, Fontaine: Editions Métamkine/Nota Bene/Sono-Concept.
Farrell, Gerry (1997), *Indian Music and the West*, Oxford: Oxford University Press.
Illich, Ivan (1971), *Deschooling Society*, London: Calder and Boyars.
Karkoschka, Erhard (1972), *Notation in New Music*, London: Universal Edition.
Nattiez, Jean-Jacques (1990), *Music and Discourse*, Princeton: Princeton University Press.
Nettl, Bruno (1983), *The Study of Ethnomusicology*, Urbana: University of Illinois Press.
Neuman, Daniel M. (1990), *The Life of Music in North India*, Chicago: University of Chicago Press.
Schaeffer, Pierre (1973), *La musique concrète*, Paris: Presses Universitaires de France.
Small, Christopher (1977), *Music, Society, Education*, London: Calder.
Song, Bang-song (1982), '*Sanjo* versus *Raga*: a preliminary study' in Falck, Robert and Rice, Timothy (eds), *Cross-Cultural Perspectives on Music*, pp. 101–16, Toronto: University of Toronto Press.
Sorrell, Neil and Narayan, Ram (1980), *Indian Music in Performance*, Manchester: Manchester University Press.
Stockhausen, Karlheinz (1963), 'Arbeitsberich 1952/53: Orientierung', in Stockhausen, Karlheinz, *Texte (Band 1)*, pp. 32–8, Köln: Dumont Schauberg.
Wishart, Trevor (1996), *On Sonic Art*, Amsterdam: Harwood Academic Publishers (second edition).
Xenakis, Iannis (1992), *Formalized Music*, Stuyvesant: Pendragon.

CHAPTER SIX

Cacophony

Robert Worby

Introduction

Noise may well prove to be the most appropriate metaphor for the twentieth century. This hundred-year period witnessed the gathering of human beings into the urban conurbations that have become our great cities, the invention of the aeroplane and the invasion of the motor car, the development of horrendous war machines and the evolution of radio, television and sound recording. Today there is more sound because there are more people and there are more ways of making, storing, retrieving and transmitting sound. Noise is with us all the time and it symbolises a world that is forever expanding and accelerating.

There are many definitions of noise: technical, scientific, legal, cultural, musical, but in common parlance noise is unwanted sound. It is the stuff of disruption, it is irritating, often too loud, ugly and unpleasant. This stuff is produced by people – it's an objectionable by-product of human activity. It's other people's radios or hi-fi, it's parties and the hammerings of home improvements, it's lawn mowing and hedge trimming. It's the peaks in the backdrop of the daily round, the spikes in the soundscape of life.

John Cage celebrated and embraced noise, when in 1937 he wrote:

> Wherever we are, what we hear is mostly noise. When we ignore it, it disturbs us. When we listen to it, we find it fascinating (Cage, 1968, p. 3).

George Steiner felt oppressed by the noise of modern culture.

> Many contexts of the decibel-culture have been studied. What is more important, but difficult to investigate, let alone quantify, is the question of the development of mental faculties, of self-awareness, when these take place in a perpetual sound-matrix. What are the sweet, vociferous hammers doing to the brain at key stages in its development ... What tissues of sensibility are being numbed or exacerbated? (Steiner, 1984, p. 433).

Jacques Attali uses noise as a vehicle for contemporary theory.

It [western knowledge] has failed to understand that the world is not for beholding. It is for hearing. It is not legible, but audible ... Nothing essential happens in the absence of noise ... for change is inscribed in noise faster than it transforms society (Attali, 1985, pp. 3–5).

Noise foreshadows and foretells. It alerts.

Cacophony

There are no agreed general definitions of cacophony. The term is often used derogatorily to denigrate music or describe any unpleasant, irritating or unwanted sound. It frequently applies to situations where many unintegrated sounds are heard simultaneously or simply to sounds that are extremely loud. Cacophony describes sounds that offend the listener and offence is displeasure, disunity and discord. There is a suggestion of unpleasantness, contention and things being out of sorts. Negativity abounds: there is no melding, no mixing, no harmony. Cacophony is conflict and difference. It implies collision: a collision of sounds, a collision of beliefs, a collision of needs.

Cacophony is a collision of sounds, and sounds, although often thought of as things, are actually very complex processes. Most of the sound we hear comes through the air, although sound also travels through liquids and solids. It moves at high speed (at the speed of sound![1]) in waves radiating out from a vibrating source. At the turn of the nineteenth century the French mathematician Fourier developed the theory that any regular complex wave could be analysed into simpler components called sine waves. Hence, as sound travels in complex waves, it too can be broken down into components of purer, less complex sounds called partials which are sine waves each with its own frequency, amplitude and duration. Just as white light can be split into a spectrum, comprising the colours of the rainbow, so a single sound can be split into a spectrum comprising the individual sine waves that, when fused together, make up that sound. Fourier never heard a sine wave because it can only be produced electronically; he was working theoretically with mathematical models of vibrations and waves, but today his theories can be demonstrated easily using audio technology. It is now possible to record a sound and then analyse it, breaking it down into its component sine waves to reveal its spectrum. Or, working the other way, it is possible to create entirely new sounds by combining sine waves according to a particular given spectrum.

So, a single sound is actually a fusion of many individual, discrete sounds (sine waves) and the way in which these sine waves combine produces the timbre of the sound, although, more generally, this might be referred to as sound *colour*. This is the physical characteristic of a sound that gives it its identity and enables distinctions between sounds. A flute, a piano and a human voice can all produce a given pitch at a particular volume for a specific duration, but they all sound different because their 'colours', their timbres, their spectra are different. In stable, pitched sounds, like those found in many traditional western musical instruments, the partial tones are combined in simple, rational relationships producing a conventionally pleasing, so-called 'musical' sound. These sounds are said to be harmonic and the partials in this instance are called 'harmonics'. They relate to the fundamental of the sound in simple, whole-number multiples. The fundamental is also the first partial.

A note on a violin provides a good example of harmonic partials. When a string is plucked and left to vibrate it will vibrate at the fundamental frequency. In the case of the note middle C this will be about 262 times per second (the frequency of middle C is about 262Hz), this is the fundamental frequency, the first partial. But within the string there are also vibrations at higher frequencies, the frequencies of the other partials, and because a violin note is perceived as a single, stable, pitched sound the partials are harmonics and are related to the fundamental in simple whole number ratios. The second harmonic is twice the frequency of the fundamental (524Hz). The third harmonic is three times the frequency of the fundamental (786Hz), the fourth harmonic is four times the frequency of the fundamental (1048Hz) and so on. This structure, this simple, whole-number relationship between a fundamental and a series of *harmonic* partials is known as the 'harmonic series'.

This produces a fabulously complex result not only because of the multiplicity of vibrations in a single sound but because all kinds of other relationships between the partials are happening simultaneously. The partials do not have equal amplitudes: generally, amplitude decreases as frequency increases so the higher partials are quieter. And they do not all decay at the same rate, the higher ones tend to fade faster, but again this is only a general rule and there are exceptions. The actual perceived pitch of the sound is a kind of aural illusion created by the brain: the harmonics fuse together to make the sound of this single violin note whose pitch is generated in the mind from several cues. This is especially true of the so-called 'missing fundamental' phenomenon. A note rich in partials may be recorded and the fundamental removed electronically – the result is that the brain still perceives the same pitch.

Here the brain is able somehow to manufacture the pitch from information it has gleaned from the partials.

When the partials of a sound are not combined in simple, rational, whole-number relationships the sound is said to be 'inharmonic'. The result is generally less pleasing the greater the degree of inharmonicity and the ear protests as it attempts to detect the simple, rational relationships found in harmonic sounds. As the ear tries to seek out the whole-number relationships several pitches may be heard within a single sound as in the case of a bell. Single, stable pitches are not present in inharmonic sounds and, because pitch is a primary structural element in conventional western music, inharmonic sounds are often considered to be 'unmusical'. Sounds that are even more inharmonic, like cymbals, triangles or gongs, have irrational partials that fuse producing great complexity without whole-number relationships making any kind of pitch detection extremely unlikely.

Combining several inharmonic sounds produces more inharmonicity creating metallic, clangorous sounds with almost no identifiable pitch. A single melodic line can be performed with bells because, as each bell sounds individually, the ear can extract some pitch information and there may be some assistance provided by the progression of the melody. But if several bells sound together the result is not a chord made of discrete pitches but more and more inharmonicity creating a dense metallic cacophony. This is caused by the collision of numerous partials in irrational relationships destroying any perception of pitch.

A sound consisting of oscillations in completely random and chaotic relationships is referred to as 'noise'. Here, the word is not used to mean irritating, unwanted sound but rather an auditory phenomenon resembling, for example, the consonants *ssh* and *fff*, the sounds of wind rustling leaves or surf crashing onto a beach. Instruments such as maracas and snare drums produce noise. In all of these examples there is no pitch content whatsoever.[2] Noise is also present in electronic circuits. It's the stuff that masks the desired signal. Static on the radio, hiss on cassettes, the sound of a stylus in a record groove (surface noise).

Noise and information

Noise will be all pervading after the 'heat death' of information. The final tepid frazzle of every bit and byte will be encapsulated in that searing hiss that jerks us awake, boggled-eyed, in front of the television set in the middle of the night. Noise – all the frequencies of the audio spectrum. Noise – the engine of the twentieth century, the ghost in the machine, the demon friend of entropy. It's everywhere; it's what we hear most. It irritates and it communicates, it enriches and it pollutes. But noise is not only sound.

Every message transmitted through every channel generates noise. Whether the channel is a telephone cable or face-to-face speech, the written word or tribal drums, noise gets into the system. A channel carries information from a 'transmitter' to a 'receiver' and in the process noise is generated. Static on the radio, ink smudges on paper and the *ums* and *arhs* and *ers* and *mms* in everyday speech are all noise. It's the stuff that disrupts the message. It's undesired information, unexplained variation, random error. It's not needed; it's not wanted; it's not *signal*. Information is both noise and signal (Moles, 1966), but it's signal that's required and sorted out because signal unlocks meaning. A receiver receives information and sorts the signal from the noise. Because noise is an evaluative term it is identified only in the receiver, the channel does not know the difference between signal and noise. Imagine that a foreign intelligence agent is sent a page from Shakespeare that is covered with pencil marks, squiggles and underlining. The page can be read in the ordinary way, as a Shakespeare text, and the marks are just meaningless irritants – they are noise. But to the agent, who knows what to look for, the squiggles highlight key words that form a message and it's Shakespeare's text that becomes noise.

In any communication system noise naturally increases. And left to its own devices it would increase to a maximum. As messages are transmitted and received and passed on noise builds up. And at some hypothetical 'end of information', at the end of all communication, at the end of all transmission and reception all that there would be is noise and a communication system in a state of maximum entropy.

Entropy

The universe is winding down. Cosmology tells us that it all started with a 'Big Bang' and is shifting to an all encompassing equilibrium where every atom will be moving chaotically at the same average velocity. Contrast will cease to exist, there will be no hot and cold, no light and dark, no fast atoms and no slow atoms. Variation and difference will be wiped out. A blanket uniformity will pervade everywhere. These theories follow from the second law of thermodynamics that says that heat only flows in one direction – from a hot body to a cold body. And the heat flows until both bodies are at the same temperature, until they both have the same amount of heat energy. Make a cup of tea; leave it for a while and it cools down because the heat from the tea flows into the environment. The tea never gets hotter with the area immediately around the cup cooling. Ice cubes chill a drink because heat flows from the liquid into the ice. Heat always flows in one direction and dissipates evenly. The steam engine turns heat into mechanical energy but it can only work when the engine is at a higher temperature than its surroundings. When all the fuel is burnt and the engine is at the same temperature as its surroundings no further useful work can be done. Here the system is at maximum entropy, the difference between hot and cold has been eradicated and there is nothing else to be done.

Everything tends towards this state of maximum entropy, chaos and randomness. An ordinary office desk naturally becomes more and more untidy. A tidy desk has low entropy because everything is in its place, clearly delineated; there is a clear difference between the items on the desk just as there is a clear temperature difference between the hot tea and the immediate environment. As the desk gradually becomes untidy chaos sets in, items are distributed randomly and entropy increases. Any 'system' has this tendency, from the whole of the cosmos to a few molecules moving around each other.

In information and communication systems entropy is manifested by noise. Entropy is low when the signal is very strong, noise is minimised and the message is clear. But no communication happens in isolation. One message refers to another, information is a complex web, signals are constantly transmitted and received and passed on. Noise builds up, signals are no longer clear and entropy increases. When entropy reaches a maximum all is chaos and communication ceases. The signal can no longer be discerned.

Entropy and western music

This model of increasing entropy maps neatly onto developments in western music, particularly in the twentieth century. Tonal music, with its primary structures centred on pitch, has very low entropy. Difference and clear delineation is created through the patterns in pitch interval relationships and scales where one note has the focal centre. The tonic in a diatonic scale is a very clear point of convergence, everything pulls towards it. All the other notes in the scale have a well-defined, hierarchical relationship to that pitch. Harmony, simultaneity of pitch in accordance with established laws, the vertical extension of the linear structure of the scale, continues this process. A listener is guided easily through diatonic music because the tonic is a constant reference point, an auditory beacon making navigation easy. Entropy is low, distinction is clear, difference is manifested in the harmonic tensions and relaxations built around the tonal centre. Here there is plenty of room for the music to be symbolic, to be programmatic and to mean something other than what it actually is – a sonic structure, a collection of sounds. Culture, memory and expectation all work together on the sound and can produce fairly predictable results – major keys equate with strident, positive feelings, minor keys are sad, diminished chords mean danger.

The pitch and duration relationships of the notes in a diatonic melody generate a clear signal because it is these relationships on which the primary structure is built. Other elements of the sound world, dynamics, timbre and the location of the sound become relatively unimportant in the structural identity of the work. The opening bars of the melody of Beethoven's Fifth Symphony can be played loudly on a kazoo, quietly on a bass trombone or sung mezzo-forte by a tone deaf rugby team but so long as the relative pitch and durational relationships remain intact it will still be recognisable as Beethoven Fifth Symphony.[3] The dynamics and timbre are redundant.

The pitch structures in chromatic and atonal music have higher entropy. Pitch relationships are more egalitarian and the gravitational force of the tonal centre is unstable or is dissipated completely. With total serialism and indeterminacy the pitch structures become impossible to comprehend with the ear alone. Timbre and dynamics have equal status with pitch and duration; what is heard is sound, not tunes or harmonies or rhythms (in any conventional musical sense). Looking back to the heyday of modernism Morton Feldman described events between 1950 and 1951 when he spent a lot of time with John Cage, Earle Brown and Christian Wolff:

> Up to now the various elements of music (rhythm, pitch, dynamics etc.) were only recognisable in terms of their formal relationship to each other. As controls were given up, one finds that these elements lose their initial, inherent identity. But it is just because of this identity that these elements can be unified within the composition. Without this identity there can be no unification. It follows then, that an indeterminate music can only lead to catastrophe. This catastrophe we allowed to take place. Behind it was sound – which unified everything. Only by 'unfixing' the elements traditionally used to construct a piece of music could the sounds exist in themselves – not as symbols, or memories which were memories of other music to begin with (Feldman, 1985, p. 48).

The traditional elements of music became 'unfixed', the relationship between these elements became unclear and chaotic, entropy increased.

No matter how the elements became 'unfixed' the aural results were the same.

> What music rhapsodizes in today's cool language, is its own construction. The fact that men like Boulez and Cage represent opposite extremes of modern methodology is not what is interesting. What is interesting is their similarity. In the music of both men, things are exactly what they are – no more no less. In the music of both men, what is heard is indistinguishable from its process (Nyman, 1999, p. 2).

Music became inharmonic and got closer to noise both sonically and in terms of information. The signals became unclear, the message was scrambled and exactly what music meant to the listening public became confused and uncertain. Indeed Stravinsky did not believe music expressed anything at all:

> For I consider that music is, by its very nature, essentially powerless to *express* anything at all, whether a feeling, an attitude of mind, a psychological mood, a phenomenon of nature, etc. ... *Expression* has never been an inherent property of music (Stravinsky, 1962, p. 53).

Noise became a powerful force in the twentieth century and its history charts the history of recent times.

The Futurists

In the years before the First World War the Futurists were proposing an 'art of noises'. They were seduced by the glamour of speed, the bustle of the city and the dynamism of the mechanical age. Youth, action, violence and rebellion fuelled their movement. They produced many manifestos and pamphlets, for theirs was the first cultural movement of the twentieth century aimed at a mass audience. Their founder and leader, Filippo Tommaso Marinetti, was a wealthy poet and skilful manipulator of the mass media. In 'The Founding and Manifesto of Futurism 1909', that was published on the front page of *Le Figaro* on 20 February that year, he wrote:

> We will sing of great crowds excited by work, by pleasure and by riot; we will sing of the multicoloured, polyphonic tides of revolution in modern capitals; we will sing of the vibrant nightly fervour of arsenals and shipyards blazing with violent electric moons; greedy railway stations that devour smoke-plumed serpents; factories hung on clouds by the crooked lines of their smoke; bridges that stride the rivers like giant gymnasts, flashing in the sun with a glitter of knives; adventurous steamers that sniff the horizon; deep-chested

locomotives whose wheels paw the tracks like the hooves of enormous steel horses bridled by tubing; and the sleek flight of planes whose propellers chatter in the wind like banners and seem to cheer like an enthusiastic crowd (Apollonio, 1973, p. 22).

These fervent portraits of industry, clamour and strength are created as much by reference to sound as to image and this is typical of the broad Futurist aesthetic that attempted to destroy the boundaries around the art forms. Similarly, a manifesto by the painter Carlo Carrà, 'Painting of Sounds, Noise and Smells', makes claims about a fantastic array of auditory effects in Futurist paintings (Apollonio, 1973). But it was Balilla Pratella who became the 'official' Futurist composer and whose work, by all accounts, was fairly conventional, employing folk melodies and whole tone scales. Nonetheless his writings (probably spiced and poeticised by Marinetti) were full of the blast and bombast of the movement and one year after the publication of the founding manifesto he produced the 'Manifesto of Futurist Musicians 1910'. This is a diatribe against the ageing musical establishment. 'I appeal to the *young*', he writes,

> Only they should listen, and only they can understand what I have to say. Some people are born old, slobbering spectres of the past, cryptograms swollen with poison (Apollonio, 1973, p. 31).

This is an archetypal youthful cry to sweep away the past, a glorious precursor to the punks of the 1970s and, in fact, to all the radical youth movements linked to pop music since the creation of teenagers in the 1950s. Pratella goes on to praise Wagner, Strauss, Debussy and even Elgar but then turns again to attack the establishment.

> The vegetating schools, conservatories and academies act as snares for youth and art alike. In these hot-beds of impotence, masters and professors, illustrious deficients, perpetuate traditionalism and combat any effort to widen the musical field (Apollonio, 1973, p. 33).

Despite his call-to-arms it was not Pratella who widened the musical field but another painter Luigi Russolo who penned the most notorious text on Futurist music 'The Art of Noises' published in 1913. The text pays homage to Pratella but quickly moves on to document the history of noise.

> Ancient life was all silent. In the 19th century with the invention of the machine, Noise was born. Today, Noise triumphs and reigns supreme over the sensibility of men (Apollonio, 1973, p. 74).

In the conclusions Russolo states that 'Futurist musicians must continually enlarge and enrich the field of sounds'. (Apollonio, 1973, p. 86). The sounds used in music had become too familiar and so:

Futurist musicians must substitute for the limited variety of tones possessed by orchestral instruments today the infinite variety of tones of noises, reproduced with appropriate mechanisms (Apollonio, 1973, pp. 86–7).

In an attempt to realise some of his ideas Russolo built a number of devices called *Intonarumori* or Noise Intoners. These were mechanical devices that were a partly sculpture and partly musical instrument. He described their construction and operation as follows:

> It was necessary for practical reasons that the Noise Intoner be as simple as possible, and this we succeeded in doing. It is enough to say that a single stretched diaphragm placed in the right position gives, when its tension is varied, a scale of more than ten tones, complete with all the passages of semitones, quarter-tones and even all the tiniest fractions of tones. The preparation of the material for these diaphragms is carried out with special chemical baths, and varies according to the timbre of noise that is required. By varying the way in which the diaphragm itself is moved, further types and timbres of noise can be obtained while retaining the possibility of varying the tone (Tisdall and Bozzolla, 1978, p. 116).

Russolo was not interested in imitating familiar sounds or symbolising objects that made sound. In many ways he pre-dated Chion's *Guide des objets sonores* (1983) and Schaeffer's idea of 'reduced listening' and the classification of sounds in his *Traité des objets musicaux* (1966). Six classifications or 'families' of noises are mentioned in the Futurist manifesto (Apollonio, 1973, p. 86):

1	2	3	4	5 Noises obtained by percussion on:	6 Voices of animals and men:
Rumbles	Whistles	Whispers	Screeches	Metal	Shouts
Roars	Hisses	Murmurs	Creaks	Wood	Screams
Explosions	Snorts	Mumbles	Rustles	Skin	Groans
Crashes		Grumbles	Buzzes	Stone	Shrieks
Splashes		Gurgles	Crackles	Terracotta etc.	Howls
Booms			Scrapes		Laughs
					Wheezes
					Sobs

The *Intonarumori* caused a sensation and were presented in salons, concert halls and theatres to riotous acclaim. The usual form of presentation was the *Serata Futurista* or Futurist Evening. This was a chaotic mixture of theatre, concert and political rally. The events were announced well in advance and the venues were always packed with an audience high on wild anticipation. The Futurists' reputation went before them, thanks to Marinetti's publicity skills, so the outcome of the evening was inevitable. Insults were hurled back and forth between the performers and the audience, fights broke out and riots ensued pouring out into the streets, bars and cafes. There were always indignant outcries in the following day's press thus fuelling the publicity machine and ensuring maximum capacity audiences wherever the Futurists went. Violence, chaos and noise spoke of the irreversible changes in society's hierarchical structures that would occur as a result of the cataclysm that would shortly engulf Europe.

Pop noise

From its earliest beginnings pop music was always more successful and enduring when it was in opposition to conventional ideas of musical sophistication. It should be a young person's music. A vibrant, rebellious din that generates perplexity, disdain or maybe even outright fear in the older generation(s). It is at its best when its virtuosity works against received notions of musicality. This was the case in pop music's humble beginnings. In Britain the skiffle groups of the 1950s utilised crude instrumentation – guitar, banjo, a washboard played with thimbles and the tea-chest bass. This was a home-made instrument constructed by stretching a string from the top of a broom pole, which stood vertically on a wooden tea-chest, down to the top surface of the chest so that the space within the chest acted as a resonator. It produced a suitable low frequency thud of dubious pitch, but adequate, in the hands of a skilful player, to give the illusion of bass. The music that these groups performed was the antithesis of the rich, suave sound produced by the Crooners and Big Bands who preceded them. Bing Crosby, Frank Sinatra and their like used microphones and amplification to integrate a soft, subtle, intimate vocal sound into large-scale, lush orchestrations penned by musically sophisticated arrangers. Here, musical sophistication is synonymous with complex harmonic structure so the relatively simple, primary diatonic harmony and pentatonic melodies of the skiffle groups coupled with the rough, raw sounds of their instruments appeared vulgar compared with the sumptuous, seductive dazzle of the previous era.

Instrumental and vocal skill also ran against the received norm. The skiffle performers were virtuosic, but in their own terms within their own invented genre. Vocalists sang down their noses producing a very resonant sound which, by conventional standards, was harsh, vulgar and jarring. It wasn't 'proper' singing, they didn't have 'good' voices.

Melodies and accompaniments were propelled by hard, fast rhythms unsuitable for dances that the previous generation had spent long evenings learning at dancing school – the fox-trot, the waltz etc. The skiffle phenomenon was driven by the idea that anyone could do it. Musical training wasn't necessary and was probably even undesirable. And lots of people did do it; the instruments were easy to obtain, there were skiffle groups on almost every street and there were ample opportunities to play in coffee bars, youth clubs and dances.

The roots of skiffle lay in American folk music. Like most post-war popular culture it was imported to Britain, mutated and then bounced backwards and forwards across the Atlantic. It started as folk music sessions in clubs where trad and revivalist jazz was predominant. Skiffle evolved alongside rock 'n' roll which had itself evolved from Black American music. This was working class culture, derided by the bourgeoisie for its apparent lack of sophistication and subtlety. It was cultural noise – jangling, harsh and irritating. British pop groups based in the major ports of Liverpool and London had relatively easy access to recordings of Black American music and rock 'n' roll which were initially brought over by people who worked on the many cargo ships and liners that regularly sailed across the Atlantic. Elvis Presley, the first white man to make a successful career singing black people's music, along with Chuck Berry, Bo Diddley and many, many others detonated the explosion of pop music. The Beatles and The Rolling Stones along with many other British groups sold rock 'n' roll and rhythm and blues back to America, and America sent back Bob Dylan, Jimi Hendrix and psychedelia.

Throughout the fifty-year development of pop music there have been periods of creative excitement alternating with periods of tedium. During periods of tedium pop music often attempts to emulate large-scale forms like opera or the orchestral suite. It becomes pretentious and focuses on conventional ideas of performance virtuosity, emphasising the idea that only the instrumental star can make music and certainly not achievable by everyone. Specialist knowledge and skills are required to participate. Skiffle/rock 'n' roll in the 1950s, acid rock in the 1960s, punk in the 1970s, techno/dance in the 1980s and 90s were classic examples of periods when things were exciting in the pop world and tedium was banished. These movements pushed pop music forward beyond the established limits. The music was underpinned by a kind of return to the basic principles of pop: anti-virtuosity, appropriation and adaptation of technology, creative experimentation and the idea that 'anyone can do it'. At these times street fashion also blossomed in the atmosphere of creativity. Young people invented new looks often based on anti-virtuosity (the ripped and torn of punk) and retro modes (the charity shop chic of the 1990s). The predominant fashion rules broke down because the 'anyone can do it' aesthetic prevailed.

Inventive pop music is generally disruptive and disturbing both musically and socially. It starts underground, a voice for the dispossessed and the misfits. It fights back, rejecting the slick marketing gloss of the powerful major record companies. The music is produced, distributed and consumed outside of the mainstream. The musicians appropriate and adapt instrumental resources that are considered rudimentary by accepted standards: the washboard and tea-chest bass in skiffle has an equivalence in the brash distorted guitars used from psychedelia to punk and the relatively simple analogue music technology and record decks that featured in early techno. In all of these cases the mainstream was represented by a rich, sophisticated sound world and the new music by a brash, vulgar noise.

Distortion, resonance and feedback (technically all very closely linked) are the powerhouses of rock music's guitar technique. The harmonic richness produced by a plucked metal string is initially amplified by pickups, mounted on the body of the guitar, which are connected to an amplifier the circuits of which are specially designed to deal with the spectrum of vibrating metal strings. There are several designs of pickup but essentially they are magnets surrounded by coils of fine copper wire. The metal string moves within the magnetic field generating a tiny electrical current in the surrounding coil which is amplified to the extent that it can drive a loudspeaker. Above a certain volume threshold the sound from the loudspeaker causes the strings of the guitar to vibrate in sympathy and this resonance builds up in a feedback loop the quality of which depends on the volume levels and the proximity of the guitar strings and pickups to the loudspeaker. The materials from which the guitar is made also have a marked effect on the quality of the sound. The whole is a very neat system; complex, sophisticated and inexhaustible but easily manipulated to great effect in the right hands.

One of the greatest virtuosos of the electric guitar was Jimi Hendrix (1942–70) a black Native American who achieved fame and notoriety after coming to England in 1966. A wild, flamboyant character this 'psychedelic voodoo child', with his mass of frizzy hair and dressed in big black hats and coloured silk scarves, terrified the white, middle-aged, middle-classes whose children were 'blissed out'[4] on the raw sexuality of his performances. The intense power of volume, distortion and howling feedback created a visceral sensory overload resembling total body immersion, a heightened drug experience or passionate sexual activity.

He was left handed but played a right-handed instrument strung for left-handed playing. In this position the volume and tone controls and the vibrato arm of the guitar were now at the top of the instrument enabling Hendrix to develop a whole new technique of controlling feedback and distortion. He used the guitar as a kind of electronic sound source although by all accounts he had very little interest in electronic music.

> On some records you hear all this clash and bang and fanciness but all we're doing is laying down the guitar tracks and then echo here and there, but we're not adding false electronic things. We use the same thing anyone else would, but we use it with imagination and common sense. Like *House Burning Down*, we made the guitar sound like it was on fire, it's constantly changing dimensions, and up on top that lead guitar is cutting through everything (*UniVibes*, 1995).

And speaking at a press launch for the album *Electric Ladyland* Hendrix spoke about the track *And the Gods Made Love*:

> You're really going to be disappointed when you hear our first track on our new LP, because it starts with a 90 second sound painting of the heavens. I know it's the thing people will jump on to criticise so we're putting it right at the beginning to get it over with (*UniVibes*, 1995).

This 'sound painting' comprises classic tape techniques of reversal and speed change. Like many other pop musicians of that time Hendrix was keen to explore the possibilities offered by the recording studio but electroacoustic experimentation was always underpinned by conventional pitch- and rhythm-based structures and, according to some critics, the music was highly programmatic.

> The 'burning guitar' effect can also be heard on the solo lead guitar at the end of the song [*House Burning Down*]. Jimi produces a 'siren'-like noise by hammering-on a flattened fifth interval between 'F' on the fourth string, fifteenth fret and 'B' on the fifth string, fourteenth fret. Whilst hammering-on these notes he slowly depresses the vibrato arm adding to the eeriness of the effect. The extreme 'motorbike'-like noise at the very end of the track was created using an echoplex [a tape echo machine] with 'regeneration' up to threshold of runaway feedback ... The 'burning guitar' isn't the only piece of programme music in *House Burning Down*. In the middle of the second verse Jimi creates a 'motorbike noise' by depressing the vibrato arm then hitting the fifth string open, then slowly releasing the vibrato arm so the note returns to pitch. The tape phasing/flanging and delay makes these effects sound all the more effective (*UniVibes*, 1995).

Hendrix's technique always embellished the mood of the song which was established through lyrics, tempo and the harmonic and melodic structures. Feedback and distortion symbolised familiar objects by emulating the sounds they produced: motorbikes, machine guns, sirens. These *things* generated meaning that resonated in pop culture at that time, they were associated with life in the western world in the late 1960s when war was raging in Vietnam and students and factory workers fought the police on the streets of Paris.

Perhaps the most glamorously vulgar pop movement to date was Punk. It erupted in the second half of the 1970s just before the Thatcher/Reagan era. Fuelled by boredom, frustration and anger it had all the ingredients of an iconoclastic new movement coiled ready to strike at the throat of a complacent establishment. The radical psychedelic experiments of the late 1960s had predictably evolved into the tedium of 'symphonic' rock, concept albums and large-scale spectacles that showcased inflated instrumental techniques. This kind of pop music took itself very seriously and the musicians wanted to be equated with the great classical composers. Some groups even made their own arrangements of popular classics in order to demonstrate their performance skills. This area of the industry was now focusing on full length LPs leaving the production of singles to glossy teenybopper bands who resorted to the extreme theatricals of 'glam rock' – sequins, glitter and impossible platform-soled shoes. Pop music had become very pretentious or extremely kitsch and was just waiting to be exploded by a bunch of pale, ill-bred, spotty youths with leather jackets, spiky haircuts and bad breath.

Like all pop music punk had precedents in America (the word itself is American, slang for 'a worthless person or thing' [*Chambers Dictionary*]). It began to show through in the extremes of White Trash Glam Rock bands like The New York Dolls and The Stooges but there were also very strong links to The Velvet Underground who had produced a powerful antithesis to the laid back, gentle sweetness of flower powered hippies in the late 1960s. This band were, and continue to be, a commanding, dominant force in the history of pop music. They made only a few records that sold in relatively small quantities but it was once said that such was their influence that everyone who heard them formed a band. The group rose to fame working with Andy Warhol in his downtown multimedia events of the late 1960s. 'Andy Warhol, Up-Tight' and 'The Exploding Plastic Inevitable' involved concentrated simultaneity: multi-screen projections of underground films, light shows, dancing with music by The Velvet Underground. The events often started routinely with one or two films. As the evening progressed the other activities were piled in so that the group played while several films, slides and lights were projected onto them; a cacophony of sensory overload. There was a lot of lascivious dancing and performers rushing into the audience screaming obscenities. The music was loud and brutal with lyrics about New York low-life, drug taking and bizarre sex. As film maker Paul Morrissey said, this was 'a completely different kind of rock 'n' roll' (Bockris and Malanga, 1983).

The sound of The Velvet Underground was particularly abrasive and the inclusion of the electric viola played by John Cale intensified this. Cale, a Welshman, was a classically trained musician who had studied in London at Goldsmiths College in the early 1960s and had come into contact with many avant-garde and experimental music figures including the composer Cornelius Cardew and the Fluxus artist George Brecht. In 1963 he went to America on a music scholarship to study with Iannis Xenakis at Tanglewood, then later went to New York where he met John Cage and, most importantly, La Monte Young. Cale took Young's ideas and filtered them directly into The Velvet Underground. Intense repetition, extended duration and extreme volume were the trademarks of Young's work at that time. With his wife and long time collaborator, the light artist Marian Zazeela, he formed 'The Theatre of Eternal Music' a performance ensemble dedicated to the exacting demands of his pieces. The works involved the establishment of a drone, often with the use of very stable sine wave generators, and the articulation of pitches harmonically related to the fundamental frequencies of the drone. Everything was amplified to maximum volume so that upper partials could be clearly heard. Young also set up sine wave generators in his loft apartment and had them droning continuously at extreme volumes.

As well as working with incredibly stable pitches and harmonics Young also worked with noise. His *Poem for Tables, Chairs, Benches, etc.* (1960) involves dragging furniture around a performance space for a very long time. *2 Sounds* is a tape piece recorded with Terry Riley, made for the dancer Anna Halprin, that comprises tin cans scraped on glass and a gong scraped with a drum stick. Cornelius Cardew wrote of the piece in *The Musical Times*:

> When the first sound starts you cannot imagine that any more horrible sound exists in the whole world. Then the second sound comes in and you have to admit you were wrong (Cardew, 1966, p. 960).

And Henry Flynt wrote:

> When the tape ends after fifteen minutes, the ensuing silence comes as a shock: silence has somehow been charged. With more

experienced hearings, the programme resolves into glissandos like the roars of animals. (It's not a blank noise piece after all.) (Duckworth and Fleming, 1996, p. 51).

During its inception the piece comprised three sounds, the third being produced by moving orchestral triangles around in a metal bucket, but Young rejected this. However, this led to apocryphal, but completely inaccurate stories of Young performing his piece colloquially known as *X for Henry Flynt* (but correctly titled *Arabic numeral (any integer) (April 1960)*) by bashing with a hammer on a bucket of nails that was amplified to the threshold of aural pain. An eminent precursor of Einstürzende Neubauten or Test Department?

John Cale had been a member of The Theatre of Eternal Music and was immersed in Young's ideas as well as those of the European avant-garde. Other New York musicians involved in early versions of The Velvet Underground had also worked with La Monte Young: Tony Conrad, Walter DeMaria and Angus MacLise. Conrad was a violinist who had played in The Theatre of Eternal Music at the same time as Cale; DeMaria and MacLise were drummers. Tony Conrad introduced Lou Reed into this circle of musicians. Reed was an archetypal rock 'n' roll guitarist playing in a band called The Primitives and Conrad, Cale and DeMaria were hired to play in the band to promote a record called *The Ostrich*. According to Conrad this song involved tuning all the strings of their instruments to the same note, a technique very close to those of La Monte Young's. This fusion of orthodox rock 'n' roll and the avant-garde was the embryonic beginning of The Velvet Underground. Reed brought in his friend Sterling Morrison on guitar and also introduced the drummer Maureen Tucker who played in a very minimal style with tom-tom beaters. Later, after the band had been adopted by Andy Warhol, the singer Nico began working with them.

While working with La Monte Young, Cale had filed down the bridge of his viola enabling him to play three strings at once, he had also used guitar strings on the instrument which he claimed gave him 'a sound like a jet engine'. This, coupled with droning, grinding guitars, dense crashing organ clusters and primitive pounding drums, all amplified to create a deluge of continuous noise, is the sound of The Velvet Underground – the seminal art rock punk band and one of the most influential pop groups ever. Their music exemplifies the deranged profanity that is New York: congested, dense and claustrophobic, with a touch of chic in the form of a seductive, European female vocalist who adds a dash of the bored *femme fatale* to the din of urban vulgarity. Here were the final deathbed gasps of modernism; not whimpers but bangs. The final shrieks celebrating the fact that the avant-garde of western culture had moved from Paris to New York. And all this just before the whole show moved back again to Europe to crank up postmodernism with the Situationist International fighting the government of Charles de Gaulle on the streets of Paris in 1968. In some ways the whole of American modernism fed into The Velvet Underground; the works of John Cage, Jackson Pollock, William Burroughs etc., had all made their mark, and what emerged was a dense, ear-splitting noise.

British punk was different from that in America. Essentially it grew from the streets, was then overtaken by an art-school aesthetic and finally became a massive pop commodity. Britain in the mid-1970s was a country of political instability, economic recession and unemployment levels that had not been experienced for many years. The post-war boom was over and the industrial era appeared to be grinding to a halt. The youth of the time had no clear future mapped out. There were no charts indicating the way ahead. Previous generations had simply followed in the footsteps of their parents or, after the war, some rode on the crest of the wave and become socially mobile. Now there was nothing and 'No future' became the anthem of punk ideology. The kids were bored, their culture was tired and pop music was dull. As often happens in times of uncertainty there was a glance backwards, a brief brush with a previous era before the blast forwards. And for a short time the 1970s brushed against the 1950s. In the desperate search for novelty some groups embraced the kitsch glamour of that time. Roxy Music, for example, with their name alone, implied a nostalgic return to the glitz and glitter of the old cinemas and dance halls. They appeared on their album covers looking like Teddy boys from outer space with slick, greasy haircuts, dazzling clothes and retro-futuristic guitars.

In this brief encounter with the 1950s and early 1960s punk music ignited spontaneously in a backlash against the pretensions and pomposity of 'progressive' rock music. The short, snappy pop song returned. The three chord trick was back – soon to be distilled into the one chord trick. Instrumentation shrunk to the basics – guitars, bass, drums – and, once again, anyone could do it. Musical training with hours of practice was unnecessary because expert technique was completely undesirable. As in the skiffle movement in the 1950s there were bands on almost every street and they began to play in pubs and clubs without the need for the massive resources on which the mainstream had come to rely. Within months the whole thing exploded. Youth had found a voice and it was used to sweep away the previous era in a great blast of *noise*.

Distortion, feedback and pounding drums drove the music at high speed. But this time complete anarchy and chaos informed the structure, gone were the considered articulations of Jimi Hendrix. Punks worked at deafening volume, hacking their songs of nihilism, boredom and discontent from great slabs of sound. Their performances were total mayhem, a 1970s equivalent of the Futurists fifty years before. Audiences careered around and bounced up and down spitting at the bands or invaded the stage bringing everything to a halt. Plugs were pulled, equipment was smashed and often everything simply collapsed in an orgy of annihilation. Wild, insane and totally compelling. Mass destruction on such a scale that anything and everything became possible.

Out of this seething entropy a more considered, informed sensibility emerged, gently assisted by one or two personalities who emerged as the 'senior prefects' of the genre. One of these characters was Malcolm McLaren the manager of punk's most visible protagonists, The Sex Pistols. McLaren created an environment in which this band could flourish. He owned a fashion boutique on the King's Road, Chelsea selling 1950s teddy boy clothes, had been well educated at Croydon College of Art and Goldsmith's College (where John Cale had also been a student) and had a keen eye for a business opportunity. Before he presented The Sex Pistols to the world he had managed the New York Dolls for a short period. At Croydon McLaren met Jamie Reid who became a friend and ally. The two of them became aware of the Situationist International, an anarchist movement of writers, artists and thinkers who railed against the capitalist spectacle of everyday life and were the intellectual powerhouses of the uprising of workers and students in Paris in May 1968. McLaren and Reid simply plagiarised Situationist art, ideas and practice and incorporated them into the prevailing punk sensibility. This injection of radical politics and art history appealed greatly to students and intellectuals and punk's art rock status was confirmed.

1970s Britain also witnessed radical change in the Fine Art world. Performance Art was emerging and there was often great media controversies about tax-payers' money being spent on activities such as those of Ddart – three men who toured East Anglia with a pole on their heads.[5] Performance Art had its roots in Futurist and Dadaist performance as well as the Happenings and Fluxus events that had grown out of the work of John Cage and others, particularly at Black Mountain College in 1952. Art colleges were experiencing some decline in interest in painting and sculpture that corresponded with an increase in interest in time based media (although the term had not been devised at that time). Students performed in non-narrative visual events, worked with sound and video (then in its infancy) and formed orchestras and rock bands. The rock bands were by no means a new phenomenon – just about every major British rock band has had at least one member who had attended art school. 'The art school dance goes on forever'.[6]

Sound, usually recorded sound, played an important role in the work of several British performance groups of this period. It was 'another layer', adding density, intensifying overload and increasing confusion. This simultaneity generated ambiguity, doubt and uncertainty. Clarity was smeared, narrative was scrambled. There were parallels with Warhol's 'Exploding Plastic Inevitable' and the multilayered realisations of John Cage's works such as *Variations IV*. But whereas Cage painstakingly constructed his works, organising each event in a piece using chance operations (thereby, he believed, leaving very little to chance in the performances),[7] the action in British performance art was often unscripted and improvised, with artists manipulating materials – their bodies, objects, light, sound – in real time. Indeed, time and process were considered 'material' just as much as concrete objects. Tape re-corders were readily available and artists made tapes. Anything and everything was recorded: speech, radio, television, music, environmental sound – *anything*. Material was mixed, arbitrarily cut and spliced and fed into the performance process. Techniques were relatively simple and chaotic compared with the meticulous operations of the established electroacoustic music studios, but the results had an equivalence with the energetic anti-virtuosity prevalent in punk. Within the fine art tradition sound became an extension of sculpture, which is not the same as sculptures that make sound.

Coum Transmissions were one of the performance groups that utilised sound. This was the name Genesis P-Orridge and Cosey Fanni Tutti gave to their performance activities just at the time punk was gestating. The subject matter of the material presented by Coum reflected a fascination with and absorption in the grim underbelly of humanity: torture, violent sexual fetishism, serial killers, Nazi death camps etc. Fanni Tutti worked as a model for pornographic magazines and one image of her inspired their 'Prostitute' exhibition at the Institute of Contemporary Arts in London in October 1976. There was a huge public outcry because of the nature of the material exhibited and the fact that P-Orridge told the *Sun* newspaper that he had spent most of their Arts Council grant on drugs. Like Malcolm McLaren he was a great media manipulator and was able to generate a great deal of attention where none was really justified. And like McLaren he realised that working within the confines of the art world, especially within performance art, would bring limited success and public recognition. Coum Transmissions had occasionally included Peter Christopherson in their work and now they added Chris Carter and together they became the band Throbbing Gristle just at the time that punk was becoming a viable commodity.

The early music made by Throbbing Gristle was a dark, chaotic cacophony. Improvised over backing tapes it comprised an arbitrary collection of lack-lustre synthesised electronics mixed with pre-recorded speech, tape loops and vocals supplemented with instrumental sounds from slide guitar, cornet and bass guitar. All processed with copious amounts of spring reverb and tape echo. A muddy, resonant din. They often employed clichéd sound effects reminiscent of cheap B-movie horror – rising glissandi washed with reverb, screams and deranged male voices fantasising about violence and murder. Looking back Cosey Fanni Tutti remarked:

> I mean TG started off as a joke in the beginning. We were quite serious about breaking down the rock 'n' roll thing, but it was tongue in cheek at the same time because we knew we were giving them a load of rubbish soundwise just to get them out of their expectation of music (Neal, 1987, p. 216).

But at the time Genesis P-Orridge seemed to take the whole project very seriously declaring:

> We're interested in information, we are not interested in music as such. And we believe that the whole battlefield, if there is one in the human situation, is about information (Re-Search, 1983).

The nature of the information in which Throbbing Gristle were interested is uncertain, as was their use for it, but there is no doubt that they were masters of control and organisation. Their appearance developed the feel of guerrilla warfare utilising camouflage jackets and military uniforms and they employed symbols, like trade marks, that bore a close resemblance to fascist emblems. Within a short time of their formation they started a record label to make available audio cassettes, videos and records. They called it 'Industrial Records' and it lent its name to the genre known as Industrial Music.

In *The Industrial Culture Handbook* (Re-Search, 1983), published two years after the formation of Industrial Records, the editors write 'By 'industrial' we mean the grim side of post-Industrial Revolution society — the repressed mythology, history, science, technology and psychopathology.' The industrial age was coming to a close in the early 1980s, its life force was exhausted and all that was left was the rotting, cadaverous hulk that had contained it. A collapsed economy left derelict factories, full of rusting machinery, crumbling, gloomy tower blocks and, for many people, a grisly daily round of dole queues, grey food and recycled television. Industrial music celebrated this closure and anticipated the coming of the digital age built on the new, electronic technology. The punk sound was constructed with loud, noisy guitars, industrial music maintained the noise but used an extended instrumental palette. The tape recorder became a commonplace musical instrument rather than a documentary tool and musicians were credited as playing 'tapes'. This practice predated the sampler and enabled any sound at all to be used for music making – a kind of punk *musique concrète*. Some bands took the materials of the dying industrial age to make music. Test Department used hammers on the redundant artefacts of the factories – huge metal tanks, sheet steel and anvils. Einstürzende Neubauten used pneumatic drills, cement mixers and angle grinders. And always these devices were amplified making bigger the sounds as they faded to nothing from everyday working lives.

Throbbing Gristle and Industrial Records were extremely influential in the creative climate that flourished during the punk era and beyond.

> Industrial culture? There has been a phenomena; I don't know whether it's strong enough to be a culture. I do think what we did has had a reverberation right around the world and back (Re-Search, 1983).

The enthusiasm for sonic exploration and experimentation, within an ethos that said 'anyone can do it', encouraged many young pop musicians to question notions of conventional musical structure – melody, harmony, rhythm – and search for other structures, other ways of putting sounds together.

The characteristics of two or more genres often 'breed' or mutate producing new styles and approaches. From the overloaded sonority of Jimi Hendrix and the aggressive, high velocity twiddlings of heavy rock came heavy metal, which itself has fragmented into death metal, speed metal, thrash metal and countless other metals. The word metal used in a musical context implies a clangorous, inharmonic din. Again, distorted electric guitar is the fundamental characteristic of the sound; distortion, crushing volume and an overbearing relentlessness. But, as usual in mainstream pop music, the primary musical structures are not that much different from those of skiffle – primary diatonic triads, pentatonic melodies and a steady, pulse-based rhythm in common time. What is different is the sound, the timbre, the dynamics and at the outer limits of heavy metal, at the edges of the genre, there are those who have abandoned the pitch and rhythm based structures and found other ways of making music. They use as their starting points the gestures, the clichés and the ethos but everything is pushed and squeezed until the pressure forces something new.

The guitarist Justin Broadrick began his work within the heavy metal genre. He played with Napalm Death, Painkiller and Torture Garden, now he is a member of Godflesh. As his career progressed the music mutated and he also pursued solo projects. Using the guitar as a primary sound source he has attempted to explore radical musical structure.

> It was a processes of taking the grossest of heavy metal riffs, feed them into the sampler, cut them up to pieces and try and get a new dynamic, a fresh sort of outlook on what people would mostly consider to be the lowest common denominator which I guess is heavy metal (Worby, 1997).

Although there is a celebration of vulgarity, crudity and what he calls 'the lowest common denominator' (it is the word *lowest* that is important here) Broadrick is well informed. Like many young musicians keen to explore the cutting edge of contemporary music he has a large collection of electroacoustic music recordings and he goes to concerts, although he feels alienated by the formality of 'classical' music presentation. Nonetheless his awareness of electroacoustic practice has informed his work.

> I discovered that beyond trying to make punk rock music, and learning my bar chord and being able to play that anywhere up and down the neck, once I'd heard Throbbing Gristle, and still being young, I realised I could make music with radios. I could turn on a short-wave radio and I could use my step-father's old analogue, echo-delay unit and feed it into that and then feed it back into it; and make my own music (Worby, 1997).

Again it was Throbbing Gristle that provided the justification for the methodology; their work gave 'permission' to Broadrick to present his findings after his explorations of what was, for him and other pop musicians, an alien sound world.

The experimental extremes of heavy metal have melded with industrial music, free improvised music and the areas where punk has invaded American minimalism, to produce noise music. This genre now incorporates a broad range of styles and techniques including loud, dense guitars, amplified industrial tools and electroacoustic instruments like samplers and record turntables but the term 'noise music' was first used in the early 1980s in New York. In those days it applied to the music that grew out of a synthesis of the art rock punk scene and downtown minimalism. Composer Glenn Branca was composing 'Symphonies' for multiple electric guitars, drums and bass. These pieces were incredibly dense and were performed at unbearable volume levels. In June 1981 'Noise Fest', a week long art and music event at White Columns, New York City, featured 26 bands. Writing about it in *ZG Magazine* Gary Zimmerman reported:

The twin sources of the music is punk and American avant-garde music ... It takes from Cage and La Monte Young the incorporation and registration of the incidental as well as the Cagean sense of being surrounded by a field of sound (an inescapable reality in New York) (Zimmerman, 1981, p. 11).

The term 'noise music' was incorporated into Industrial Music and today it also includes the outer edges of techno and other popular genres. The DJ culture of the 1990s unifies an historic throwback to the early *musique concrète* works of Pierre Schaeffer and the classic postmodern notions of appropriation, made easy with the availability of the sampler but actually started with the tape recorder in the late 1970s. In Japan, where 'noise bands' have thrived and then migrated to Europe and the USA, Otomo Yoshihide uses turntables, guitars, samplers and home-made electronics to make music that is a mixture of free jazz, *musique concrète* and extreme techno. He plunders, scrambles and reconstructs film scores, easy listening and jazz. His techniques are self-taught, eclectic and idiosyncratic.

Most influence comes from French musique concrète, Pierre Schaeffer and Pierre Henry. Also, there was some kind of rock stuff like Pink Floyd, always tape effects. Mostly contemporary composer's tape work, also Japanese '60's music. I really loved music when I was a teenager but I had no idea about how to play any instruments. My father is an electric engineer. Naturally, I knew how to make an analog system from my father. My mother was a big fan of jazz and rock. So, between my mother and father ... (Gross, 1998).

Resonance, feedback and distortion are a crucial ingredient in noise music and, it would seem, in all radical pop music. Distortion is accumulation, overdrive and mutation at the limits of a system and these extremes bring about change, be that in sound or in society. Distortion and feedback in sound cause partials to pile up and collide like molecules in a hot gas – chaos, randomness and entropy are manifested in noise. Noise *is* entropy; it signifies closure, the end. When society is pushed to the limits, when change is necessary and imminent, when the end of an era is reached noise blasts through every strand of culture, humanity and life.

The control of noise has made individuals, companies and governments rich and powerful. The suppression of noise has enabled the generation and efficient transmission of information by those who regulate, command and rule. But cacophony, dissonance and noise have flourished in our times, they have become weapons with which to fight complacency, indifference and lethargy and have made the music of the twentieth century a fabulous celebration of all that drives us into the future.

So to return to Jacques Attali: 'Nothing essential happens in the absence of noise' and 'for change is inscribed in noise faster than it transforms society'. (Attali, 1985, p. 3 and p. 5). Noise and cacophony have flourished in our times. Din is ingrained in our lives.

Notes

1. About 330 metres per second.
2. Although the degree of randomness of the vibrations can be constrained within set limits resulting in 'coloured noise' – noise within frequency bands. Drums are a typical example; we can order them from low to high without any individual drum having a specific pitch.
3. Played on muffled timpani it was the call signal ('V for Victory') for radio broadcasts to occupied Europe in the Second World War.
4. A fashionable phrase taken as the title of an examination of popular culture, *Blissed Out: The Raptures of Rock* (1990) by Simon Reynolds and Bill Albert (UK: Serpents Tail).
5. 'For this piece of work a 150 mile circumference circle was drawn on a map of East Anglia. Using existing roads and pathways a route was walked as close to the circle as possible. Average 23.5 miles a day. Pole worn at all times en route' ('Confessions of a Pole Walker' by Ray Richards of Ddart in *Extremes Magazine*, Vol. 1, 1976). This performance piece caused outrage at the time: a venomous article appeared in *The Sunday People* and questions were asked in the House of Commons.
6. 'Things May Come and Things May Go, but the Art School Dance Goes On Forever'. Title of an album by Pete Brown and Piblokto. (Harvest Records SHVL 768). The catch-phrase 'the art school dance goes on forever' was adopted by Fine Art practitioners during the 1970s.
7. Personal communication with the author 1989.

References

Apollonio, Umbro (ed.) (1973), *Futurist Manifestos*, London: Thames and Hudson.
Attali, Jacques (1985), *Noise – The Political Economy of Music*, Manchester: Manchester University Press.
Bockris, Victor and Malanga, Gerard (1983), *Up-Tight. The Velvet Underground Story*, London: Omnibus Press.
Cage, John (1968), *Silence*, London: Marion Boyars.
Cardew, Cornelius (1966), 'One Sound: La Monte Young', *Musical Times*, 107 (no. 1485), pp. 959–60.
Chion, Michel (1983), *Guide des objets sonores*, Paris: Buchet/Chastel.
Duckworth, William and Fleming, Richard (eds) (1996), *Sound and*

Light: La Monte Young and Marian Zazeela, Bucknell Review, Vol. XL, Number 1, Cranbury, NJ: Associated University Presses.

Feldman, Morton (1985), *Morton Feldman Essays*, Kerpen: Beginners Press/Walter Zimmermann.

Gross, Jason (1998), 'Otomo Yoshihide – Interview by Jason Gross', on http://www.furious.com/perfect/otomo.html (consulted March 2000).

Moles, Abraham (1966), *Information Theory and Esthetic Perception*, London: University of Illinois Press.

Neal, Charles (1987), *Tape Delay*, Harrow: SAF Publishing. .

Nyman, Michael (1999), *Experimental Music – Cage and Beyond* (second edition), Cambridge: Cambridge University Press.

Re-Search (1983), *Industrial Culture Handbook*, (*Re-Search* Issue 6/7), San Francisco: Re/Search Publications.

Schaeffer, Pierre (1966), *Traité des objets musicaux*, Paris: Editions du Seuil.

Steiner, George (1984), *George Steiner: A Reader*, London: Penguin.

Stravinsky, Igor (1962), *An Autobiography*, New York: W.W. Norton.

Tisdall, Caroline and Bozzolla, Angelo (1978), *Futurism*, New York: Oxford University Press.

UniVibes (1995), Univibes: The International Jimi Hendrix Magazine, Issue 20 (November 1995), Enniskeane (Ireland).

Worby, Robert (1997), *Cacophony Now*, BBC Radio 3.

Zimmerman, Gary (1981) 'Noise Music', *ZG 81 Magazine*, No. 3.

PART THREE

New places, spaces and narratives

CHAPTER SEVEN

Art on air:
a profile of new radio art

Kersten Glandien

Introduction

When art is on the move, definitions become blurred. This is true for radio art too; in fact, the changes in and around radio in the course of the twentieth century have made this condition the rule rather than the exception.

Ideas about using radio in an artistic way are as old as the medium itself. But, in the last two decades of the millennium, radio has taken on a new lease of life, generating new concepts, new approaches, new claims and new questions. Not only have the traditional art genres of radio work – *Hörspiel*, feature, radio theatre, sound poetry, electronic and electroacoustic music – bred further mutations and with them a new climate of interest, but also entirely new radiogenic forms have emerged. Artists coming from the visual world have found themselves increasingly attracted by the possibility of working with sound – eventually rediscovering radio as an appropriate medium for such work. In the fields of performance art, improvised music and multimedia new concepts and forms have appeared, which have lent themselves to or have been adopted by radio. All this has turned radio once again into a focal point of cultural interest. In times when new technologies have radically challenged the prospects of all artistic forms and genres, many artists and musicians have left their traditional discourses, venturing into new realms and creating new publics, dimensions and spaces. In the course of this migration radio has been rediscovered as a fruitful field of operation. Artists have looked for new auditive formats in this relatively old medium, making innovative use of its transmission technology and crossing over from telepresentation into telecommunication. From their side, adventurous radio producers have engaged with the new stream of activities by fighting for institutional space, working to create a forum for unconventional forms and assisting artists directly to deploy radio's unique media potential.

As a result of these changes, a field of widely varying activity and experimentation has been opened up, so diverse that no one has really been able to name it or nail it down. It was in this unsettled situation that the term 'radio art' was coined – a term sufficiently vague to accommodate the vast variety of forms on offer. Radio art first referred, perhaps, to the arrival of sound in the art world, but was immediately extended to embrace all unusual radiogenic experiments in other fields. Whenever definitions were attempted, they turned out to be either pragmatic or merely itemising.[1]

However, the vagueness of the term did not diminish its practicality. On the contrary, it helped facilitate communication and exchange between producers, artists and organisers whose interest in sound and work profiles otherwise significantly differed. At the same time this terminological indistinctness was evidence of a considerable lack of critical reflection, historical awareness and self-understanding. For a field in the making this is hardly surprising. Even at the beginning of the 1990s, when the development of the sound arts was well under way, there existed very little critical, historical or theoretical writing about radio art or sonic art-forms in general. Gregory Whitehead complained in 1991 about the 'numbing absence of critical discourse' (Whitehead, 1992, p. 253) and Douglas Kahn declared in 1992 the 'study of the relationship of sound and radio to the arts ... [to be] ... open to a full range of investigations, including the most general' (Kahn, 1992, p. 1).

Working backwards in time – looking for the landmarks of sound art, radio, media and technology – broadcasters, theoreticians and artists alike sought reassurance in history to establish their positions. Early evidence, such as the manifestos of the Italian Futurists, the intriguing sound poetry of the Dadaists and Orson Welles's radio-theatre work seemed as welcome to them as such later manifestations as Antonin Artaud's Theatre of Body-without-Organs (Artaud, 1974; see also Weiss, 1995), Glenn Gould's *Idea of North* trisonata (Page, 1984), German *Neues Hörspiel*, electronic music and *musique concrète* and the sound experiments of John Cage[2] or Mauricio Kagel. Detected sources of reference seemed to be as manifold and various as the perspectives taken by radio art itself and they continue to expand today as new forms emerge – *sound bricolage* being a recent example. In the space of the last ten years a considerable amount of textual groundwork on radio art has been completed so that we are now able to refer to some standard anthologies[3] and a fair number of theoretical and factual contributions on specific topics and events. These are the work of producers, radio enthusiasts, artists and the occasional academic and have appeared in books,[4] magazines,[5] catalogues,[6] conference documentation, radio publications and on the Internet[7] – mostly widely scattered and hard to locate.

In practice, sound arts emerging from various disciplines found their way into the most obvious sound medium at hand: radio, intending to utilise the magic channels for their own ends. In marginal programmes on public radio, in the small outposts of independent stations, in group projects and through the activities of enthusiastic radio mavericks, a wide range of radiogenic sound art was amassed and broadcast. All these initiatives were pluralistic and without a common aesthetic denominator and had the cumulative effect of rethinking radio in its institutional, medial and sonic aspects.

Radio: sound

In the early stages radio helped to bring into being the emancipation of sound. In the first two decades of the twentieth century and in a general atmosphere of technical invention, artistic experiment and social upheaval, an overall dissatisfaction with traditional art concepts and their inability to address changing social and cultural conditions grew steadily stronger in the artistic community, generating a craving for profound artistic change, radical statements and novel inspirations. Many of these inspirations were provided by radio. As the first solely acoustic medium in which every visual dimension was entirely absent, it found itself in a pioneer position, challenging the growing dominance of visuality characteristic of our age. Sound, once taken from its environmental context, its place of origin and means of generation, lost its self-evidence (Bruisma, 1990, p. 89) and gained an independent sonic existence in and beyond music. As a discrete entity, it became material for artistic exploration. This was made manifest in numerous texts (Luigi Russolo's *L'arte di rumori* (Russolo, 1986), in sound poetry (Kurt Schwitters, Victor Klebnikov), sound compositions (Antonio Russolo, Filippo Tommaso Marinetti), through the invention of new instruments (Luigi Russolo's *Intonarumori*) and in the incorporation of non-instrumental sounds into musical works (by Erik Satie and George Antheil) – to name but a few.

Radio engaged in this process with its own means. Through the use of audio amplification and recording and transmission technology, it proposed a new way of presenting music and speech: out of thin air. A disembodied sound reached listeners in their homes, first out of headphones and then loudspeakers. Radio also informed a new way of listening; one without direct visual references. Broadcasting speech and music at first separately through the same channel, radio soon started to fuse them into a new form. In 1924 *Hörspiel* was born, when in *Zauberei auf dem Sender* (Radio Magic) Hans Flesch succeeded in mixing text, sound and music into a single piece, establishing therewith a genre that would find a permanent place in German Radio programming. In this way, the new medium, with its capacity for combining music, sound and text, not only created its own genres but also challenged the autonomy and aesthetic orthodoxies of each individual component.

In the mid-1960s Paul Pörtner described both his *Schallspiel* (Soundplay) and his altered situation as author thus:

> [Soundplay is] a collage of voice and sound effects taken through a series of electronic manipulations until the sound effects begin to speak, the voice to drip like water and shatter like glass ... I trade the desk of an author for the studio of the sound engineer, my new syntax is the cut, my product is recorded over microphones, mixers and filters on magnetic tape, the principle of montage creates a playful composition (*Spielwerk*) out of hundreds of particles (Paul Pörtner quoted in Kahn and Whitehead, 1992, p. 331).

This combination of music, noise and text has been an important aspect of sound development from the early days, and still is: indeed radio art has often been generalised in these terms. Listening, for instance, to the sound pieces compiled by Heiner Goebbels in the early 1980s (discussed below) or American mixology aesthetics in the 1990s, makes it abundantly clear how potent this old radio art trinity still is.

After the Second World War, studio technology advanced the process of sound exploration. Public radio found itself at the heart of this development as it established experimental recording studios all over Europe. In this way, it assisted the development of sound work in two very different directions. The *Atelier de Création Radiophonique de Radio France* gave room to Pierre Schaeffer for his experiments with *found sounds*, and in the *Studio für Elektronische Musik* at North West German Radio (NWDR – later West German Radio, WDR) Robert Beyer, Herbert Eimert and Karlheinz Stockhausen generated the sound material of their compositions wholly synthetically, exploring the possibilities of sound building inherent in the latest electronic technologies. Informed by very different aesthetic concepts and working towards very different ends, composers and engineers pushed the frontiers of sonicity through their exploration of tape manipulation, new electronic processing devices, synthetic sound generation and multichannel diffusion.

The involvement of European public radio with these two major strands of post-war composition – *musique concrète* and *elektronische*

Musik – led German composer Dieter Schnebel to claim that these kinds of music 'came out of radio art' (Schnebel, 1994, p. 5). Yet, as advanced and influential as both of these endeavours were, they still remained within the conceptual boundaries of modernist music, since they continued to insist on working with abstract sound[8] – that is, sound that refers exclusively to itself. Even though Schaeffer took to the environment to find his sonic material – his *objets sonores* – he still focused exclusively on their non-referential usage. The aesthetic compulsion to music and the fact that this pioneering work was realised under the exclusive – and at the same time restrictive – conditions of expensive studios in public institutions, marked both of these projects.

In the late 1960s and through the 1970s, experimental radio work followed its then established routes of experimental *Hörspiel*, feature and new music. In the Studio Acoustic Art at the WDR (Cologne), for instance, radio art experiments started in 1963 with experimental acoustic literature, sound poetry (*Neues Hörspiel*) later moving with a similar aesthetic over to experimental music. 'In treating language and sound effects as concrete material, it made possible the same kind of aesthetic reaction associated previously only with music.' (Cory, 1989, quoted in Lander and Lexier, 1990, p. 98).

Yet, the creative potential of radio and its studio facilities – exemplified by the work of Pierre Schaeffer, Karlheinz Stockhausen and their associates – was increasingly lost in the course of technological advancement, especially with the advent of live electronics, digital technology and home studio recording. These developments gave sound exploration its major turn, liberating artists and musicians from the restrictions of public radio institutions at a basic structural level, since sound engineers and radio producers no longer had to mediate between technology and artist, and time restrictions and the limitations of prescribed radio formats no longer applied. This last point was critically addressed by Glenn Gould in his concept of 'contrapuntal radio' (Gould, 1992, pp. 190–91), which challenged the linear structure of radio documentation.

The changed conditions of technological accessibility liberated individual work from public conventions and gave experimental sound work outside the radio an enormous boost, commencing in the early 1960s and peaking by the 1980s. People from all sorts of backgrounds who would never have had the privilege of using the facilities of public radio now became interested in working with sound. As a result, not only would the aesthetic spectrum of sound work change rapidly and fundamentally, but also many sound artists would begin to choose more intuitive and experimental ways of working than had previously been possible, opting rather for an openness, an unfinished quality in their 'final' pieces.

Under these new circumstances an interest in sound spread widely into various areas of artistic work. While the *Hörspiel* was originally situated between literature and music, many fresh inspirations for sound art now came from the world of the visual arts. Stimulated by the cross media experiments of Fluxus and the performance arts of the 1960s, artists and musicians started to combine visual and auditive elements into sound sculptures.

Sculptors expanded their work with plastic materials towards its sonic qualities. The sonicity of glass, metal, stone and wood formed the basis for their sound pieces. They took the position that 'all objects have a sound component, a second shadow existence as a configuration of frequencies.' (Viola, 1986, p. 43). Thus the very specific sound signatures of sculptural objects and materials became a source for the exploration of the affiliation between sound texture, resonance and their natural carriers. Artists understood sound as 'matter' and sought to mould sound, by giving it a *sculptural* structure. Pieces like *Small Music* by the German artist Rolf Julius (Julius, 1994) are reminiscent of Marinetti's vision of being 'seduced by the vibration of a diamond or a flower' (Marinetti and Masnata, 1992, p. 267). Other artists would expand their sculptures by giving them a sonic dimension. Such sound sculptures – still or moving – were made either to emit sound by themselves, or to react to the actions or movements of the public.

In the second half of the 1960s artists started to venture away from the sonicity of the sculptural body or material and into space. When Max Neuhaus created one of the first sound installations, his *Drive-in Music* (1967/68), he wanted to arrange sounds in space and leave it to the listener to place them in his or her own time (Neuhaus, 1975, p. 34). Sound installations, unlike sound sculptures, work with the physical dimensions and acoustic properties of a concrete space, so it is the space that is to be experienced through sound. Consequently, they are typically site-specific. Dutch artist Paul Panhuysen, for instance, transformed spaces into instruments by installing long strings that would pick up the resonant frequencies of the room. These sound resonator installations explore the impact of sound onto space and space on sound. In Alvin Lucier's installation *Empty Vessels* (1997) six microphones, placed in the openings of six glass vessels, record the sound of the space they are in, which is then played back into the same room via six speakers – only to be immediately rerecorded together with the disturbances caused by the public and so on, creating a constantly changing sound loop.

Often sound sculptures and sound installations include the public by delegating the initiation of sound or the form of its perception on to the activity of the listener. These works would be silent until some movement or deliberate operation triggered the sound. In many of Christina Kubisch's installations visitors have to discover the sounds using headsets by moving around in electromagnetic sound fields (Kubisch, 1990, pp. 69–72). Their audio experience relies entirely on their personal activity. Depending on a dialogic relationship of audience and piece, this encounter dissolves the opposition of art/artist and recipient. A compendium of the enormous variety of forms that both sound installation and sound sculptures can take was recently assembled for the *Sonambiente Festival* in Berlin in 1996 (Akademie der Künste Berlin, 1996).

A special form of sound installation was created through radio itself by transmitting sound from one place to another, altering sonic perception of the new environment. Such transmissions can span enormous distances. The *Sound Bridges* of Bill Fontana between *Cologne and San Francisco* (1990)[9] and *Cologne and Kyoto* (1993) for instance, were realised by transcontinental broadcasting via satellite with the help of WDR (Cologne).

Sound sculpture and sound installation exemplify the merging of formerly very different and autonomous artistic disciplines and the abolition of the delimitation between the conventional temporal and spatial arts.[10] Artists started to commute between visual and audio genres. Thus the migration towards sound sculpture and sound installation occurred from various sides – music, performance and visual arts.

Not all of these works lend themselves easily to radio. Not only because of the missing visual dimension but also often by virtue of the sonic material used or the site-specificity of the sonic experience. Canadian artist Gordon Monahan came across this problem in his experiments with the doppler effect, using swinging speakers. He refers to sound effects that elude recording:

> there is a section in the piece that does deal with the particular space ... That is the actual sonic impact of resonant frequency in the space to a kind of pressure-pulsation happening. When you try to record that, you get modulation on the diaphragm of the microphone. You can't get a true representation of that on the recording. (Monahan, 1987, p. 143).

Still, quite a few sound installations have a vivid sonicity that can be remixed and prepared for an exclusively auditive experience – on CD, or for that matter radio.[11]

Another contribution towards the expansion of sonicity came from inside music. Since Russolo, and later Cage, had declared the autonomy of sound by 'using sounds not as sound effects, but as musical instruments', the way was cleared to 'make available for musical purposes any and all sounds that can be heard' (Cage, 1968, p. 4).

In recent years new developments in performance art and improvisation have depended extensively on sound. In particular, portable electronic sound technology such as turntables, samplers, effect units, tone generators and so forth – either used on their own, or together with other musical instruments – made possible an immense diversity and individuality of aesthetic approaches and stimulated a whole plethora of sonic events.

Japanese musician and performer Keiji Haino, for instance, tackles the polarity of the sound spectrum and its perception. In his performance with amplified sound on the electric guitar he exposes the audience to extreme physical volume, overstepping the pain threshold and driving the listener literally out of the room. On other occasions, however, in delicate percussion performances with body movements in the dark, an audience has to strain to follow the sound as it hovers at the limits of audibility.[12]

Many performers use spoken language, singing voice and the resonances of their bodies as sonic source material. Performing her semi-autobiographical one-woman-musical O Little Town of East New York (Hirsch, 1995) singer Shelly Hirsch combines all three elements into a seamless and highly individual texture. The precedent for combining sung and spoken texts was most famously set by another New York woman performer, Laurie Anderson, who also broke new ground by inventing her own electronic instruments.[13]

New technology forged an important link between traditional musical skills and the technology of sound generation and processing. The Studio for Electro-Instrumental Music (STEIM) in Amsterdam designs bespoke sound technology for performance artists. English violinist Jon Rose has been working at the interface between computer processed and instrumental sound for many years using a customised interactive electronic bow made by STEIM. Michel Waiswicz, on the other hand, converts body movements into sound employing electronic gloves (The Hands). Midi controllers, photo-electric cell devices and mini-radio transmitters are all used to trigger electronic sound systems and release pre-prepared and digitally stored sounds or, more recently, to sample live sound. Indeed many new, sometimes quite eccentric instruments have been invented and developed in the process of improvisation and performance employing recent technologies (for instance Don Buchla's Lightning), not to mention electronic body armour and biofeedback systems.

The use of live electronics is now well established in all kinds of new improvisation, turning this traditional field of instrumental music into a resourceful area of technologically driven sonic creativity. But 'high tech' seems also to have heightened the interest in 'low tech'. *Sound bricolage* may be the youngest form of sound exploration. Its practitioners, often with little or no artistic background, but very interested in generating sound through technical devices, compile sonic trash and hi-fi debris in their bedrooms and home studios. German bricolagists like Bernhard Günter[14] or Boris Hegenbart, for instance, explore their fascination with microscopic audio phenomena, producing fragmented pointillist pieces. While the Swiss duo *Voice Crack* (Andy Guhl and Norbert Moslang) use everyday objects – 'cracked everyday electronics': radios, turntables, calculators, dictaphones and game machines – manipulated in novel and expressive ways, controlling them with light, body movements and their voices.[15]

As these electronic bricolages rely largely on intuition and fragmented micro-sonicity and defy structural preconception (composition), they seem to have very little in common with conventional forms of electroacoustic music. But even the latter has seemed unable to withstand change. Exposed to experiments in other fields, the general orthodoxies of the electroacoustic trade began to crumble when its self-identification through abstract sound and legitimated musical structures was undermined by referential sounds taken from natural and urban environments, or by text and 'open' structures (exemplified, for instance, in the work of Canadian composers Robert Normandeau (Normandeau, 1990) and Christian Calon (Calon, 1990; 1998)). In this field computer and sampling technology allowed not only for work with new sound material, but also new working methods – such as 'Composing by Ear'[16] or cinematic approaches[17] – as well as new forms of presentation and collaboration.

Sampling technology itself introduced a completely new aesthetic, suddenly making it possible to recycle our entire recorded history, not only providing an enormously expanded sound continuum, but also supporting work methods formerly strongly taboo in avant-garde music. After all, selecting fragments of existing recordings and 'merely' collaging or montaging them, subverts all established aesthetic concepts based on artistic originality, authenticity and material-immanent progress. Such new approaches still meet strong and disproportionate resistance, as John Oswald's[18] plunderphonic pieces – and the concept they embody – impressively confirm.

All these different developments in sonic arts were not only fuelling radio art, but radio itself was becoming a sound source or an instrument for musical performance, and was used by many composers and performers – most famously in John Cage's *Imaginary Landscape No. 4*, where twelve radios are to be played by twenty-four players at given frequencies and volumes under the timing instructions of a conductor. In 1985 American performer Nicolas Collins made a piece by mixing samples from FM and AM transmissions at the time of the performance (Collins, 1986). This strategy of live-mixing sound directly from the ether reappeared in the 1990s, notably in the work of Robin Rimbaud (alias Scanner) who modified it for mobile phone scanners. Indeed, as early as the 1960s amongst a whole generation of improvisers and musicians, radio was in common use as a chance-driven instrument and is still fully integrated into the work of English guitarist Keith Rowe, for instance.

The extension of abstract into environmental sound not only concerned sound producers, but also opened up a number of questions about our way of listening – for instance to sounds which we might normally not listen to or simply take at face value. Canadian sound researcher and composer R. Murray Schafer explored this problem in the 1970s through his idea of soundscape – the sonic fingerprint of a place. He called for a battle against sound pollution (*Ear Cleaning*) and advocated a new way of listening (Schafer, 1977). Hildegard Westerkamp, taking up the idea of experimental listening and acoustic ecology, sought 'to make radio a place of environmental listening by broadcasting soundscapes that listeners experience in their daily lives' (Westerkamp, 1994, p. 88). This strategy was quickly adopted by sound artists all over the world who recorded the soundscapes in which they lived or which they encountered in their travels, passing on these sonic imprints to listeners everywhere.

Finally, we should not fail to mention one last soundfield which despite its long tradition has, like *Hörspiel*, proven infinitely resourceful: the sonic dimension of the human voice – and in particular the relation between speech and sound, as explored in many and varied ways since early experiments by Dadaists and Futurists with sound poetry and acoustic literature. Many of today's new approaches, for instance, defy author-centred, message-oriented concepts by mixing text-splinters of various origins from high and popular cultures, by creating an understanding of complex texts through misreadings (for example Heiner Goebbels's *Despoiled Shore* (Goebbels, 1984)) or by developing new forms of associative storytelling (Gregory Whitehead, Jackie Apple). Text and language-based soundworks also provide a strong ground for culturally and socially engaged radio work.

All these very different approaches to sound, and the enumeration here must remain sketchy and incomplete, make for a whole encyclopaedia of unconventional aesthetics. However, these activities emerged and flourished largely outside radio. With new technologies designed for flexible and individual use, sound arts gradually developed their own independent existence outside the big institutions. And, as they challenged the conventions of the artistic fields from which they came, they needed also to build up new means and new networks of propagation. In the 1980s and 1990s, radio became an option again for many artists in their search for larger audiences. In taking these outside works in, radio now found itself in a new role, as a patron for a whole catalogue of stray sound works. It was then that the term radio art (used by Kurt Weill as long ago as 1926 (Weill, 1984)) caught on as a mode of understanding and reference between producers and sound artists from different countries and aesthetic orientation. Henceforth, radio would gather and produce works in an extremely pluralistic and open-minded way, providing them both with a forum and with wider recognition. Thus radio art became a hybrid – inclusive rather than exclusive – and consequently not to be 'determined by negation'.

It is important to note that nowadays there is hardly any Sound Art on radio that could not survive without it. Sound arts have all found themselves their own formats, modes and territories, be they on CD, the Internet, sound galleries or performance venues. And as the genres float, so do the specialisations: many sound artists now work in several different genres simultaneously. New technology with its different formats allows a piece to exist in various incarnations and perhaps as a number of somewhat different pieces. Such flexibility is linked to an artist's familiarity with different media. A piece might be produced in a home studio, offered to the radio, pressed onto CD and then integrated into a live performance, or it might begin as a sound installation with the sound element released as a CD, which is then played on the radio; so the sound realises 'other existences', independent of the original installation with its attendant visual and spatial attributes. Even complex live events or telecommunication projects with live sound-mixes may later be successfully remixed for CD – as was the case with Patrizia Jünger's Hör-promenade *Transmitter – First to Second Nature* (Jünger, 1996). In such ways pieces are in constant flux, changing shape according to the context and occasion in which they appear. It can happen that a single work exists as a stereo production, in DVD 5.1, as a concert piece, part of a video collaboration, dance performance or multimedia event.

This wide range of formats points to a crucial problem that radio encounters when attempting to present such diverse works: its own technological limitations. In a way, such technical difficulties make it all too obvious how far – on a technological level – sound explorations have moved away from radio as a medium. New digital technology allows for greater clarity, fidelity, extreme dynamics and an ever-widening range of frequencies, providing a continually expanding field for sound artists of all provenances to experiment with. They will test the limits of audibility or even physical bearability of sound. Low-frequency effects, for instance, feature prominently – and not only in popular music. Live performances might rely on the immersion of the audience in the sound where spontaneous head movements can be vital to the final experience. Live performances with tone generators and controlled electronic feedback, for instance by Sachico M and Otomo Yoshihide, depend on such factors and are incomprehensible to radio. Such forms must always present extreme difficulties to a medium based on *distance and strict directedness*, rather than *immersion and diffusion*. Thus the essence of live soundworks which depend extensively on the acoustic qualities of the space or the active perception of individual listeners is inevitably lost when recorded or broadcast.

Sound compression on the radio reduces dynamic range. Since the aesthetic of both recorded and live sound pieces often work with drastic dynamic changes, radio is simply unable to transmit them. 'Such broadcasting shows no dynamic shadings or phrasing. It does not breathe. It has become a sound wall.' (Schafer, 1977, p. 95). Something similar is true for radio's stereo effect which cannot mediate full spectrum multichannel diffusions. This longstanding problem (one only has to think of the *Acousmonium*)[19] becomes even more evident today as we are familiarised to multichannel audio in Dolby Digital 5.1 or SDDS 7.1[20] as cinema standards – or the sound capacities of 24,000 watt in Imax-centres. Such sound deficiencies we find in other media too, for instance when sound travels through the Internet. The sound quality of Real Audio suffers even more than that of radio, because of low sampling rates and high data compression. These are reasons why 'most radio artists reject the Internet'.[21]

Well aware of the shortcomings of radio technology, sound engineers have worked for decades to overcome them by way of simulations. In fact, simulating virtual spaces has become one of the major playing fields of sound engineering. Such a fascination with virtual spaces becomes even more curious in the light of the lack of suitable real spaces for sound events. In this regard the direction pursued notably by Karlheinz Stockhausen to create new spaces for new sound work has been disappointingly neglected.

However, sound technology is moving rapidly. Digital radio will become the norm in the next few years. Artists working with sound and radio are fully aware of the problems of reproduction involved and weigh the advantages and disadvantages of having their pieces presented in radio space. The same is true of radio art programmers and presenters. This may be one of the reasons why the latter sometimes turn their backs on the 'magic channels' and head towards spatial or live events, presenting radiophonic pieces in surround sound spaces – observatories, for instance, or set up sound galleries, such as the *Klanggalerie* of the Free Berlin Radio (SFB) – or become involved in large-scale performance events or festivals, such as ORF Kunstradio: *Ars Electronica*; WDR Studio Akustische Kunst: *Ars Acoustica*; SFB Internationale digitale Radiokunst: *Gala of the Prix Europa*; RAI Audiobox: *International Festival of Sound Experimentation*. Radio art producers constantly work in:

> Sound Spaces of Radio beyond the boundaries of radio. In the process, various media-forms of presentation are employed, for example the loudspeaker concert, the live performance, the space-sound installation, the sound film with integrated loudspeaker concert, the simultaneous radio and television broadcast, urban sound sculptures broadcast live on the radio etc. (Schöning, 1999).

They set up 'live on air, online, onsite-sound-installation',[22] art projects which take place simultaneously in different media and different spaces and deploy audiovisual intersections.

Considering all these recent developments in the relationship between sound and radio, radio art today has to be regarded as one of many sound art formats. In this respect Nicholas Zurbrugg has described the current phase of sound creativity as 'post-radiogenic' – following the pre-radiophonic and 'purely radiophonic' phases. In this third, most recent phase he defines sound art through the combination of 'sound, music, speech and image, colour and gesture in both real time and studio time in various technological broadcasts, installations and performances' (Zurbrugg, 1988). On radio, however, sound art inevitably filters through very specific institutional and media channels.

Radio: institution

As the medium radio appears in various institutional formats, radio art finds itself in various different contexts. This is especially true of Europe and Australia, where public radio still plays an important role. As a well-established institution, it has international contacts and the financial and administrative power to realise and host big events, run international competitions, hand out prizes, commission unusual or extravagant works and organise festivals. On top of this, radio has access to a substantial and largely guaranteed listenership.

——When sound art became ubiquitous, producing and presenting more and more works outside the context of radio, adventurous producers and programmers in public radio stations took note: 'independently produced audio-tapes began to emerge from the artistic community and demanded to be heard on the radio' (McLennan, 1995/96). Building on this growing interest in experimental sound and radio work in the 1960s and 1970s[23] producers initiated, at first occasional and then regular, radio presentations, covering a wide range of experimental sound art: Australia: ABC *The Listening Room* 1988; Austria: ORF *Kunstradio* 1987; Germany: WDR *Ars Acoustica* 1968 (continuously, with a changed profile) and SFB *International Digital Radio Art* 1992; Italy: RAI *Audiobox* 1982 (following *Fonosfera* 1978/79). As time passed, these special programmes became established centres of international radio art.

However, setting up such special programmes inside public radio did not proceed without encountering severe institutional problems. After all, every institution inevitably establishes a certain aesthetic profile with its own formative templates – and in most public radio stations, programming is dominated by news, information and entertainment. By presenting innovative and experimental sound works, the new radio art programmes constantly overstepped established limits and challenged the aesthetic orthodoxies of radio institutions. Although the aesthetic formats of *Hörspiel* and feature had long been recognised in public radio programming, the new radio art found itself under constant attack. Such discrimination was and is expressed through legitimisation pressure, budget cuts, being placed lowest on any institutional priority list, wholesale dismantling of perfectly viable programme structures (recently experienced in Austrian radio by ORF *Kunstradio*), erasing entire programmes (RAI *Audiobox*, September 1998) or ignoring new radio art altogether (a solution for which the British Broadcasting Co-operation is so infamous).

Things got worse when public radio was faced with competition from commercial stations, now also fighting for their listeners' favour. As broadcasters gave in to mainstream listening – renouncing their former claim to education and enlightenment and cutting budgets for experimental work – radio art became an early victim of discrimination, easily dismissed for being too élitist. Stressing the argument that radio had to 'serve' its audience, radio administration began to judge successful programming by way of ratings: applying the lowest common denominator standard of mass appeal.

In response to these developments, and particularly since in many countries radio art on public stations was not even an option, other outlets for experimental sound work were urgently required. Radio art found itself in the company of many other marginalised genres, social issues, topics and forms, discriminated against by the institutional politics of public radio and looking for alternative radio outlets. Radio guerrillas work on the outskirts of the radio landscape – at 'the low end of the radio dial' (Breitsameter, 1999) – either having to broadcast within a legally restricted transmission radius (e.g., college and community based stations in Canada, the United States and Australia) or for a limited period (stations with a Restricted Service Licence). Other radio enthusiasts opt for the underground – surfing as airwave pirates offshore[24] or on land in forbidden waters. Some exit radio altogether, finding other channels through which to distribute and exchange their works and ideas.

In all these cases radio is understood as a tool either for social and political intervention or for emphasising a cultural difference discriminated against by corporate power. In many community and college stations such a direct communicative aspect stands at the top of their agenda. Their mission is to produce radio for a specific community, take up internal issues of communal life and address their own specific concerns. Other stations deal in marginalised or ignored topics which otherwise find no place in a politically and culturally regulated broadcasting environment.[25] Here the idea of 'democratising the radio' is often evoked as a call to oppose the concept of radio as a unidirectional voice of power (however populistically packaged) in which information flows from the public station to the single listener, with no feedback facilities and no cross links between receivers. 'The horror lies in the "structure of communication" or – to say it more simply – in the material and/or immaterial cables. If one could reverse the cables, the horror would be rectified.' (Flusser, 1998, pp. 73–4). Then radio could be turned into a bi- or multi-directional instrument, a network of connections that could facilitate a telematic exchange between all participants.

The idea of a 'democratic radio', already suggested in the 1920s by Brecht (Brecht, 1993, pp. 15–17) and others, re-emerged in the 1970s in the 'free radio movement' with community stations like Radio Alice in Bologna – itself a product of the deregulation of the airwaves in Italy – which subsequently inspired independent radio initiatives all over Europe.[26] Alternative programming, community interests and the artistic use of radio can come together on such a territory. Much of American radio art with its profile of high cultural and social engagement –

contrary to art- and intellect-based European radio art[27] – fits this communicative framework very well, entering the social discourse of independent stations on grounds of content or as part of alternative, interest-bound programming. The balance between community interest and art experiments could even tip towards radio art, if the community happened to be interested in experimental sound endeavours – as we find it for instance at WLUW Chicago (the station of Loyola University) or New American Radio (New York).

Similar interests in 'free radio work' are expressed in even more informal ways, this side of or beyond official radio frequency regulations. Where regulations tolerate low frequency transmissions, this technology can become the basis for radio experiments and wider radio networking. Tetsuo Kogawa has been experimenting with low frequency transmissions in Japan since the early 1980s. He built mini-FM transmitters which can be used for 'different models of radio on college campuses, housing complexes, coffee shops and bars, stalls at street fairs, local offices' (Kogawa, 1994, p. 290), that is for microwave transmissions in urban areas. By networking these mini-stations, the covered area of communication can be expanded. Tetsuo Kagawa's concern with changing 'the nature of communication between those who speak and those who listen' takes an extreme turn when he suggests 'the same number of transmitters as receivers' (Kogawa, 1994, p. 291).

Going beyond the boundaries of national radio legislation, many pirate stations were formed around some special interest – such as styles of music or ignored social or political concerns. Many marginalised groups think it worthwhile to risk violating official airwave regulations in order to communicate with like-minded listeners or express opinions on controversial issues which would otherwise have no chance of an airing on officially censored mass media. For instance, a group of women in Galway, Ireland overcame 'their fear of being penalised for talking or singing into a microphone', because they wanted to exorcise 'the sense among woman of starvation, of never being listened to' (D'Arcy, 1990, pp. 319–23) and were finally heard via telephone links across three continents. Amsterdam radio pirates who have operated in different formats since the early 1980s started to experiment with the medium itself. Stations such as Radio Dood, later Radio Patapoe with a heady combination of very little money and a lot of time and enthusiasm, embraced an unorthodox, mixed programming, accommodating a 'carefree experimentation with sound' (Lovink, 1993, p. 115).

All these alternative broad- and narrow-casting initiatives show that there is an interest and a place for radio outside publicly imposed mass media formats – and that radio art can be part of it. However, in order to pursue a solely art-oriented course, artists have also found ways outside official or unofficial radio institutions. In 1973 two English artists, William Furlong and Barry Barker, founded *Audio Arts* (Furlong, 1994). Conceived as a kind of sound magazine, it made use of the then growing availability of the audio cassette to produce and distribute radiophonic work. What was originally conceived as an aural documentation of the vigorous debate about the form and purpose of art, soon became a complex and comprehensive body of sound work of all kinds. Rod Summer's *VEC Audio-Exchange*, on the other hand, adopted a mail art exchange format to produce audio collages on cassette from the contributions of friends and collaborators. From 1978 to 1983 this exchange produced sixteen one-hour programmes and found a wide distribution (Summers, 1990, pp. 235–40). Other editors of sound art publications, such as those of the audio-cassette magazine *Tellus* (created in 1983 in New York City) 'perceived a need for an alternative to radio programming'[28] and made commercially available unusual recordings in the cross-over field of visuals, music, performance and spoken word.

A critique of dominant radio practice with a high emphasis on radio art was realised by independent initiatives such as *Radia 89.9FM* and *Radio Rethink* (1992 at the Banff Centre for the Arts in Canada) (Augaitis and Lander, 1994), by the English Restricted Service Licence-stations *Hearing is Believing* (Liverpool, 1995)[29] and *Resonance FM*, (London, 1998).[30] All these temporary stations with small transmission ranges set out to explore the creative dimension of radio as a medium. They presented pre-recorded audio pieces and live events, commissioning artists and musicians to create special works – and inviting theoreticians, critics, producers and artists to discuss the state of radio art under current institutional conditions. They considered radio 'as a medium for critical intervention in today's culture' (Augaitis and Lander, 1994, p. 1).

A sharp shift in independent radio activity came with the commercialisation of, and later the introduction of audio to the Internet. As technology provided an audio link through the World Wide Web, the possibility of global audio transmission became a welcome alternative to official and unofficial airwave battles. Webcasting has considerably shifted media reality. Despite shortcomings in audio technology on the net, such as time consuming downloading and even hard signal compression in *Real Audio*, making for poor sound quality, the net freed sound art at a stroke from radio-space, institutionalised formats, fixed broadcasting times, places and limited transmission ranges. It made sound art available on a global scale, free from territorial limitations and national restrictions. Moreover, the Internet liberated radio art from any institution or collective body. In the last few years thousands of radio stations have gone online and some independent stations, like New American Radio,[31] formerly forced to offer their programmes to public networks, have switched from broad- to net-casting precisely to avoid endless problems with large and indifferent institutions.[32]

The net entwines in a single strand the media of transmission, production and reception at the level of the user. It makes it possible to present sound art, as well as to *archive* it. In public radio, sound works were produced by and for radio; they were broadcast and then stored away in radio archives, so that availability was strictly limited to the actual time of airing and the transmission range of a particular station. The establishment of *Real Audio*-archives on the net, and the presentation there of new sound art projects improves accessibility to sound works (both past and present) and on a global scale.

Downloading audio files and recording in MP3 format has made pieces of nearly CD quality universally available both for listening and as source material for further processing – whenever, wherever. The consequences for our audio landscape, institutions and property questions are unquantifiable; it is impossible to imagine or assess the eventual effect on our audio landscape. But one thing is already clear: the Web with its potential for openness, interactivity, multi-directedness and accessibility, defies the very concept of media-democracy, since its structure subverts any political idea based on majority representation.

In addition to all this one needs to consider that the Internet is not only an autonomous medium but one attached to most existing media bodies as well. Public radio stations are using it more and more as a welcome addition to their existing facilities, since the Internet is able to graft itself onto all manner of existing media and to be used by individuals and public institutions alike. Thus, formerly autonomous media become hybrids, merging with other media until they will all finally unite in an endless streaming of public and private data flying through digital channels. This hybridisation of media is already underway and will profoundly change radio, both the medium and the landscape. It will integrate the old one-way street into a multidimensional superhighway network, eventually collapsing medium and institution into one another.

Radio: medium

Understanding radio art in its media-specificity requires us to adopt a different perspective from the aesthetic, sound-centred or institutional ones we have employed so far. For this, radio has to be situated in the wider framework of contemporary electronic/digital media and their cultural effects. In this respect, radio cannot be understood merely as 'extended acoustic space' (Schafer, 1977, p. 91); rather, 'radio-space is a wave-space' (Braun, 1999, p. 4), an abstract inaccessible space which may only be entered virtually, by tuning into a given frequency. When any work of sound art is submitted to this electronic space (in other words, when broadcast) it takes on a new life, determined by the medium. Every broadcast work is thus subjected to major transformations through the technical configuration of the medium, its coding/decoding system and the properties of the audio equipment at the listener's end. Since, under these conditions, dynamics, fidelity, signal-to-noise ratio and timbre are highly variable, the work as a fixed and unalterable entity inevitably vanishes and the author of a work no longer has any influence on its final sound, or indeed what happens to it. In contrast to an acoustic or acousmatic concert hall presentation, a composer or performer giving their work up to the radio has no opportunity to create the conditions for its ideal reception, since both the technological and environmental conditions of radio listening are essentially unpredictable.

At the same time, radio-space disconnects a work, its author, performers and auditor from any common place of experience and event. This space is equally absent for all participants. Moreover, listening conditions are not fixed by the conventions of common behaviour – as would be the case in a concert hall or at any communally experienced real-time event – but are dependent on the way radio fits into a listener's daily routine. Listening may be distracted or incidental, or it may be focused but not in radio real-time (as when listening to a recording taken from a broadcast, for instance). Often, it is just one of several simultaneous activities. Thus, radio sound meets the listener on his/her own terms while 'the sound environment generated by radio merges potentially with the sound environment at a given location' (Braun, 1999, p. 5). This generates a highly fragmented perception, one that is not programmed into the work but imposed upon it by external conditions. The listener cultivates a selective form of perception characterised by non-linearity, disruptiveness and partiality, so that the same work will take on many different forms, depending on listening strategies and contexts. These tendencies in radio listening coincide with other fragmented, pointillist forms of perception associated with various types of musical and sonic creations.[33] Indeed, many sound artists take the variability of today's sound media into consideration from the outset by producing works which are themselves fragmented and changeable, planning and realising a single work in several different versions and formats.

Since radio is not a shared space between creators (authors and performers) and audience, and lacks a commonality of experience, all direct communication is eliminated. Every radio experience rests on the distance between the component parts of a formerly integrated artistic process. Not only are artistic creation, sonic execution and listening completely separated from one another, but radio listening itself is an extremely lonely occupation, though this is usually camouflaged by the comforting and familiar voice of a presenter and the common belief in the 'listening community'. Cut off from the source as well as from each other, radio listeners have to accept whatever comes out of their speakers.[34] Here communication and information are profoundly disconnected.[35] The missing cross-links between receivers and the lack of feedback facilities underpin the authoritarian and non-communicative structure of traditional radio broadcasting. This distance between the radio components is not coincidental; it is immanent in the medium itself. Yet, under the conditions of increasing global interaction and communication, a uni-directional media structure seems to become increasingly insupportable. For this reason artists and producers continually seek ways to challenge and overcome this distant nature of radio in both directions: vertical – between producers, artists and listeners; and horizontal – between listeners or artists themselves. They promote new concepts of working in and with radio.

ORF-Kunstradio, for instance, addresses radio as part of the recent media shift by making it productive for telematic projects. Through events such as *Horizontal Radio* (1995) and *Rivers and Bridges* (1996)[36] it explored radio's capacity for global networking. By using radio in conjunction with telephone, fax, computer and the World Wide Web, the projects created an integrated electronic system, linking people in radio stations and studios across three continents in lengthy, continuous radio art sessions. Such telecommunicative events became concerned less with the 'transmission of "aesthetic" products and more with [...] the creation of a network situation' (Breindl, 1997, p. 10) in which sound is transmitted immediately to be re-used as source material for some new sonic activity, a situation in which sound artists, engineers and producers can interact over long distances. Senders become receivers, and receivers senders. In reference to Marinetti's concept of *La*

Radia (Marinetti and Masnata, 1992) and his anticipation of 'a world-wide net of live radio lines' (Grundmann, 1994, p. 131), these projects occupy a special place in today's radio art landscape by stressing an aspect of radio not centred on sound. By cross-connecting radio stations, studios and now – by courtesy of the Internet – private persons on a global scale, such telematic events exceed the traditional centralised scope of national public radio by pursuing forms of bi- and multidirectional worldwide interaction. Audiences are witness to an instantaneous, simultaneous process of artistic exchange where the 'overall work ... cannot be grasped, either by the active participants (artists/ engineers) or by the audience at the various places' (Grundmann, 1993). These telematic initiatives suggest changes in sound art creation and perception that go beyond modernist concepts of authorship, ownership, artistic self-expression through the production of unique works and 'truthful' perception. They advocate new ways of art making – not defined by work but *process*; not through the polarisation of creator and receiver, but rather through *communication* and *interaction* between them. Once connected to other media, radio becomes part of a telecommunicative structure that is non-linear and goes way beyond simply 'reversing the cables'. These networking strategies open up new ways of genuine media *communication*.

All these changes find their ultimate expression in the Internet where all uni-directionality and hierarchical forms of communication are potentially abolished. Its network structure opens up new possibilities for communication as well as art making, since artist and listener alike are involved in the same dynamic system where 'every (artistic) act ... is an open action' (Breindl, 1997, p. 9). Sound works and splinters are floating through cyberspace, changing their sonic specifications and waiting to be appropriated, sampled and transformed. This requires a wholly new self-understanding from the producers of such telematic art, since artistic as well as commercial ownership is fundamentally threatened by digital sound technology (hard disc recording, CD burners, MP3 players) and global availability. Telematic work is an offer for exchange. Artists and businesses alike will have to come to terms with these new technological and cultural facts. Moreover, despite changing the way sound art is made, the new medium also challenges the identity of sound art itself as an art exclusively for the ear: sound work will be irresistibly drawn towards visuality, since the computer screen shouts out for it.

Although the final outcome of all these technological changes is difficult to predict, an aesthetic shift is definitely underway. By way of the Internet, for example, sound work becomes a genuinely individual enterprise; it can originate in anybody's bedroom and have at the same time a universal presence – and still be open to change and exchange. However, it remains to be seen how this polarity of active sender and passive receiver will be resolved. Obviously the Internet will not suddenly turn every passive sound consumer into an active sound producer. But decentralised networks, interconnected at all levels will provide at least the possibility for both simple reception and active engagement.

Given, on the one hand, the rapid development of digital technology and the subsequent changes in media structure and, on the other, the hybridisation and expansion of art forms and processes, the consequent cultural transformations are bound to effect radio art. Current projections range from the hope that, once new media take over radio's traditional information and entertainment functions, radio itself might be freed for experimental work, all the way to predictions of 'the end of radio'. Although history repeatedly shows that old media are not simply replaced by new ones, it is still not easy to predict what form the changes underway will eventually take. Sound art, however, seems to thrive on all these developments – its theoretical reflections constantly chased and surprised by the enormous creativities they are facing. May theory draw comfort from the fact that everything has already moved on!

Notes

1. 'RadioArt is audio art produced in or transmitted by radio' (Breitsameter, 1998).
   'RadioArt is an electroacoustic genre, which fluctuates in the indistinct realm between *Hörspiel*, new music, sound installation, soundscape, performance art and experimental pop, and which creatively and artistically handles the entire spectrum of the world of sound, the equal juxtaposition of noise, music and speech' (Breitsameter, 1999).
   '... a rare amalgam of different radio forms ranging across new music, acoustic art, environmental soundscapes, performance works, radiophonic features and documentaries' (Ravlich, 1998).
   'Acoustic Art is a melting pot of heterogeneous elements ... a world of sounds and noises – from the real acoustic environment or artificially produced. And a world of speech, speech tending toward phonetic sound, inflection and music, the universality of tones ... a symbiosis of these speech and noise worlds and their acoustic organisation by means of electronic technology' (Schöning, 1997).
2. Cage (1968); see also Hagen (1997).
3. Lander and Lexier (1990); Kahn and Whitehead (1992); Strauss and Mandl (1993); Augaitis and Lander (1994).
4. For example Schafer (1977) and Page (1984).

5. *Musicworks*: Radio-Phonics, 53 (1992); *Neue Zeitschrift für Musik*: Radiokunst, Heft 1 (1994); *Resonance*: Retuning Radio, 5(2) (1997).
6. Akademie der Künste Berlin (1996).
7. http://thing.at/orfkunstradio
    http://thing.at/texte/
    http://thing.at/orfkunstradio/THEORIE
    http://tunix.is-bremen.de/~hagen/.
8. See Simon Waters's contribution to the current volume (Chapter 3).
9. The first sound bridge in the history of radio (Fontana, 1994).
10. As established in the eighteenth century (see Gotthold Ephraim Lessing, *Laokoon*, 1766) and dominating the modernist discourse ever since.
11. For instance Kubisch (1995) (CD).
12. See for instance Haino (1993) (CD).
13. For instance the Tape Bow Violin (1976) and the Viophonograph (1975), both together with Bob Bielecki.
14. For example Günter (1999) (CD).
15. Annual Festival of Experimental Music, LMC London, programme notes, 1996.
16. See Glandien, Lutz (1994) (CD).
17. Robert Normandeau, 'Cinema for the Ear', conference script (unpublished).
18. See Chris Cutler's contribution to the current volume (Chapter 4).
19. Multichannel sound diffusion system conceived by François Bayle in 1974.
20. New surround sound standards for cinema diffusion.
21. Interview with Helen Thorington, July 1998 (unpublished).
22. ORF Kunstradio, *Immersive Sound* (Bregenz, Austria, 1998).
23. By *ACR* at Radio France, *Radiophonic Workshop* at the BBC, *Studio Akustische Kunst* at WDR, Milan *Studio di Fonologia Musicale* at RAI.
24. 1960s in Europe; most famously Radio Caroline went on air off the English coast in 1983. See Strauss 1993 pp. 123–8.
25. Eco (1994). Listen also to KPFA, Caifornia and Alternative Radio, Boulder, Colorado.
26. See Guattari (1993) pp. 85–9 and Eco (1994) pp. 167–76.
27. Interview with Helen Thorington, July 1998 (unpublished).
28. Tellus: http://harvestworkss.org/tellus/.
29. See *Hearing is Believing* (1995) (CD).
30. Run by the London Musicians' Collective. See: *Resonance* (Magazine and CD) (1997) and (CD) (1998).
31. http://turbulence.org.
32. Interview with Helen Thorrington, July 1998 (unpublished).
33. See Glandien, Kersten (1997).
34. Particularly since the technology of sound art production and radio transmission are for most listeners incomprehensible which makes most of us sound-illiterate. See Flusser (1998) p. 76.
35. See Kittler (1993).
36. Sodomka/Breindl/Math/x-space, *State of Transition* (1994). The first project which incorporated the Internet as a medium of communication into the structure of a live-radio performance.

References

Akademie der Künste Berlin (ed.) (1996), *Klangkunst*, Munich and New York: Prestel.

Artaud, Antonin (1974), 'Pour en finir avec le jugement de dieu', (1947) in Artaud, Antonin, *Œuvres complètes*, 13, Paris: Gallimard.

Augaitis, Diana and Lander, Dan (eds) (1994), *Radio Rethink: Art, Sound and Transmission*, The Banff Centre for the Arts: Walter Phillips Gallery.

Braun, Reinhard (1999), 'Paradoxe Räume – Mediale Effekte. Elektronische Räume als öffentliche Räume?'. Gained from http://thing.at/texte/06.html (consulted July 1999).

Brecht, Bertolt (1993), 'The radio as an apparatus of communication', (1926) in Strauss, Neil and Mandl, Dave (eds) (1993), *RadioText(e)*, New York: Semiotext(e) no. 16, pp. 15–17.

Breindl, Martin (1997), 'Lo-re vs.hifi: Kunst Internet', *Positionen* 31 (May, 1997), pp. 9–13.

Breitsameter, Sabine (1998), 'Resonance FM roundtable', London, 4 July 1998.

Breitsameter, Sabine (1999), *Geräusche am Rande der Skala: Radiokunst in den USA*, radio programme of the Deutschlandradio Berlin.

Bruisma, Max (1990), 'Notes of a listener' (1985), in Lander, Dan and Lexier, Micah (eds) (1990), *Sound by Artists*, pp. 88–96, Toronto and Banff: Art Metropole and Walter Phillips Gallery.

Cage, John (1968), 'The future of music: Credo' in Cage, John, *Silence*, pp. 3–6, London: Marion Boyars.

Cory, Max Ensign (1989), 'New radio drama as acoustical art' (1988), in Kostelanetz, Richard (ed.), *Esthetics Contemporary*, pp. 405–14, Buffalo: Prometheus Books.

D'Arcy, Margaretta (1990), 'Playing in the airwaves', in Lander, Dan and Lexier, Micah (eds) (1990), *Sound by Artists*, pp. 319–23, Toronto and Banff: Art Metropole and Walter Phillips Gallery.

Eco, Umberto (1994), 'Independent radio in Italy', in Eco, Umberto, *Apocalypse Postponed*, pp. 167–76, Bloomington: Indiana University Press/London: British Film Institute Publishing.

Flusser, Vilém (1998), 'Bilderstatus', in Flusser, Vilém, *Medienkultur*, Frankfurt/Main: Fischer.

Furlong, William (1994), *Audio Arts: Discourse and practice in contemporary art*, London: Academy Editions.

Glandien, Kersten (1997), 'Music machines: spirits raised by us …', in *The Angelic: A Catalogue*, pp. 22–7, Bologna (1997).

Gould, Glenn (1992), *Vom Konzertsaal zum Tonstudio*. Schriften zur Musik 2, München/Mainz: Piper/Schott.

Guattari, Félix (1993), 'Popular free radio' (1978), in Strauss, Neil and Mandl, Dave (eds), *RadioText(e)*, New York: Semiotext(e) no. 16, pp. 85–9.

Grundmann, Heidi (1993), 'Some aspects of telecommunication art in Austria', gained from http://thing.at/orfkunstradio/THEORIE/grundmanntheorie.html (consulted July 1999).

Grundmann, Heidi (1994), 'The geometry of silence', in Augaitis, Diana and Lander, Dan (eds) (1994), *Radio Rethink: Art, Sound and Transmission*, pp. 129–39, The Banff Centre for the Arts: Walter Phillips Gallery.

Hagen, Wolfgang (1997), 'Silencetechno: Cage und das Radio' in *Step Across The Border. Neue musikalische Trends – neue massenmediale Kontexte*, Karben: Coda.

Kahn, Douglas (1992), 'Introduction: Histories of sound once removed', in Kahn, Douglas and Whitehead, Gregory (eds), *Wireless Imagination*, pp. 1–29, Cambridge, Mass.: MIT Press.

Kahn, Douglas and Whitehead, Gregory (eds) (1992), *Wireless Imagination*, Cambridge, Mass.: MIT Press.

Kittler, Friedrich (1993), 'Geschichte der Kommunikation', in *On-line. Kunst im Netz*, Graz: Steirische Kulturinitiative (1993).

Kogawa, Tetsuo (1994), 'Toward polymorphous radio', in Augaitis, Diana and Lander, Dan (eds) (1994), *Radio Rethink: Art, Sound and Transmission*, pp. 287–99, The Banff Centre for the Arts: Walter Phillips Gallery.

Kubisch, Christina (1990), 'About my installations', (1986) in Lander, Dan and Lexier, Micah (eds) (1990), *Sound by Artists*, pp. 68–72, Toronto and Banff: Art Metropole and Walter Phillips Gallery.

Lander, Dan and Lexier, Micah (eds) (1990), *Sound by Artists*, Toronto and Banff: Art Metropole and Walter Phillips Gallery.

Lovink, Geert (1993), 'The theory of mixing: an inventory of free radio techniques in Amsterdam', in Strauss, Neil and Mandl, Dave (eds), *RadioText(e)*, New York: Semiotext(e), no. 16 pp. 114–22.

Marinetti, Filippo T. and Masnata, Pino (1992), 'La Radia', (1933) (tr. Sartorelli, Stephen) in Kahn, Douglas and Whitehead, Gregory (eds), *Wireless Imagination*, pp. 265–68, Cambridge, Mass.: MIT Press.

McLennan, Andrew (1995/96), 'The Listening Room' (radio programme promotion material).

Monahan, Gordon (1987), 'Speaker swinging' in Lander, Dan and Lexier, Micah (eds) (1990), *Sound by Artists*, pp. 140–45, Toronto and Banff: Art Metropole and Walter Phillips Gallery.

Neuhaus, Max (1975), 'Programme Notes', York University, Toronto, in: SoundWorks (Ostfildern, 1994), vol. 1.

Page, Tim (ed.) (1984), The Glenn Gould Reader, New York: Alfred A. Knopf.

Ravlich, Robyn (1998), 'Sound signatures', in Sounds Australian, 52, (February–March 1998).

Russolo, Luigi (1986), 'The art of noises', in Russolo, Luigi, The Art of Noises, (1913), (tr. Brown, Barclay), Monographs in Musicology no. 6, New York: Pendragon Press.

Schafer, R. Murray (1977), The Tuning of the World, New York: Alfred A. Knopf.

Schnebel, Dieter (1994), 'Gedanken zur Radiokunst', Neue Zeitschrift für Musik, Heft 1/1994, pp. 4–5.

Schöning, Klaus (1997), 'On the archaeology of acoustic art in radio', in Klangreise: Studio Akustische Kunst 155 Werke 1968–1997, pp. 12–21, Köln: WDR.

Schöning, Klaus (1999), 'Sound spaces of radio' at Musica Scienza '99, Roma.

Summers, Rod (1990), 'VED audio exchange', in Lander, Dan and Lexier, Micah (eds) (1990), Sound by Artists, pp. 235–40, Toronto and Banff: Art Metropole and Walter Phillips Gallery.

Strauss, Erwin (1993), 'Pirate radio pirates', in Strauss, Neil and Mandl, Dave (eds) (1993), RadioText(e), New York: Semiotext(e) no. 16, pp. 123–8.

Strauss, Neil and Mandl, Dave (eds) (1993), RadioText(e), New York: Semiotext(e) no. 16.

Viola, Bill (1986),'The Sound of One Line Scanning', in Lander, Dan and Lexier, Micah (eds) (1990), Sound by Artists, pp. 39–54, Toronto and Banff: Art Metropole and Walter Phillips Gallery.

Weill, Kurt (1984), 'Radio and restructuring of musical life' (1926), in Hermand, Jost and Steakley, James (eds), Writings of German Composers, pp. 262–5, New York: Continuum.

Weiss, Allen S. (1995), 'From schizophrenia to schizophonia: Antonin Artaud's to have done with the judgment of God', in Weiss, Allen S., Phantasmic Radio, pp. 9–34, Durham, NC: Duke University Press.

Westerkamp, Hildegard (1994), 'The soundscape on radio', in Augaitis, Diana and Lander, Dan (eds) (1994), Radio Rethink: Art, Sound and Transmission, pp. 94–97, The Banff Centre for the Arts: Walter Phillips Gallery.

Whitehead, Gregory (1992), 'Out of the dark: notes on the nobodies of radio art', in Kahn, Douglas and Whitehead, Gregory (eds) (1992), Wireless Imagination, Cambridge, Mass.: MIT Press.

Zurbrugg, Nicholas (1988), 'Sound-Art, Radio-Art and Post-Radio Performance in Australia'. Lecture at the symposium 'With the eyes shut' at the *Steirischer Herbst 1988*, gained from http://thing.at/orfkunstradio/THEORIE (consulted July 1999).

Recordings

Calon, Christian (1990), 'Minuit', in Calon, Christian, *Ligne de vie*, Empreintes Digitales: IMED-9001-CD.
Calon, Christian (1998), 'The Ulysses Project', radio piece, Deutschlandradio Berlin/SFB.
Collins, Nicolas (1986), *Devil's Music*, Trace Elements Records, TE-1013 (LP).
Fontana, Bill (1994) 'Ars Acustica – Ohrbrücke/Soundbridge Köln–San Francisco', (CD) Wergo: WER 6302-2 286 302-2.
Glandien, Lutz, 'Scenes From No Marriage' (1994) (CD booklet), ReR Megacorp: ReRC LG1.
Goebbels, Heiner (1984). *Hörstücke*, (CD), ECM Records: ECM 1452-54 513 368-2.
Günter, Bernhard (1999), *Univers temporel espoir* (CD), trente oiseaux: TOC 991.
Haino, Keiji (1993), *Watashi Dake* (CD), PSF: PSFD 38.
Hearing is Believing (1995), Hearing is Believing/Video Positive: lmtd edition.
Hirsch, Shelly (1995), *O Little Town of East New York*, (CD), Tzadik: TZ 7104.
Jünger, Patrizia (1996), *Transmitter – First to Second Nature. From Riverbed to Inundation* (CD), ANIGMA: acoustic arts (part of the 'Rivers and Bridges' project of the ORF-KunstRadio).
Julius, Rolf (1994), *Small Music CD. Vol 1, White, Yellow, Black*, NADY: SM-1001.
Kubisch, Christina (1995), *Sechs Spiegel* (CD), ED.RZ 10003 Paralelle 3.
Normandeau, Robert (1990), *Lieux inouïs*, Empreintes Digitales: IMED-9002-CD.
Resonance 5(2) (1997), RES 5.2 CD and 7(1) (1998), RES 7.1 CD.

CHAPTER EIGHT

'Losing touch?':
the human performer and electronics

Simon Emmerson

Preface

For millennia sound and music have been products of mechanical action, extended in scope through mechanical technology. By harnessing the power of string, wind and solid objects, humans have sought greater range of sonic expression through direct bodily action. Electricity and electronic technology have allowed (even encouraged) the rupture of these relationships of body to object to sound, replacing them with a range of options from the entirely cerebral to the totally immersive (Emmerson, 1995) . What is it to be 'live' in electroacoustic music?

Since the inception of the electroacoustic music field in the decade after the Second World War so-called 'mixed' electroacoustic music (instruments and tape), 'live' electronic music (using processing of sound produced by a performer) and more recently 'real-time' computer music have all attempted to reconcile some aspects of these ruptures of human cause and effect (Emmerson, 1994b; 1998). The advent of the Internet extends this still further; now we can have apparently 'live' music in a virtual space performed by composer/performers to an audience neither of which has physical boundaries. Indeed the distinction of composer, performer and audience may cease.

This chapter examines some key approaches to this evolution of the last fifty years; some see it as a problem to be solved, others as an opportunity to be exploited. There are no definitive answers.

Introduction

A motivation to write this chapter comes as I see a conflict emerging within electroacoustic music. On the one hand we have the clean, smooth surfaces of an increasingly sophisticated genre based historically on developments from *musique concrète* and the French tradition.[1]

In this approach, stunning accuracy and clarity create quite extraordinarily detailed sound images and landscapes. There is often a strongly synaesthesic component – or at least a tendency to invite the listener into 'apparently very real' spaces (albeit ones that might exist only in dreams!). The medium is transparent, how the sounds have been created, stored and are presented to the audience should in no way intrude between the intentions of the composer and the listener.

This approach stands in a very uneasy relationship with genres stressing an often noisy bricolage, sometimes improvised, often 'urban' in feel, dense, industrial and often lacking in 'real space' perspective (that is, depth). Sometimes, too, the 'sound' of the medium is overtly part of the presentation – whether vinyl, analogue or eight-bit.

The second of these approaches has, to an extent, baffled the followers of the first. It was assumed that improved sound quality, extended processing possibilities including realistic 'sense of space' algorithms, would lead inevitably towards a technical Nirvana where synthetic and concrete, virtual and real, would be seamlessly manipulatable. A rejection of such a path and its glittering prizes was seen as perverse, even Luddite. It is, in part, to such thinkers that this chapter is addressed.

'Indicative fields' (Smalley, 1992)

My first task is to examine in detail an article which I believe to encapsulate brilliantly a tradition of electroacoustic working which has become dominant within much of the acousmatic music developed from the French tradition.[2] Denis Smalley's article 'The Listening Imagination: Listening in the Electroacoustic Era' (Smalley, 1992) extends classical Schaefferian (Schaeffer, 1966; Chion, 1983) thinking into a coherent examination of the relation of sound to human experience – a move away from an over puritan abstraction towards a rehabilitation of the real world and its attributes.[3] While such relations had been true in practice (within this particular tradition) for many years, the article appears to explain at a stroke why certain sound types have specific functions within electroacoustic music of this genre.

I shall then propose a substantial extension to these ideas in an attempt to see why some radical alternatives seem to be so incomprehensible within the model. It may be that such an extension is untenable and that a newer paradigm may be needed.

We must first review the outline of Smalley's position. I will concentrate on his idea of 'indicative fields'.

Nine fields are identified. Three are archetypal: gesture, utterance and behaviour. These fields are original universals. Human utterance and the consequences of gesture have traditionally provided the sounding models for music. The behaviour-field is concerned with sounding relationships in space and time, which can be considered analogous to certain modes of human relationship, observed relationships among things or objects, or human-object relations. The six remaining fields are energy, motion, object/substance, environment, vision and space (Smalley, 1992, p. 521).

In the succeeding elaboration in this article, Smalley consistently relates several of these fields to the human body:

> Broadly defined, human gesture is concerned with movement of the body and limbs for a wide variety of practical and expressive reasons (Smalley, 1992, p. 523).

> Utterance is the second archetypal indicative field, and like the gesture-field it is directly linked to the human body (Smalley, 1992, p. 525).

Behaviour is not specifically related to the human body but is nonetheless very much grounded in the individual's understanding of a solid physical (mechanical) universe. He states:

> It may refer to human behaviour deduced from the utterance-network, to relationships in and among the networks of object/substance, environment or vision. The fields of energy, motion and space are inevitably strongly implicated (Smalley, 1992, p. 526).

He goes on to examine this field (behaviour) under three subheadings: *dominance/subordination*, *conflict/coexistence* and *causality*. The first two pairs of oppositions almost suggest a sentience (a consciousness) behind the metaphor of description. While it is true that primordial forces in the universe can show conflict, coexistence, dominance or subordination there is a sense in which these terms are profoundly rooted in our observations of the behaviour of objects around us. This is reinforced in the notion of *causality* which

> although it exhibits attributes of the two paired oppositions, needs separate consideration. Causality in this context does not refer narrowly to physical gesture. It is more concerned with one sound acting upon another, either causing the second event to occur or instigating change in an ongoing sound (Smalley, 1992, p. 527).

The energy-field 'is associated with the creation and release of tension which, as we know, is at the source of the gesture-field.' (Smalley, 1992, p. 528). The term 'tension' is specifically a mechanical attribute (much present in muscular energy). He continues:

The energy-field depends on the motion-field ... Since motion is integral to temporal experience all types of non-musical motions can have musical counterparts (Smalley, 1992, p. 528).

Object/substance is self-evidently a physical metaphor:

actual sounding materials can be used, simulated or alluded to ... stone, glass, ceramics, woods, metals, skins, etc., which can be subject to gestural play ... objectness can be deduced from types of motion that suggest analogies with the motion of objects ... objectness can be attributed to morphologies without reference to real materials as long as there is some semblance of a plausible gestural origin (Smalley, 1992, p. 529).

The next field – that of *environment* – is in the first instance interpreted literally. Smalley refers to human and animal utterance and to the 'sounding objects and textures of the environment'. It is precisely here that I shall argue (below) for a 'Trojan horse' kind of reappraisal which may spread out into the other indicative fields and networks. The penultimate field is that of *vision*.

Every field discussed so far contributes to the visual indicative network. It is true to say that vision is at the very basis of the gesture-field, and that the energy motion trajectory is unimaginable without its visual correlations (Smalley, 1992, p. 530).

What he describes as a consequent 'weaker, voluntary, associative synaesthesia which will vary in consciousness and activity among listeners' (Smalley, 1992, p. 530) is once again inextricably a product of a sensory appreciation of the physical world (sight).

The final field discussed is the *space-field*. This he divides into three aspects. The first two are traditional notions of space with physical dimension: those of composition (the 'sound image' of the piece as composed); the second that of performance and public presentation. The third aspect 'concerns the affective interpretation of space – how the listener experiences and feels about space' (Smalley, 1992, p. 531). It is this third 'psychological' space which we will re-engage and develop here also.

This emphasis may be said to be 'Piagetian': the idea that human development is rooted in the physical senses and that we have evolved primarily to explore through these senses (Piaget, 1969). This paradigm remained unassailable until the advent of recording, telecommunications and electronic synthesis. It must now be re-examined.

The initial impact of recording in the last part of the nineteenth century was thought of as profound and yet some of the consequences are only just becoming apparent; the telephone dislocated in space the

cause of sound from its perception, to which recording added dislocation of time.[4] In the early part of the twentieth century the first synthesis
removed the need for the mechanical causality[5] of sound altogether.
These three dislocations effectively modified all the standard relationships of body to sound – it did not replace them altogether, but extended
and challenged them.

This challenge has taken some time to develop. At first, the new
media of recording, communication and sound synthesis remained
strongly integrated within the prevailing 'physical music' paradigm.
Recording and music telecommunication aimed at ever higher 'fidelity'
with each technical improvement – fidelity to an idealised recreation of
concert hall experience. Even synthesis remained within this performance tradition, more often than not basing its models on existing musical
instruments and performance practice within traditional (physical instrument) ensembles.[6]

The transition from recreation to creation with this new technology
which started in the 1920s and 1930s was to gather momentum in the
period after stabilisation in Europe from about 1948. The classical
rivalry of *musique concrète* and *elektronische Musik* addresses two of
these dislocations directly: the French group turning the turntable (and
the act of recording) around into a creative and productive force, the
German group idealising the synthetic power of the new technology;
while both groups came under the umbrella of institutions of our third
dislocation – radio, articulating the need for a new kind of diffusion of
a music 'which could only be heard over loudspeakers'.[7]

Causality

How do I *know* that the cause of the sound I have just heard is a 'bang
on a can'? There are two components. The generalisation of my immediate experience to others. If I have experience of sound production for
myself then I can deduce the causes of sounds even when invisible. This
is learnt in early childhood; the voice is recognised immediately, followed by an increasingly wide vocabulary of sounds.

But there is also an entire class of sounds to which I cannot have
regular access as (physical) producer: environmental sounds in the broadest sense. Some are 'natural', whether inorganic (wind, water, thunder)
or from other life-forms (bird, animal), while some are 'cultural' and
human-made (street and urban sounds, electrical motors, building sounds,
construction sounds etc.). Of course, some of the properties of these
sounds can be related to those we know and have learnt to make

ourselves (they are simply 'larger' versions), but others we need to learn through other means.

The philosopher Braithwaite discusses how we come to understand the *cause* of an event. He distinguishes what he calls 'regular concomitances' ('a concomitance of properties in the same thing or event' (Braithwaite, 1968, p. 308)) from *regular sequences, regular simultaneities* and *regular precedences*. Given the spatio-temporal continuity of the former it is easier to grant the status of 'cause' to the relation – 'I hit an object and it sounds'. We know and can perceive the continuity Braithwaite alludes to. The evidence for causality is sufficiently high for us to make the assertion.

But in the latter group the relation is looser. Perhaps we are observing at a distance – maybe even acousmatically. But in this group we may not have direct access via other senses; we *observe* and make judgements. Braithwaite asserts a particularly empirical philosopher's position: 'Scientific laws will be taken as asserting no more (and no less) than the *de facto* generalizations that they include' (Braithwaite, 1968, p. 10). The basis for us assuming the relation (for us sound, but for him anything) 'A causes B' will be the observation of persistent regularities and our generalisations from them. We can never be *absolutely sure* about any such causal relation; but we gain sufficient knowledge to be 'happy' with the statement: 'Lightning causes thunder'.

This second group then suggests less certainty concerning the origin of sounds. Modern science has supplied the causal explanation linking lightning to thunder, but it required other information – not immediately available to a lay observer and itself the result of scientific enquiry into the behaviour of gases – to make the link secure. These larger chains initially rest on repeated observation ('thunder always follows lightning') and generalisation rather than immediate tactile knowledge.

My object here is not to pursue an investigative programme in philosophy but to facilitate a shift in focus from examining the causalities of the physical world which have directed our 'Darwinian' evolution to those which include the dislocated experiences described above including most importantly those whose immediate source is the loudspeaker.

Learning involves consistency. The same action must produce the same result. In the world of physically produced sound this enables increasing nuance to be learnt. Crude distinctions are learnt in early childhood – I hit harder to produce a louder sound. Then as objects become more specific, a musical instrument for example, the effects may be more subtle. I begin to feel – I need not be able to express it in words – the changes that minute differences in breath pressure, embouchure, finger position etc., bring about as I painstakingly practice an instrument. In so far as the new media involve reproduction of our existing experience (or possible experience) there is little problem. The best electronic musical interfaces ('controllers') preserve and even extend what F. Richard Moore (1988) has described as 'control intimacy' – a useful notion which combines consistency of behaviour with sensitivity – and it should not be necessary to use a highly energetic gesture to produce a 'just noticeable difference' in a sound quality.

We learn quickly to decode the origins of physically produced sound and its surrogates on radio, television and in recorded form. But once the medium becomes the tool of production rather than reproduction the matter changes radically.

Extending indicative fields?

There are two fundamental points to be made which may be read clearly in the above summary of Denis Smalley's exposition. One has been highlighted already: the firm embedding of his thesis within a primarily and dominantly physical universe. This world certainly has 'agencies' for action which operate within (most of) the indicative fields but which do not, as agencies, possess a 'culture'.

In this view the human body has learnt about sounds first through interacting physically with the world to produce sound or second, through hearing sound produced elsewhere but of assumed mechanical origin.[8] Whereas I will not suggest that this will disappear there are two developments which alter fundamentally this mechanical learning paradigm: the ubiquitous loudspeaker present in many young human lives from birth[9] and the presence in the immediate environment of sounds produced electronically.

But more subtly and less overtly stated, Smalley's 'indicative fields' idea appears to remain firmly within the nature side of a binary nature-culture paradigm; that is, the relationship appears to be between a learning 'I' and a physical world 'out there'. This is idealised into an assumed learning curve which seems to ignore that the very subject under discussion – electroacoustic music (or at least acousmatic sound) – is itself present in the very environment in which these archetypes are being learnt. The least we must do is to examine the effects of this cultural dimension; one that is not at all absolute but exists in a 'real' and developing time and space. In what way does this influence or alter the 'mechanical' (primordial) idealised model? We may have to extend this idea to include more 'cultural' fields.[10]

This transformation is paralleled in the move away from 'nature-as-opposed-to-culture' approaches within ecology, with the emergence of integrated models which see not a binary divide of urban and rural but a complex interdependence. While this chapter will not claim to have presented such a holistic theory, I wish to suggest this paradigmatic shift as necessary to our understanding of the acousmatic world.

New objects and substances

Just as in the physical world we saw the relationship between sounds we could produce ourselves and 'large' sounds of the environment, so in the new acousmatic universe we have sounds which we appear to be able to make ourselves and those beyond our comprehension.

For example, a particular type of electronic sound was typical of the first generation of computer games. The simple morphology and spectral type was in part a product simply of economy – computing power was not to be wasted on unnecessarily complex sound production. But such sounds gained an immediate social dimension: they always had a precise semiotic function with respect to the game they 'inhabited', indicating simple moves or more complex outcomes. The ubiquity of such games added another level of signification: the sounds entered the urban soundscape for both the individual and the collective memory.

The strong link of such sounds to function we know (or are taught) is arbitrary; any sound might have been chosen,[11] there is no physical causality involved. Yet there appears to be (as above) 'regular sequence', an action on screen produces a sounding result – every time. While superficially similar, and allowing the same kind of learning as for the physical object or instrument, the effect on memory may be fundamentally different.

While Smalley (following Schaeffer) might hear a mechanically produced sound that indicates (even remotely) 'metallic substance hit with great force in a vast space', the indicators for our computer game sound when similarly lifted out of its accustomed context cannot be articulated in quite the same way. Such a sound might, using the existing indicative field indicators, be classed as a 'remote' or even 'dislocated' surrogate with respect to several of them. That it might not be related even remotely to physical sounding models would make it (in Smalley's terms) 'unviable'.[12]

But the sound is not heard 'in abstract' if included in a composition. Indicative fields seem to leap into operation unannounced – we need not actively engage them (although we can choose to concentrate on a chosen field). In this case the field suggested cannot but have a real-time dimension. A first descriptive response might be 'Space Invaders level 2, annihilation sound'; this is a generalisation of the experience 'this sound is similar to that which always occurs at a particular point while playing Space Invaders'. This apparently resembles the phrase (in description of a 'metallic sound') 'this sound is similar to that which always occurs when I hit a metallic object with great force' but is, of course, much more context specific.

A first field indicator described this way (assuming such an extension to the original idea of indicative field is accepted) then leads to additional indicators which may also be clearly shared experiences and not merely autobiographical.[13] For example, aspects of the sound may indicate the particular 'space' in which the game was most often played, the machine and feel of the controls, joysticks, physical posture and gestures. These are, of course, considerably more context and history-specific than the generalised fields drawn from experiencing the sounds of the physical world, but have sufficient persistence to have been assimilated into sonic memory with these specific connotations.

It might even be that such fields come into operation to a greater extent when the 'primordial' ones (as described by Smalley) prove unhelpful. Leigh Landy reports an example of what might be the result of this emergence of context-specific fields which have the power to act retrospectively:

> It was in the early 80s that a small group of "punks" ... attended an electronic music concert in which a couple of Gottfried Michael Koenig's electronic pieces from the 60s were performed. These works are highly original. They are also pretty loud. The "punks" were in ecstasy and most attending ... after their initial surprise, finally understood why (Landy, 1991, p. 165).

Koenig's electronic pieces are often generated using what is known as 'non-standard synthesis' including forms of algorithmic composition, usually involving the direct generation of waveforms according to stochastic laws.[14] In many ways the resulting sounds and structures could not be further from the sounding models referred to by Smalley[15] and appear to inhabit a space without real dimensions, flat and alienated. And yet at a different level they can appear to 'refer to' and model the stochastic processes of urban existence – loud, noisy and arbitrary. And, as Murray Schafer has pointed out, such soundscapes are increasingly devoid of perspective and subtlety, becoming increasingly flat and monochrome.

> The hi-fi soundscape is one in which discrete sounds can be heard more clearly because of the low ambient noise level ... In the hi-fi soundscape, sounds overlap less frequently; there is perspective – foreground and background ... In a lo-fi soundscape individual

acoustic signals are obscured in an overdense population of sounds. The pellucid sound – a footstep in the snow, a church bell across the valley ... is masked by broadband noise. Perspective is lost. On a downtown street corner of the modern city there is no distance; there is only presence. There is crosstalk on all channels (Schafer, 1977, p. 43).

It is perhaps in this strange way that algorithmic composition may sneak into our discussion. This is perhaps an area most remote from the view of the acousmatic so eloquently articulated through the idea of the indicative field. In the first instance any such compositional 'system' was seen as anathema to the ear-based approach of the Schaefferian tradition.[16] The use of, for example, chaotic or fractal generation procedures often created crude results through naïve mapping procedures from number to sound. I do not intend here to attempt a rehabilitation of these.[17] However, that is to ignore the integration of certain algorithmic procedures into our everyday world. We *hear* the results of deterministic yet chaotic processes all around us: from control systems in buildings to computer noises, to the resulting 'noise' of the World Wide Web. These are steadily becoming their own 'indicative fields'.[18] An algorithmic process of generation may then – unexpectedly, without necessarily the intention of the composer – relate to a 'sounding model' in some process in the real world.

In a profound sense, this was predicted by Iannis Xenakis whose works move to and fro across what appears to be a divide between those having a clear sonic metaphor in the real world (the 'mass sounds' of *Pithoprakta*, the arborescences of *Cendrées*) to those apparently embedded firmly in mathematical abstraction[19] (the *ST* series or *Nomos Alpha*) (Xenakis, 1992). As a believer in the 'deep' relationship of science, mathematics and other symbolic systems to music he has never accepted this divide.

> The artist-conceptor will have to be knowledgeable and inventive in such varied domains as mathematics, logic, physics, chemistry, biology, genetics, paleontology (for the evolution of forms), the human sciences and history ... Moreover, the time has come to establish a new science of "general morphology" which would treat these forms and architectures within these diverse disciplines ... The backdrop for this new science should be the real condensations of intelligence; in other words, an abstract approach, free from anecdotes of our senses and habits (Xenakis, 1985, p. 3).

As we become more aware of the industrial and information processes that surround us and regulate our every moment such abstractions may 'discover' ever more concrete manifestations. We begin to observe – more precisely to hear – such processes around us. New *kinds* of sounding models emerge based on the complexities (even, literally, the chaos) of urban life. Thus a new generation of composers may see an apparent lack of perspective *as the new perspective*.

But the newcomer is potentially invading old territory also. If the youngest of listeners learns a wide variety of 'instrumental' sounds only from the presets of a synthesiser, the sounding models from which they originate may cease to be learnt. Here a very different kind of process may be at work. The ear quickly learns to differentiate by sound alone: we soon realise to our surprise that this is a classic case of 'reduced listening'. The relation of the verbal phrase 'bowed string' to an actual waveform emanating from a loudspeaker may be retained but based upon an entirely different experience. The user may never have experienced a bowed string demonstrated to his/her aural, visual and tactile senses. The 'old' route – verbal description of physical phenomenon is applied to sound produced – is replaced by a conventional (that is, agreed) label (of the 'preset'). Such labels will, of course, remain reasonably close to those originally given through physical observation for a long time to come – at least until 'bowed strings' have disappeared! But the degree of arbitrariness of these labels may be seen in their progressive removal from the known and familiar ('bowed string', 'flute') through the vaguely known ('shakuhachi') to the 'joke sound effect' ('Mount St Helens').[20]

The user has no means of knowing that this is what we have previously described as 'reduced listening', indeed the phrase becomes progressively meaningless. The synthesiser might become the sole source of the sound produced; not just of the one sound but the potentially infinite many. Schaeffer's language is further inadequate to describe this object as it ceases in his terms to 'be' an instrument at all.[21] Such experiences leap over the phenomenological reduction demanded by Schaeffer straight into the world of directly perceived timbre: a 'flute' is a 'flute' is a 'flute' – that is, not necessarily a sound produced by a flute.

Ideas and technology as possible fields

In conclusion to this part of the discussion we have to face up to the possibility that we may slowly but steadily move away from physical agency as the basis for learning the indicative fields used for the interpretation of acousmatic sound and music. If this is the case then other 'fields', mapped in a more fragile way to the experiences of the industrial, information and urban soundscapes may emerge. For example, the 'ideas' of stochastics, chaos and noise have already found their real-world expressions. I do not mean that stochastic, noisy and chaotic algorithms in composition will suddenly gain greater comprehensibility (they may or may not) but that these aspects of the soundscape may, without us necessarily being conscious of their presence, form associations of the type described in Smalley's discussion. And finally, technology itself, may become a reference field, drawn attention to as a crucial signifier; the acousmatic veil torn down and the transparent means of production and dissemination become the subject of the discourse.

Live electronic music?

In Emmerson (1994a) I discussed the relationship of two terms which I felt had become dangerously confused. The term 'real-time' had been introduced into music through computer applications to refer to near instantaneous processes. These could refer to sound synthesis, sound modification or sound diffusion. Progressively any electroacoustic performance which involved such resources 'on stage' was described as 'real-time'.

This description absorbed within its generality the older term 'live electronic', used first for the treatment of acoustic instruments using the analogue resources of an earlier era.[22] This strand of work maintained the human performer firmly in the centre of focus – most usually performing an acoustic instrument (or voice) for modification, but also possibly playing an electronic instrument. The members of the Stockhausen ensemble in the 1960s, for example, would treat 'live' the sounds of the electronium, other synthesisers such as the EMS Synthi AKS, or use short-wave radios as instruments.

There was also what the French termed 'mixed' music, combining instrument (or voice) and electroacoustic sounds (originally 'on tape'). Here the focus was balanced between the fixed performer (albeit with some limited mobility through amplification and sound projection) and the usually multi-speaker electroacoustic diffusion. These two approaches – 'live electronic' and 'mixed' – could, of course, be combined.

But another completely different approach to the use of technology in concert performance concerns using the calculating power of the computer to generate musical material ('events') during the performance. Such an approach was made radically easier following the advent of Midi in the early 1980s. Simple events (often just 'notes') could be specified easily and rules for their sequence and combination defined and applied with sufficient speed for the process to appear instantaneous. With more sophisticated interfaces emerging throughout the 1980s and 1990s this has led to the development of *interactive* performance and composition systems in which performer and machine (or even machine and machine) can respond to each other 'spontaneously'[23] on the concert platform. These systems are all referred to as 'real-time' – but not all of them are 'live'.

For some of these systems the audience can have no idea what 'cause' has resulted in what musical 'effect'. The loss of appreciation of human agency within the sound world loses our immediate sense of the 'live'. But before we see how the extension of indicative fields (above) might effect our sense of human presence I want to review the first decades of live electronic and mixed music in terms of the relationships between the human performer and the sounding result.

In many ways the instrument is an extension of the body; instrumental gestures are extensions of vocal and physical gestures. The relationship to dance, work and the rhythms of everyday life has never been far beneath the surface of music – even a music such as western art concert music which has moved steadily away from body rhythm towards more esoteric concerns.

These are the origins of a major tension within contemporary organology: the instruments we have today are the product of a mechanical technology largely finalised by the mid-nineteenth century. The twentieth-century western musical world has seen an unprecedented expansion in 'permissible' sound typology even before the advent of electronics into the mainstream. We may observe this in several ways within the tradition: the extension of both harmony and timbral complexity in the first part of the century, in tandem with the extension of instrumentation to include, most notably, new percussion instruments. While the first wave of this expansion was based on existing performance practice, a renewed interest in the period after 1950 led in some quarters to pressure to develop new performance practices: so-called 'extended techniques'. This has remained a relatively underdeveloped field. Wind instrument multiphonics, for example, have some universally agreed specifications, yet the dream of 'extending' all instruments has hardly been realised.[24] The invention of entirely new instruments has been a further stage in this development but has remained firmly embedded within an 'experimental' tradition, producing no long-lasting new inventions.[25]

The contribution of mixed electroacoustic music to this development is important – and has shown up some of the inherent difficulties (even contradictions) in this enterprise. A classic 'acousmatic' style is usually severely disjunctive with the tradition from which western instrumentation emerged. Pitch is seen as a subset of timbre and not necessarily an important one at that. Harmonic development is often replaced by more complex *timbral* relationships. The first step we might observe in trying to overcome this incompatibility is towards treating the instrument as 'sounding body', exciting its resonances and eliciting other sounds through a variety of techniques, most of which we might describe as 'extended'. In short to re-create it as a source of *objets sonores* to complement in quality those which have been pre-prepared in the electroacoustic part. Ironically, the causal link which the listener may have – instrumental gesture to sound – may be broken; the extraordinary sounds created from our 'familiar' instrument may not *seem* to come from it. The instrument aspires to the condition of the acousmatic.

But this is the nub of the problem; the instrumental sound remains in practice anchored to the instrument. It is impossible to diffuse the amplified instrumental sound in the same manner as the electroacoustic sounds. The composer is often unsure whether to try to 'free' the sound from source, to let it separate and have its own life – as that would undermine the vestiges of its relation to the live presence – or to leave it ambiguously stationary. Hence the live performer sometimes has the uneasy feel of a persistently real and recognisable intruder into a dream.

Conversely, there are composers who have attempted a rapprochement from the other side. The reintroduction of an 'instrumental' gestural world into the electroacoustic part is also a possibility. This is seen by some who espouse the acousmatic cause as a betrayal of the ideals of the medium. The tape hints at being a mere substitute 'accompaniment'. This approach has often resulted in apparent 'super-instruments', virtuosic and ghostly counterparts to the live performer who interact with an apparently superhuman (and sometimes robotic) force. Within this approach the live instrumental part is often more traditionally composed and a clearer anchor 'centre stage' with which the electroacoustic part takes issue and acts as 'surrounding' – itself often more clearly anchored[26] – without overt diffusion around the space.

A perfect balance of the two has rarely succeeded yet an early example remains a universally acclaimed exception. Stockhausen's *Kontakte* combines piano and percussion with electroacoustic sound. The instrumentation continues the composer's preoccupation with the continuum between pitch and noise. Of all instrumental families the percussion group has least reliance upon pitch within its enormous timbral range. The piano, due to its polyphony and pedal control of resonance, can create such densities of pitched sounds that more complex objects emerge. As John Dack points out:

Kontakte presents intricate networks of relationships whereby differences between instrumental and electroacoustic practice and theory can appear simultaneously to conflict and support each other (Dack, 1998, p. 86).

The instrumental parts and the electroacoustic part in those sections of the work when it is most in 'contact' with the instrumental sound world articulate an apparently improvisatory and complex flux and exchange, maintaining the non-metric rhythms and density characteristic of the 'modern' music of the period. Thus, that both the live instrumental and the acousmatic parts aspire in some senses to the other results in the contact intended: the very opening gesture in which a metal beater is drawn in a circular gesture upon the surface of a tam-tam creating a sound which blends in with a similar (though extended) sound on tape is a paradigm example. The tape 'emerges' from the live.

The 'live electronic' field had as many subdivisions. The processing of acoustic instrumental and vocal sounds in performance may be divided into two: time and frequency domain. The two may be combined. The relationship of performer to sounding result is at issue here. The situation for the listener is very different for solo (or small group) than ensemble performance. For the small group the relation of loudspeaker sound to original (if absolutely no element is pre-recorded) is usually quite clear; if time delays are used the delay times are (for technical reasons) usually within short-term and always within medium-term memory. Frequency domain changes were clearly subtractive (filtering) or the generation of somewhat predictable side-bands (amplitude and frequency modulation). In all these cases the performer's gestural contour was usually preserved. There was rarely any acousmatic dislocation. An exception involved re-enveloping and extension of the sound; a sound without its attack often loses cues for recognition, delayed or extended in other ways it can lose a degree of its source bonding.[27] In the transition to digital processing techniques little changed in the first generation – experimental music had in general moved away from live electronic music towards real-time interactivity (without the acoustic sound of the live performer) in the early 1980s. The advent in the late 1980s of fast real-time processing of both the sounds and 'events' of live performance has moved towards healing the breach – especially as processes such as those developed by Miller Puckette, Cort Lippe and Zack Settel become available at more modest cost.[28] A final discussion concerns *interface* – the human–computer relationship.

Interfaces

The need for human–computer interfaces more sensitive to the needs of performers is emerging as the most important new field of research. Two approaches have emerged in the final years of the century: devices which track and measure physical action (sometimes known as 'controllers') and those which analyse the sound produced in performance through processes such as pitch and envelope tracking, real-time spectral analysis and measurement of noise components; the results of this analysis are converted into a suitable format for the control of sound production or processing.

The first group has existed since the earliest developments in electronic music (a keyboard is a simple controller). Notwithstanding the impetus given to this development by Midi and the subsequent development of, for example, guitar, wind, string, piano and percussion Midi-controllers, the limitations of the Midi protocol itself has frustrated their further development (F. Richard Moore, 1988).

The second group had to wait (at least for wider dissemination outside of research organisations) for the speed and power of the computers of the 1990s. Such real-time analysis processes came even more quickly up against the timing and information density limits of the Midi standard and most such systems use Midi only at the final stage of output.[29] The target of either of these two approaches[30] was the same: to control a versatile synthesis and sound processing system.

But an interesting divide has emerged in research into new interface design. One approach retains tactile feedback to the performer through strings and membranes under tension, spring-loaded paddles and joysticks, objects of familiar or newly developed elastic and plastic solids. Transducers 'read' this interaction from within the device. Another group avoids such elastic feedback while preserving tactility: measuring pressure, velocity or direction for example via transducer pads built into other objects, such as gloves, clothing, chairs, the floor. The performer may only partly be aware of the action taking place (perhaps through a change in the sound).

But there is also the possibility of remote sensors which never come into contact with the performer, using ultrasound or light beam systems[31] to detect proximity or movement. In addition, biophysical interfaces, which have remained on the fringes of experimental music throughout both analogue and digital developments, may yet move to the forefront of music interface technology.[32]

Extending the 'live'?

My own definitions of 'the live' have, as with Smalley's 'indicative fields', been anchored firmly in the domain of the physical. My definitions have related strongly to just those 'Piagetian' developments alluded to in my discussion of those fields. The apprehension of live presence was taken to be the product of a mechanical causality in which I could somehow 'work out' that there was live agency in the production of something I had just heard. Furthermore I associated that live agency with a specific role within the music, continuously informing its continuity through gestures I could *hear* as part of or extensions of the human repertoire of sound production. Occasionally this strongly realist position could be extended: a human could perhaps surrealistically 'play' a thunderstorm, where an instrumental gesture could be perceived in articulation or other aspects of the sound's evolution. But the smallest of anchors had to remain to the possibility of human causality in a physical sense. I rejected, therefore, actions such as triggering preset algorithms or soundfiles as being 'live' in this sense.

But I must now perform the same critical functions upon this supposition that I did earlier for indicative fields. In a universe of loudspeakers and urban 'noise' I can no longer simply assume that a child learns through audio-mechanical means alone to recognise human presence. But I am going to argue for a modification to these views in a very different way.

Loudspeakers today are most often used to project yet further evidence of human presence into every aspect of our lives. The ever present background music, talk and news creates an ideal community around us which we believe to be 'live'. The paradox for the composer could not be greater. The loudspeaker is the predominant communicator of the age: the telephone, the computer loudspeaker in addition to the radio and television. And most material heard through it indicates some aspects of human presence – whether alienated, fake or (even) real.

The reassertion of humanity over such new soundscapes has come in unexpected ways. Let us generalise the desire for live aspects to remain in music making to the desire to have a reflection of ourselves as real sentient beings somehow 'within the music'. In some cases we rejoice in the community of the performance, in others we revel at the virtuosity, feel challenged by the possibility of human error – with a hint of the voyeur when catastrophe strikes. In all circumstances the live performer was 'another one of us' even though glorified and separated the other side of a theatrical proscenium. This entire argument existed within the mechanical/physical universe I have continuously alluded to. The soundscape over which humans claimed control was acoustic. How then has an equivalent demand for recognition of human presence been articulated in our electroacoustic (and largely acousmatic) world? Attali has identified this ubiquitous pseudo-socialisation:

> It ['background noise'][33] slips into the growing spaces of activity void of meaning and relations, into the organisation of everyday life ... everywhere, it signifies the presence of a power that needs no flag or symbol: musical repetition confirms the presence of repetitive consumption, of the flow of noises as ersatz sociality (Attali, 1985, p. 111).

To date we have been faced with an overwhelming lack of influence over what we have received through the loudspeaker. And herein lies the first assertion of human action: *choice.*

The very technology that brought us the dislocation of recording from live performance has now enabled us to shift the focus: I am asserting the possibility of 'playing' the loudspeakers. This might seem no different from the activites of every electroacoustic composer who revels in the use of an 'orchestra of loudspeakers'. But here the materials of the 'play' come from those forming experiences which surround us. At its crudest 'channel hopping' is the most primitive assertion of this choice which has as its increasingly sophisticated offspring the areas now known as 'plunderphonics'[34] and the more experimental 'turntablism' of the club DJs.[35] The act of wilful change and choice is often quite vicious in its application. The original recordings which are the material of this new music may have been constructed with due respect to language, melodic shape, balance and 'beautiful sound'; but as the subject of these arts of collage the material is ruptured from its pretence at 'representing a performance', hacked up and fragmented with deliberate disregard for these original niceties, while preserving just enough of them to allow a degree of identification with their human origin. It is almost a revenge by the artist against the previous lack of control over the ubiquity of the loudspeaker, a reassertion of creativity and authorship.

> Therefore, in the final analysis, to listen to music in the network of composition is to rewrite it: "to put music into operation, to draw it towards an unknown praxis," as Roland Barthes writes in a fine text on Beethoven. The listener is the operator. Composition, then, beyond the realm of music, calls into question the distinction between worker and consumer ... (Attali, 1985, p. 135).

In like manner a shift in listening habits towards 'sampling' the music at venues[36] shows another aspect of this shift to 'listener as creator (or at least controller) of experience'. The increase in interest throughout the arts in sound installations, site-specific artworks and environments also shifts responsibility substantially towards the individual visitor for the final experience. The introduction of interactive technologies also gives further power away from the 'author'.

Thus once again we see not a simple extension of the idea of 'the live in the music' – deduced as we have seen from our knowledge of the physical universe – but a shift of focus now that the loudspeaker has become the source of new experiences. We no longer assert our human presence only through hitting, scraping and blowing the objects around us, but through reasserting our power over the new medium – and using *it* as source.

To do this we need clearly to perceive that the medium *is* the medium, that is far from making it transparent (as our acousmatic artists have previously advocated) quite the opposite is the case. For anyone to show you that constructive power has been 'regained' over the loud-speaker, you must clearly recognise the sources as those associated with the loudspeaker with all its connotations. We draw attention to it; it must be recognisably an artefact.

Recognisable recordings are but one obvious and controversial possibility. But then so are some of the more obvious techniques of the medium: looping has been with us since the dawn of *musique concrète* – from *sillon fermé* through the tape loop to the byte-specific definitions in the digital sampler. In addition that actual quality of the medium may be highlighted: vinyl itself has qualities of bandwidth, audio compression and surface noise which may be recognised – even when finally mastered in the highest quality digital format. To paraphrase Roland Barthes (1977) the 'grain of the voice' – which gives it such characteristics and personality – has become the 'grain of the recording' with which we now assert our independent choice and creativity.

Conclusion

The assertion of human presence within music produced by and through technology will take many different forms as humans become increasingly alienated from purely physical sound production. We have examined two streams within this process. Some will carry on representing humanity within the music when produced – the inherited role of the human performer on stage for us to hear. The 'amplification' of human gesture made possible with the new interfaces may create distorted giants of unreal proportion – but we may recognise them at least.[37] But second, we have seen the possibility of a music of technology with the clear imprint of the human *will* rather than the human *presence*. As composer, performer and listener distinctions can blur, choice and construction within the act of listening become the act of composition itself. When this is repeated on each occasion we may see it as an essentially live and sentient activity.

This writer, at least, hopes that the two approaches will not lose touch with each other.

Notes

1. Though purists note that the idealised notions of *écoute reduite* and *objet sonore* have given way to a more liberal approach to including the sound origins.
2. Especially (interestingly) outside France itself; for example, Canada (both the Quebec French tradition and the World Soundscape Project group (Vancouver)), Sweden, the UK, and many offshoots.
3. The article does not address the 'real world'/synthetic divide *within the music* (see Wishart, 1986), but how we relate the spectromorphology of *any* sound to a possible *indicative field* (q.v.).
4. The mixed metaphor – 'dislocation of time' – is significant; the mapping of time onto space is a characteristic of western modernism.
5. Except that of the loudspeaker to which we shall return.
6. This generalisation must not detract from the extraordinary exceptions of the Theremin, aspects of the *Ondes Martenot* and other early experimental interfaces; nonetheless the overall paradigm remained firmly based on the keyboard model. The *Telharmonium*, too, was heard by telephone – another premonition of contemporary distribution.
7. The title of a series of radio broadcasts by Stockhausen on the WDR (Cologne) 1964–66: 'Kennen Sie Musik, die man nur am Lautsprecher hören kann?' which reviewed electroacoustic music from several traditions, published as Stockhausen (1971).
8. Of course Smalley refers often to apprehension of sounds produced synthetically (electronically); but throughout the indicative fields and networks discussion he refers almost exclusively to the world through physical/ mechanical metaphors.
9. Or before, from playing music to women in pregnancy to contact transducers which transmit stress reducing pseudo-heart beats.
10. As a first stage in establishing a continuum of natural and cultural fields, perhaps.
11. Although a closer hearing reveals that many are remote surrogates of real physical sounds – sometimes of games of previous eras.
12. He writes: 'Many a listener's problem can be related either to the loss of tangibility created by the severance of direct gestural ties, or to the difficulties in comprehending the remoteness of new surrogacy' (Smalley, 1986, p. 83).

13. A field can only exist if shared amongst a large community of understanding.
14. The *Funktion* series, for example.
15. And are certainly extremely remote in sound quality from the post-concrète genre referred to in the opening paragraphs above.
16. Schaeffer referred to the composers to enter the GRM from 1957 as 'This generation, visibly liberated from their serial straight jackets' (Schaeffer, 1973, p. 31).
17. Partly victims of the 1980s obsession in some quarters with event-based algorithms following the invention of the Midi protocol.
18. I am crudely lumping several together here which will surely become more clearly differentiated in future.
19. That is not to say the mathematical abstraction *could* not be related to processes in the real world just that it does not *sound* like it. I am arguing here that this distinction is fluid.
20. I remind the reader I refer to synthesiser preset labels in these points. 'Mount St Helens' was a sound effect preset on the DX7 synthesiser, a landmark in the evolution of named presets. Interestingly younger users may no longer understand the volcanic reference.
21. An instrument being precisely that which gives coherence and identity to a group of sound objects (Schaeffer, 1966, chapter 13).
22. There was an explosion of such work in the 1960s although precursors in the USA (Cage most notably) can be dated back to the early 1940s.
23. The evolving 'Voyager' project of trombonist/composer George Lewis is a case in point.
24. A series from the University of California Press, 'The new instrumentation', included volumes on double bass, flute, trombone, clarinet and guitar.
25. That is not to underestimate the influence of these usually one-off devices on attitudes to timbral composition and performance practice.
26. There is a possible paradox here. The 'apparent' instrument (on tape) may need to be more definitely anchored in order that spatial movement within it may more clearly be heard. Javier Alvarez's *Papalotl* (piano and tape) is a good example.
27. The guitar feedback techniques of Jimi Hendrix are a case in point.
28. The MAX/MSP environment is but the first and has already led to an explosion of possibilities in this field. For a discussion of such an environment from the view of an improvising group see Casserley (1998).
29. In recent interfaces from both Steim (Amsterdam) and MIT (Cambridge, Mass.) the internal resolution of the tracking far exceeds the Midi bandwidth. The advent of such as real-time C-Sound may see the end of Midi within such systems.
30. A combination of both approaches (performance action and signal analysis) has been used in the some devices.
31. Interfaces developed for special needs performers and composers have pioneered combinations of these approaches. In the UK, the Drake Music Project, for example, has made extensive use of these.
32. The systems of David Rosenboom and Alvin Lucier are well documented cases in point. These are sometimes erroneously described as 'biofeedback' processes – some are, some are not. They use biophysical controllers to control an outside system.

33. Attali heads the section 'Background Noise', but it is clear throughout the chapter that he refers to background music as *noise* in this sense.
34. See Chris Cutler's contribution to the present volume (Chapter 4).
35. Robin Rimbaud ('Scanner') with *Spring Heel Jack* on nine turntables (ICA, London, 20 March 1999), for example.
36. In the sense of moving between spaces, listening for a while, moving on and being sociable. The term 'concert hall' is no longer applicable to these small 'club venues' which are often taken over for such presentations.
37. From Galileo to D'Arcy Thompson (1961), engineers have pointed out that we cannot simply ignore *absolute* size when we scale the proportions of a model. The bones and muscles of a human scaled to twice the size would not function effectively. Fleas can jump many times their height while elephants cannot even jump.

References

Attali, Jacques (1985), *Noise – The Political Economy of Music*, Manchester: Manchester University Press.

Barthes, Roland (1977), *Image-Music-Text*, London: Fontana/Collins.

Braithwaite, Richard B. (1968), *Scientific Explanation*, Cambridge: Cambridge University Press.

Casserley, Lawrence (1998), 'A digital signal processing instrument for improvised music', *Journal of Electroacoustic Music* 11, pp. 25–9.

Chion, Michel (1983), *Guide des objets sonores*. Paris: Buchet/Chastel.

Dack, John (1998) 'Strategies in the Analysis of Karlheinz Stockhausen's *Kontakte für elektronische Klänge, Klavier, und Schlagzeug*', *Journal of New Music Research*, 27(1–2), pp. 84–119.

Emmerson, Simon (1994a), 'Live' versus 'real-time', *Contemporary Music Review*, 10(2), pp. 95–101.

Emmerson, Simon (1994b), '"Local/field": towards a typology of live electroacoustic music', *Proceedings of the International Computer Music Conference 1994*, pp. 31–4, San Francisco: International Computer Music Association.

Emmerson, Simon (1995), '*Live* Performance: How do you know it's me you're listening to?', *Report No. 16: Report from an Electro-Acoustic Music Conference (March 1995)*, pp. 9–15, Stockholm: Royal Swedish Academy of Music.

Emmerson, Simon (1998), 'Acoustic/Electroacoustic: The Relationship with Instruments', *Journal of New Music Research* 27(1–2), pp. 146–64.

Landy, Leigh (1991), *What's the Matter with Today's Experimental Music?*, Chur: Harwood Academic Publishers.

Moore, F. Richard (1988), 'The dysfunctions of Midi', *Computer Music Journal*, 12(1), pp. 19–28.

Piaget, Jean (1969), *The Mechanisms of Perception* (tr. G.N. Seagrim), London: Routledge and Kegan Paul.

Schaeffer, Pierre (1966), *Traité des objets musicaux*, Paris: Editions du Seuil.

Schaeffer, Pierre (1973), *La musique concrète*, Paris: Presses Universitaires de France.

Schafer, R. Murray (1977), *The Tuning of the World*, New York: Knopf.

Smalley, Denis (1986), 'Spectro-morphology and structuring processes', in Emmerson, Simon (ed.), *The Language of Electroacoustic Music*, pp. 61–93, Basingstoke: Macmillan.

Smalley, Denis (1992), 'The listening imagination: listening in the electroacoustic era', in Paynter, John; Howell, Tim; Orton, Richard; Seymour, Peter (eds), *Companion to Contemporary Musical Thought*, pp. 514–54, London: Routledge.

Stockhausen, Karlheinz (1971), 'Elektronische Musik aus Studios in aller Welt', in Stockhausen, Karlheinz, *Texte zur Musik (Band 3)*, pp. 242–87, Köln: Dumont Schauberg.

Thompson, D'Arcy Wentworth (1961), *On Growth and Form*, Cambridge: Cambridge University Press.

Wishart, Trevor (1986), 'Sound symbols and landscapes', in Emmerson, Simon (ed.), *The Language of Electroacoustic Music*, pp. 41–60, Basingstoke: Macmillan.

Xenakis, Iannis (1985), *Arts/Sciences: Alloys*, New York: Pendragon.

Xenakis, Iannis (1992), *Formalized Music*, Stuyvesant: Pendragon.

CHAPTER NINE

Stepping outside for a moment: narrative space in two works for sound alone

Katharine Norman

I believe we have a need for a new kind of literature to explain works of art for sound, one that listens differently to what is going on and allows for subjective interpretation as a valued tool. In my personal interpretation of the two works I have chosen[1] – by Paul Lansky and Luc Ferrari – I have found more resonances in the varied narratives of fiction, in particular the rich, multilayered diversity of the novel, than in music. This chapter itself explores fiction and non-conventional presentation as a vital way of illuminating narrative in two works for sound alone.

Stepping outside
'Things she carried' – first movement of *Things She Carried* by Paul Lansky

The movement begins with a loud, fairly low-pitched note, recognisably of electric guitar origin. Then a female voice announces the title of the movement (which is also 'Things she carried') in a matter-of-fact way. Slow, guitar-like drones continue, and a steady rhythmic patterning commences on percussion, continuing throughout most of the movement. Whilst this is going on the speaking voice lists a series of objects, those likely to be found in a woman's pocketbook or handbag. Some time after the voice has stopped the music fades.

There is, of course, far more to it than that.

1
A few seconds into the piece, a female voice announces the title. Although the loud guitar note which opened the movement decreases in

amplitude at this point, the voice is not unequivocally at the forefront of the texture. There are no clear clues as to either what, or who, the voice represents or its function here: it could be that of a radio continuity announcer, a narrator, or someone about to read a poem. It could be an actor playing any of the above. Regardless of this dilemma, in annunciating a title the voice initiates the expectancy of an ensuing narrative of some kind, albeit one that does not yet claim a genre.

2

The 'guitar' notes amble in slow, consonant intervals around a central pitch. They are generally lower in amplitude than the speaking voice, though not always. It should be relatively easy to relegate these aimless drones to the 'background' as an attractive aural wall-paper, but there remains a disquieting sense that something isn't 'right'. Wall-papering is difficult when the dimensions of the hypothetical space are impossible to gauge. Several familiar listening cues as to space have been 'corrupted' by the way that sounds are presented. For instance, the electric guitar sound is compromised on at least two counts, proximity and timbre: the long notes have rather too large and mobile a timbre for a 'real' guitar, some sounds are less guitar-like than others; subtle differences of reverberation and a lack of attack on some of the notes indicate that the sound might emanate from a distant point in a large space, on the other hand fluctuations in amplitude sometimes hint at precisely the opposite.

3

The 'gamelan'-like percussion pattern starts pottering around pleasantly when the voice comes in. The sound is immediately and unnervingly 'close': if this were a 'real' instrument our understanding of its proximity to our listening ears would be informed by the small sounds that close-mic-ing picks up and the resonance created by the space. But these sounds – like the guitar notes – have a tendency to treat the stereo field to a game of spatial hopscotch. Their timbre is more reminiscent of pots and pans than gongs and bells, yet these kitchen implements are perfectly tuned and played with machine-precision accuracy. There is nothing new, now, in the hyper-perfection of quantised, synthetic timbre from which 'human' intervention has been somehow miraculously erased, but there is something that doesn't ring true in the conflicting spatial and timbral signals implied individually by this patterning, the guitars and – as will be discussed further – the nature of the speaking voice. They refuse to sit down together. Nevertheless, the innocuous timbres, harmonic predictability and the static rhythmic patter contribute to a relaxed feel and a sense that, though something will happen soon, there's no hurry.

4

The piece is framed, the title is announced. Let action commence – 'and now, Radio 4 presents *Things She Carried*, starring Hannah Mackay'. Imagine the scene: as the guitar soundtrack fades we'll tune in to the foreground sound of a bag being emptied, perhaps a few contextualising mutterings from the female character and the scraping of wood against a tile floor. A room, a bag, a table, a chair, a woman sitting down . Safe in the knowledge that we are now equipped with the requisite clues for visualisation – since in radio drama the audience is asked to provide the set – we can settle back as the action (even a monologue is active internal dialogue) unfolds before our ears and inner eye.

We can almost see it. Right?

ASIDE: The lure of the open door

Perhaps paintings can have a soundtrack too, if we broaden our definition to include the internal music of the observer's response in looking at a work of visual art.[2] Lansky is not unaware of that possibility, drawing analogies to Vermeer's *The Love Letter*, in alluding to what he is trying to achieve.

> You're standing in front of Vermeer's painting, *The Love Letter*. Looking through a doorway, you see a woman holding a lute. She has just been handed a letter by another woman ... You could invent a different story [to 'explain' the painting's subject] each time, and it wouldn't matter. What does matter is the way the painting creates a vibrating moment – the consequence of some things that might have happened – and the way you, the viewer, experience the painting through that imagined moment (Lansky, liner notes to *Things She Carried*, 1997).

In trying to pin down the potent attraction of *trompe l'oeil* painting, Baudrillard attests that it is our appreciation of the *un-realness* of the depiction that 'lures' us into being seduced by the painting's charm. In his view it is the *absence* of a dimension which creates this sense of 'almost but not quite' and gives the image its strength. Our senses are mystified so that we are at once aware that we are not seeing a real object, but are attuned to the 'immanence' of the real.[3] By extension we might judge that *trompe l'oeil* attunes us to the immanence of the real sense of – in this case – seeing. We know we are looking at a painting but, in our mystification, respond as if we are looking at the objects depicted, rather than their depiction. This latter subtle variation of *trompe l'oeil* reception, I suggest, need not be confined to visual works, and has important implications for our response to narrative in sound.

To use Vermeer's *The Love Letter* as an example: the composition of the painting is, indeed, 'as if' seen through a doorway, and is typical of his work in this respect. The composition is framed, in addition to the physical frame, by the frame of the door in the painting itself. We look through, we see. We could almost be there.

Almost.

The painting is not concerned with *trompe l'oeil* objects but has an element of *trompe l'oeil* with regard to *seeing*. By inserting the frame of the painted doorway within the frame of the painting Vermeer lures us into believing that we are 'seeing through his eyes' or perhaps that he has somehow 'stepped out' of the painting and has joined us in seeing – that the story of the painting, in these terms, exists now, in our time. The skewed composition – a partial view through a doorway, off-centre, deliberately 'un-composed' – exploits a visual 'trick' or lure that film and TV has cheapened and done to death: consider the numerous schlock horror movies where we 'see' through the unseen villain's eyes as he stalks his unsuspecting prey, or the hand-held shaky camera movement exploited by numerous 'real life' documentaries or cop shows. Vermeer is more subtle – he doesn't paint his paintbrush into the scene. This is a *trompe l'oeil* with regard to experience rather than recognition and, though he does not 'lure' us into thinking we are seeing the 'real thing', he does lure us into thinking we are *really* seeing the thing. That is, that our seeing is unmediated, in the present, and it is happening now. In terms of narrative the painting conflates third and first person voice, and is ambiguous in tense: he saw it and we see it; he is seeing it, and we are seeing it. And we are seeing it – just a trick of the (narrative) 'I' – under the impression that the act of seeing is unmediated by the painter's brush. Yet we are at no time convinced that this is not a painting. This appreciation of the 'artefact', as Baudrillard suggests, offers a more satisfying and involving experience than the 'perfection' of virtual reality which, as he puts it, can 'expel the reality out of reality'.[4]

The absence of dimension that Baudrillard identifies as empowering the painted *trompe l'oeil* is the absence engendered by the lack of real three-dimensional space. The two-dimensional painting seeks, instead, to magically create an illusion that should – that must – be recognised as just that in order to acquire its alluring mystery. The space which things occupy defines their reality – and this is no less true of sound. So, is there a comparable nuance of aural *'trompe l'oreille'* in which we can be lured into the experience of, not 'hearing the real thing' but of 'really hearing the thing', in which we can be gripped by the same illusion in relation to listening to sound? I would argue that while a great deal of energy has been expended on theories relating to the notion of hearing sound objects as 'real' (or by reversal, 'not real'), the notion of 'real' listening in a work of 'fictional'[5] sound art is underexplored. Yet the conviction that when we listen we are 'really hearing' the narrative before us is a powerful tool. Once convinced of this, the narrative can travel to all sorts of unreal places and rely on us coming along for the ride, and even doing the steering. And, like *trompe l'oeil,* the power of this tool emerges from an absence of dimension.

5

Wrong. (To pick up the narrative thread).

This piece does *not* encourage our visualisation of an imaginary stage set. We are *not* supplied with the necessary aural clues to point towards visual objects – chair, table, bag, woman. The list of 'things' is not illustrated with any audible 'evidence' – nobody audibly unwraps the chewing gum, shakes a bottle of pills or (and more of this later) places coins on a table. However, although we should not underestimate the relevance of this sonic absence, the use of overt visualisation clues is arguably more often an optional 'extra' to sound's narrative – their removal does not constitute an absence of natural dimension in Baudrillard's sense. In this example of sound art the dimensional absence, I would argue, comes – as with the visual equivalent – from the 'removal' of real space.

We already know that Lansky's space isn't real. Everything about it *lacks* 'virtual' reality – this is not a '3-D' environment. Surround-sound assumes our ears are at the focal point of its virtual reality, it places us (literally) in a passive armchair listening position: we recoil in our seats as the freight train bears down on us, or the plane passes over us. Lansky's presentation of *trompe l'oreille* hearing (as opposed to *trompe l'oreille* things) is encouraged by its lack of '3-D' reality. Fixed spatial boundaries – and by implication a fixed flow of time – are the *absent* dimension. Just as in *trompe l'oeil* painting it is the obviously 'unreal' surface that provides the lure, here it is the removal of the real acoustic space and its replacement with something that doesn't 'make sense' in real terms that both 'spaces us out' and lures us in.

6

Filtering out the 'reality' of any sense of place is extraordinarily difficult. It is not enough to turn the volume down. Record a woman speaking in a room and, however much you remove every scrap of extraneous noise or ambience, you will still have a recording of a woman speaking in a room. It will just be a different room – even if it is the dead 'non'-room of a radio studio (perhaps the most recognisable space of all).

In order to obliterate space, time and place, something has to step in to muffle the loud silence of reality's departure. So, bring on the giant guitars that, in Lansky's space, provide not the hyper-reality of film music's emotional colour-wash, nor the unlistened-to sedative of musak, but a music which heightens the absence of dimension.

ASIDE : A different space

In the radio play music can serve as both outer and inner space, to accompany both scene-changes and 'internalised' thought. In cut and dried cases the music is indeed 'incidental' in that it amplifies events in a foreground narrative, in a similar manner to the emotional narrative supplied by music in film. Whilst in radio plays background music frequently comes to the fore, takes over for a few seconds or carries on while the drama continues it generally subscribes – unless chosen for particularly specific ends – to the conservative norms for the genre; it is harmonically regular, predictable, illustrative (in terms of mood) and has no long-term goals.

Watching a film we have no difficulty in creating separate spaces for 'seeing' and 'listening' to narrative and 'hearing' music. Indeed, often we are listening to music without even consciously acknowledging the fact. The rescued kid gets a big close-up hug and a cheesy crescendo from surging strings triggers our emotional empathy to such a point that tears are inevitable. But it's well-nigh impossible to *listen* to two things at once without a visual (or visualised) narrative without trying to relate one to another in the same conceptual space. In a musical work we can certainly prioritise as to 'importance' – the lead guitar, the solo violin, the loud acousmatic gesture – but only in relation to the other sounds we hear, at the same time.

Lansky's piece has a slightly more interesting hold on the division between background and foreground *musical* gestures, partly precisely because it both exploits and undermines some of the 'easy' listening foibles of incidental music and the solo/accompaniment relationship traditional to many forms of abstract music. It places us in a listening 'comfort zone' in which we might feel at ease with the seemingly unchallenging harmonic and timbral ambience. The guitars and percussion are 'music' in conventional terms whilst the voice isn't. This background music plays tricks, and raises questions as to what might be meant by 'background' in the context of a work such as this, for sound alone. To be in the background means to occupy a different space from the foreground.

7
There is more to speak of.

Given that this is patently not a radio play or a straightforward recitation, we might expect a defined relationship between voice and 'music accompaniment' to emerge: either she starts to rap, breaks into song or the percussion should start to do something a darned sight more interesting. If it's that rather uncomfortable hybrid, poetry recited over music, the voice should be an up front recitation, situated apart. But the voice is definitely part of it – whatever 'it' is: the sound of the speaking voice is subject to just enough sonic processing and manipulation to bring disembodied voice and 'music' into the same strange, unquantifiable space inhabited by extremely large guitars and a hyperclean-living percussion section.

The use of the voice in this movement fuels interesting dilemmas as to genre. The composer describes the work as a 'musical portrait of a woman' in a similar way to the Vermeer he refers to (which, like *Things She Carried*, is anything but a simple likeness). Whereas many of Lansky's works use deliberate obfuscation to enhance the 'hidden' meanings inherent in the timbres and rhythms of natural speech, this voice presents words that are, for the most part, completely intelligible. Indeed, a measured recitation of a list of mundane objects, read by a softly-spoken, attractive voice provides a peculiarly one-dimensional perspective that borders on monotony. This would serve well as a means for focussing on sonic content – lifting the material into the abstract plane of acoustic metaphor (think of Normandeau's *Spleen*, for instance, an acousmatic masterpiece in this vein) but here it is verbal meaning that matters. It is the subtle complexity of what is going on in the use of voice, text and narrative perspective that gives this movement – and the whole work – conviction as a work of fiction for sound alone.[6]

8

The opening section of the text (which divides broadly into 'verses', with 'things she carried' serving as a recurring refrain) is spoken in normal, if measured, tones. The sound is quite 'realistic' in that there is none of the overt comb-filtering that characterises much of Lansky's previous work with speech (though – perhaps as a gentle, even unconscious, aside – the text describes a comb at length) but there is a great deal more going on.

Each short phrase is presented as a close layering of very slightly different versions of the same spoken material. The small delay, a deliberate spatial 'spread' between the simultaneous voices, and the minutely detuned timbres all heighten the disembodiment of the voice. Though delay or reverberation has almost become the norm for indicating a move from foreground present to internalised thought or 'dream state' in radio and TV, this is far more subtle. Although each component 'voice' is separately audible – but only just – the aural effect is undoubtedly that of a single 'real' voice observed simultaneously from very slightly different perspectives; the aural equivalent, perhaps, of looking in one of those hinged mirrors that offers a three-way reflection from left, right and centre.

In terms of narrative voice, too, we are engaged in a game of magic mirrors in which we hear, alternately, a voice, a reader, a character, the eponymous 'she', or ourselves listening. Sometimes – contorting ourselves in front of grandmother's dressing-table – we catch an enchanting glimpse of all our reflections at once.

ASIDE: stepping outside for a moment

In a novel the author, as narrator, can assume an omniscient viewpoint, or can write from the point of view of a particular character – either in the first or third person or by slipping, by various devices, from one to the other. So the narrative voice in fiction can shift imperceptibly back and forth between different points of view, different 'points in space', different minds. It is possible to direct narration as if from a hypothetical 'reader' who observes external action without knowing the inner thoughts of the characters, and with whom we – as actual reader – can identify. Similarly, self-conscious (and, dear reader, by their nature 'fiction-conscious') asides to the invisible audience can allow a narrator to 'step out' of the text for a moment. The way in which words are presented – in particular the subtle ambiguity of free direct speech[7] – can place the reader in a state of flux with regard to where they are currently situated in terms of tense (or time) and point of view (or place).

In drama there is, generally, no narrative voice[8] since drama is action and dialogue played out before your very eyes and ears. Instances of 'narrative voice' within a play are quite unusual, because it is difficult to convince an audience that the play is no longer the thing. A character can play the role of narrator from within the plot (often, in an interesting piece of cross-pollination, acting out on stage the *invisible* 'voice-over' narration that more often occurs in film.)[9] But when a character on stage 'steps out of character' he or she 'steps in' to another, equally 'acted' role. It is *very* hard to convince an audience that a character has 'dropped the act' in making an aside – the fool is still 'in character' when he tells us a joke – though performance art, in particular, plays with appearing to dissolve these boundaries.

In dramatic art, rather than literary fiction, an audience – those 'within hearing' – can be asked to cross the divide and become 'present' in the play: one could argue that when Hamlet soliloquises, the stage extends to encompass the auditorium as the audience 'joins' him, each member of the audience playing, at that moment, the character of Hamlet's internal listening – 'really listening' to his thoughts. So when we applaud Hamlet, we applaud our own perform-ance too.This kind of involvement, perhaps, is comparable to the kind of 'real listening' that, I suggest, is enabled by Lansky's spatial lure. Once hooked, we are gently inveigled into different narrative relationships to both the sound of the voice and the words spoken.

9

The voice – as with the guitars and percussion – is a mobile entity.

The manner of speech is measured but fairly natural. Significantly, there are no extraneous 'human' sounds. The voice is placed, rhythmically, within the surrounding texture – the transparently composed placing of the vocal fragments assures us that the voice inhabits the same ambigu-ous place as guitar and percussion, and takes its time from their measure. The 'she' of the title is still uncreated; she is neither here nor there because neither 'here' nor 'there' has been defined with any reliability. 'She' might be the omniscient narrator looking down, or a third-person character musing as she holds up 'a comb, a fine comb, a broken comb' then, quietly and fading towards a resolution, 'three pens and two pencils'.

'Things she carried'.

'A cheap comb, a comb with several teeth missing'.

This minor shift in the text invites our evaluation and possibly kickstarts mental journeys (what kind of person would keep such a comb, and why?). It is accompanied – using the word reservedly now – by a shift in the guitar-like sounds, which dissolve into a quieter, warmer ambience. As a result, the voice moves further forward on our listening 'stage'.

'Three pens and two pencils', again; but this time the voice is in the foreground, louder and definite in tone. She – narrator, reader, reciter? – has reached centre stage in our listening. She is still separate. Her world is a third-person narrative, apart from our first person listening. She is 'inside our head' but we are not inside hers.

ASIDE: Feeling tense

There can be no narrative without tense whether that tense is past, present or a fluctuating no-man's-land between the two. A narrative – at least in the English language – requires the inclusion of verbs in order to proceed through time, in order for things to 'happen' convincingly. The deliberate obliteration of tense is difficult to achieve, and is perhaps more usually the province of haiku's encapsulated images or the deliberate opacity of found-object sound poetry. Even so, it is very rare to find narration with no time at all.

Perhaps, in the same way that, as Lansky suggests, a painting can invite the viewer to create their own story (or stories), poetic imagery can invite the reader – by their subjective response to its allusions – to create their own temporal narrative and set their own clock running. But in general, once the narrative clock is ticking, careful engineering is required in order to move back and forth in time. Consider a common device in film: we hear a character in voice-over, telling a story from her past. As we listen we see the past happening on screen before our eyes – our eyes share her internal memory. Then, by a simple closing in of the shot, we 'enter' the memory and the past becomes present. The characters on screen take over the dialogue in their present, the voice-over fades. This kind of shift of focus is a simple device, regularly exploited in film, and sometimes literature, since visual (or visualised) information can help us go with the flow. There is a temporal counterpoint between two media – the aural 'past' and the visual 'present' – and we can easily isolate one tense at a time. It is much harder to appreciate that kind of separation in works for sound alone since – as with any 'single media' work – the nature of the material is elemental. There is certainly a counterpoint between the work and our reception of it but – especially in the case of sound-art – within the work tense can be usefully entangled with the abstract 'no time' of musical process.

10

Up until this point there has been no tense to this narrative other than that of the intermittently repeated 'things she carried', a phrase which tentatively imbues the list of objects with a reported past and keeps us at a comfortable listening distance.

But, during the course of two lines of text there is a seemingly minor shift where, I suggest, everything changes. From this point forward, we – listening – know that nothing will be the same. Though there is no verb, these lines are in the present tense. Hannah Mackay's expertise – and Lansky's use of it – is such that a couple of subtle vocal inflexions take our listening from then to now.

'Change purse with one dollar and coins'
A brief sigh, an inhalation on the word 'change', then the smallest of pauses before the word 'coins'. It's the first audible breath in the piece and the implication of human presence couldn't be louder.

She is looking at the coins. They are in front of her – we now know this. The disembodied narrative voice has gone, instead we are listening to – no, *with* – a first person narrative, speaking now.

'Change purse with a dollar and 25, 35, 45 cents.'

She counts the change deliberately, pausing as she lays out the coins – '...25...35...45 cents'. We don't hear the coins – in fact it is essential that we don't for then the work would tumble into the kind of 'radio play' genre that is the least of its concerns. Instead we are there, inside her head, listening – *really* listening – to the music of her thoughts.

After a pause in which we can only contemplate we hear her voice again – 'Things she carried'. Whereas the first time around this was merely the title of the piece, now we are together, *really* listening, and she is there. The voice speaks to us, the volume and placing of the sound is close to our listening ears – she has looked up to tell us something in an explanatory aside. She has entered our listening – and we have entered hers – just as we look through the door by way of Vermeer's sight.

And things sound different from the inside. When the voice returns the processing is more apparent. The real (almost) unprocessed voice is layered with versions of itself that are blurred and sonorous rather than clearly intelligible as speech. Now the distinction between processed and unprocessed is apparent – a division between verbal meaning and emotional association is implied, indicating the personal narrative of 'feeling' within the character with whom we now listen and through whom we hear. The emotional highs and lows that accompany inward reflection are often unpredictable and inconsistent, similarly, the balance between music and meaning fluctuates here. For instance, the phrase 'a packet of homeopathic insomnia tablets' is heavily processed and tuned – possibly by some poignant association on her behalf – while 'rumpled kleenex' – perhaps a very ordinary and expected thing to find in a bag – is set up front, sounds 'real' and appears emotionally insignificant.

The voice stops, but the sound of her time and place continues for quite a while. And all the while we are still with her in the listening space that she, too, continues to inhabit. The sounds we hear are the sounds of inward listening. And we are still listening with her when the next movement starts ('Things she noticed'), we are still in her thoughts as her story continues to unfold.

The twist of narrative time and place that takes place in this piece is achieved not by words – not by verbs, tense or descriptive language – but by a narrative sensibility with regard to the composition of *sound*.

For a moment
Presque rien avec filles by Luc Ferrari

The activity of listening can make us vulnerable; by apprising us of associations that we might not expect, or want, to encounter, or by prising all kinds of emotional resonances from the depths of our memory banks. This is no less true whether we are listening to Mozart or the cry of a newborn baby. But at least, listening to either *Eine kleine Nachtmusik* or a child's bedtime wail, we know which listening clothes to put on: we understand the boundaries of the experience. Perhaps the kind of trivial sampling trick that produces a chorus of dogs barking the National Anthem is mildly amusing because it makes a play on the discrepancy between these two listening attires. At the other extreme, it can some-times seem as if the proffering of listening 'theories' to delineate the abstracted timbral gestures of acousmatic music is an attempt to fit us out with 'musical' clothes of a predetermined style.

Well, in these terms Ferrari's *Presque rien avec filles* forces us to run around naked half the time. Once, at a concert, I observed someone listening to this piece with an ostentatious display of boredom and watch-glancing frustration. His behaviour partly indicated he was try-ing – and trying *very* hard – not to listen. The piece evidently didn't sit well in a concert situation, but this particularly obvious discrepancy between one listener's expectations of a 'tape piece' and what he actu-ally got, made me wonder about what might be contributing to his 'being bored' so angrily. He was left waiting – for something that didn't turn up. And, as Adam Phillips remarks 'in this familiar situation, which evokes such intensities of feeling, we wait and we try to do something other than waiting, and we often get bored – the boredom of protest that is always a screen for rage' (Phillips, 1994, p. 82).

Or course, it all depends on what you're waiting for. *Presque rien avec filles* breaks all the rules of engagement for both abstract music and, what might be construed as its counterpart in this context, a straightforward recording of the natural environment. At times it has a beat, yet in some respects it is an amorphous anecdotal fabric made of soundscape recordings. There are overtly *musique concrète* gestures and acousmatic abstraction, but there are also birds, wind, and distant gunshots. There are words, but there are no easily intelligible phrases. There is no story. Or rather, there are as many conflicting stories as you care to make. This is a piece that defies – that *defends* itself against – any revelations through formal analysis, and refuses to acquiese to a single genre other than being a 'work for sound alone'.

At many levels *Presque rien avec filles* draws attention to the several boundaries it fails to respect: those between music and sound, between coherence and confusion, between subjective and quasi-objective analysis – and between listening and being bored. The transgressing of boundaries is always risky, since it can place us with our feet in unknown territory. And we should beware of this, for if you accidentally step on the cracks between the paving stones, a bear will come and eat you up – there's a danger of a nasty surprise. But, for me, what makes *Presque rien avec filles* an interesting study in narrative terms is that by stepping on the cracks 'accidentally on purpose' it makes us aware of the space between, for a moment – and surprises are not all bad.

The intent of this piece seems deliberately opaque and alienating, and yet it rails against attempts to decipher it in other than subjective terms. The structure is an aural hotch-potch of disparate sections and sudden juxtapositions. Events don't seem to 'go' anywhere, and yet many things happen without apparent rhyme or reason. There's no point scrabbling to pin down the facts since facts, in Ferrari's world, are slippery events. So, to hell with both bears and boundaries; perhaps a personal approach to his sonic fiction is all that's left in terms of useful explanation. And a subjective, disjointed plurality is common practice in that epitome of the inclusive form – the novel. As a form, the novel can fruitfully accommodate all kinds of genre 'transgressions' – from letters, diary entries, and travel writing, to poetic imagery and even factual journalism. Just possibly there might be intimations that works for sound alone can have more allegiance to the literary than is audibly apparent. And that would be worth waiting for. So listen dangerously, up close and personal.

SOME KINDS OF NOW

Last Spring they had moved to a new house. She hadn't wanted to. Even now she lies in bed each night trying, with increasing despera- tion, to retain her image of the old house by cataloguing its details. With the child's inherent conservatism she longs to keep things 'the same', and so she drags her half-asleep consciousness on an internal journey, forcing herself to remember – the blousy red flowers on the sitting-room wallpaper; the little varnished pile of coins that served as a magic doorstop in the study; the hall carpet with its mysterious cobweb patterns; the smooth perfect rail of the banisters; the big tree in the back garden, that creaked against the wind like a ship at sea.

Third-person narrative by omniscient narrator who is privy to the memory and emotions of a character within the text. The 'now' is that of the character who is observed. We are not explicitly aware of the narrator as a persona. Fiction – could not happen in real life.

Actually I made most of that up (did you believe me?). Well, on reflection it is mostly true, but the facts get a little more Proustian in the re-telling and poignancy has been laid on thick. Some facts have been changed to aid the flow. The memories have been infiltrated by a general comment on child behaviour in the third sentence, and a rather lame simile near the end. Of course, the purpose has also changed. Thirty-odd years ago a petulant kid in a strange new home wanted a 'security blanket' memory to grasp hold of. Now I'm older, sitting at a distance, in a different chair – and there's an audience.

First person confessional aside by 'the author': a narrator self-consciously aware of the reader and the text. Implication of veracity – a false 'truth'. A shift in chronology ('thirty-odd years' ... 'I'm older') brings time forward. Now, it appears, the narrator is stepping out of the text and speaking 'to camera'. The first paragraph is, in retrospect, revealed as a fiction.

And that was fiction, of course.
    Yet even as I write this I find that I, too, can still take my internal journey around my own childhood home. And now, led back by details, I have retrieved the differing sensations of the cold tiles on a kitchen floor, stale air in a fusty conservatory, and the rough bark of a towering ash, warm under my small hand.

Fiction. Now a new narrator implies that the time of writing is 'now': 'as I write this' claims the authority of *real* truth for the last paragraph and also draws the reader back to the 'real' time of writing – *before this was made fiction*. The authority of 'truth' is accentuated by the fact that now the reader is being invited to share a private moment of reflection, apparent fact in contrast to the preceding fiction. The narrator who speaks is 'the true author'. The second paragraph is, in retrospect, revealed as a fiction.

And that was fiction too, of course.

And that was fiction, too, of course.

And that was fiction too. Of course! – pure fabrication, knocked together to illustrate a point about shifting narrative voice. Such shifts of inflection can merrily play havoc with our evaluation of the difference between fictional truth, fictionalised truth and the 'real' truth of non-fiction. Now I am telling the truth. But beware of the cracks: a change of font is an unreliable test of authority.

Presque rien avec filles is subject to similar unreliability in its transitions; between different narrative presences, and between where 'fiction' ends and 'truth' begins. One ostensibly straightforward narrative voice is the actual sound of the composer. At times we hear foreground sounds that are undeniably evidence of a human presence – breathing, movement and, just twice, a male voice. We deductively construct the narrative voice of 'the composer' who moves – now – in the natural landscape, listening, and recording material for his piece. Except that this *is* his piece that we are listening to. Like a dream within a dream, in which we wake to find we are still dreaming, Ferrari's apparent presence within his own piece provides an invasive irritant that draws attention to boundaries we might otherwise not have noticed.

Listen ...

At about 3:40 a male voice – a single word (*perhaps 'vont', I can't be sure*), quite loudly in the foreground. Unexpected. And then the sound of someone moving –

the composer?

In retrospect it's as if the opening minutes of the piece were just an overture to something that will now unfold more clearly. But instead he pulls across the curtain and ushers in a more 'realistic' section of outdoor, natural sound. A forest or mountain landscape filled with the sound of the wind in the trees, birdsong and open space.

Much later, the sound of feet moving over the undergrowth, and again the crunching and scrabbling that indicate small sounds of movement writ large by proximity. The foreground sounds of breathing and the rustle of movement.

At the very end of the piece, his voice again.

To me the words sound (possibly) like 'caché dans la main' – 'concealed in the hand'. If so, this is perhaps an explicit reference to the microphone, the act of recording and of his 'being there'. But, whatever he says – and it doesn't really matter – his voice is a reminder of his continuing presence.

and then a faint female voice speaking to a companion in the land-scape to which he listens, his breath audible to us but not to her.

The woman who speaks to her companion is a distant part of the 'now' of the observed landscape of Nature. Her voice is almost blown away on the breeze. It is his nature, and hers – but she cannot hear him listening.

The sound of his breath, and of his feet moving – in the landscape. Finally, the sound of his breath again – but moving inside, into a room acoustic without any sounds from the natural landscape. Indoors.

In the different 'kind' of now we now inhabit, the 'real' composer is making the piece, or listening to it. Making it up now – as we listen.

Each entry of 'the composer' comes as a minor surprise – like meeting a friend in the street, though we knew they lived in the vicinity. At these points – most noticeably when he actually speaks – we are suddenly aware of the difference between the 'first-person' fabricated 'composer' and the apparently unmediated natural environment. When he was absent, we were not especially aware of the absence – we did not *hear* the absence. When he comes back, we notice he wasn't there – and we perceive the difference: bumping into our friend we yell – 'hello! I haven't seen you for *ages*!' rather than 'there you are!'. And the friction between absence and presence reveals something in the space between: while absence and presence are jostling together, another voice is made explicit for a moment, that of the piece itself. We notice that which is usually taken for granted – the compositional equivalent of the authorial voice of the novel. The tantalising, barely perceived, awareness of a separate 'personality' who relates the text we read is precisely the voice that gives the novel the authority of being (for the duration of our reading) 'true'. An authorial voice is part of the novel and cannot be perceived as distinct from the work itself just as, recorded inside the landscape, 'the composer' is an elemental part of *Presque rien avec filles*.

But it is not Ferrari's voice, or movement, or his words that, ultimately, reveal the 'authorial voice' of the piece – it is the moment at the end of the piece when we hear him 'outside' the natural environment. We have been prepared for the sudden shift by the friction between hearing 'the composer' in the landscape and hearing the landscape alone. But the last few seconds of the piece, where we hear 'him' in a different acoustic with no 'outdoor' ambience, show 'the composer' divided from his text. The ending of a piece is a powerful moment, and this disruptive revelation places all our 'memories' of how the piece 'went' at risk – it's as if we've peeped behind the scenes and seen how it's done. Things will never be the same, no matter how many details we try to remember.

Some music ...

Now the beginning.

Now a low drum slowly beating, gradually emerging as an almost regular pulse. The timbre is muffled and indistinct, but quite loud.

Now, over the drum, there's a hissing, flanged sound – it is looped repeatedly, almost three to a measure. An intensification of volume and timbre. But some kind of 'real-world' environment – birds, thunder, wind? – seems to be leaking through from beneath the surface.

Now a change – to a less regular drum beat. A new, harsher flanged sound that could be processed wind or thunder. Then a higher-pitched sweeping sound over this. Again, repetitions over the drum beat. The sounds move, panning left to right. 'Off stage' sound interrupts and comes forward for a few moments – something dark and thundering.

Now a new section, *più mosso*: a metallic hammering sound moving left to right in a regular rhythm, plus a quicker pulse – like a rather energetic bird that can keep time. Possibly a dog barked a couple of times – somewhere in the distance, outside.

Now everything stops. A male voice utters a single word, (perhaps 'vont', I can't be sure), quite loudly and 'to audience'.

Ferrari's authorial games are just one aspect of an extraordinarily disruptive ethos. An ethos which values insecurity, subjectivity, and choosing to be lost.

This opening passage of *Presque rien avec filles* functions primarily as abstract music: its formal processes are clear – extremely simple in fact – and though the timbres are fairly complex, the way they are orchestrated is easily comprehended. Though the music is not explicitly programmatic, there is something ritualistic, perhaps processional, about the repetition over a slow drum beat. It goes on for nearly four minutes. Listening to this as the opening of an abstract work we might have certain crude expectations – namely that it will probably get louder and louder and then there will be some kind of bang. The tam-tam player is counting furiously, or the drummer has both sticks poised. In this world time and place are measured in pulse and pitch. All the indications are that this stuff is music, so we listen accordingly.

But although this passage might seem conventional on the surface, it is engaged in an under-the-table battle with sounds that don't ask for 'musical' listening. Whenever musical phrases stop for a breather some ambiguous sound from the real world leaks through – as if the music is screening some neighbouring eyesore that, though it can't be removed, can at least be concealed from view.

There's another problem: the expected 'bang' doesn't happen. The tam-tam player stands idle and instead we get a brief utterance from 'the composer' to introduce a natural, outside environment, dripping with birdsong, the resonance of wind in the trees and echoes from the hills. These sounds invite – require – a different listening; more than that, they appear to defeat musical listening. It's just one thing after another.[10] Our evaluation of 'what this work is' is undermined. The opening minutes commit us to musical listening – despite a few dodgy moments – and then, just when we'd got comfortable, the carpet is pulled from under our feet. Of course, the piece can't pull that trick twice since we're now wary, ready to hop from one foot to another. But the bang will come – later – when we're least expecting it.

In narrative terms these juxtaposed passages perhaps reveal the difference between one kind of literary variety and another. Turning the page we find the next chapter starts with an epistle. But although the narrative is deliberately fractured, we are not yet lost.

Some more music ...

In the natural landscape, almost nothing going on: one ear on Ferrari in the foreground and the other on the sounds of birds and the wind. Here's a dog – a hot dog, panting for a drink. A bit too close – and the sound pans from right to left, the repeated sound of his panting becomes a regular pulse. And then he's gone. Some very distant gun shots.

[... ...]

In the natural landscape, *almost* 'almost nothing' going on: one ear idly listening to the familiar natural landscape, the other noticing that distant gun shots have started. Perhaps they're shooting birds. Was that a cuckoo? Forty seconds later the landscape seems to have started tapping its feet – short gestures that sound a bit like the guns, bits of cuckoo and a little plink occasionally. Some of those timbres came out of the percussion cupboard. The texture is gradually getting more complicated and louder. Music.

[... ...]

In the natural landscape, almost music going on: those fragmentary sounds have become less shy; louder and there are more of them. The 'musical' patterning they make is clearly distinct from the continuing natural landscape. Just then a fragment, suddenly, of a female voice 'mmm ...', speaking in the landscape.

———————

We've been listening to two worlds, attending at one moment to the sounds of a natural landscape and at other times to a distinctly 'musical' structuring. With two rule-books open on our laps, we're able to mix and match, and to appreciate the contrast between the (apparently) natural landscape where things just happen, and the (apparently) musical landscape where things are composed and need to be deciphered. The fragments of sound that become 'notes' for a more rhythmically structured patterning are drawn from the natural environment, or sound as if they could have been, and the composed rhythms infiltrate the natural rhythm of the landscape before coming to the fore as 'music'. We appreciate the sounds of the natural environment in their new role as musical objects – a cuckoo makes an interesting ostinato, guns are quite convincing as percussive instruments – and we appreciate the two 'varieties' of listening. Unlike the opening of the piece, 'music' here arises out of the natural landscape. The trick now is to somehow detach this music from the surrounding landscape without removing either from view. It's as if a juggler has picked up some objects from the kitchen table, and now delights us with an increasingly daring display of throw and catch. But it's only natural that he'll drop the pepperpot eventually.

With a bang ...

In the natural landscape, almost nothing going on: one ear on Ferrari in the foreground and the other on the sounds of birds and the wind. Here's a dog – a hot dog, panting for a drink. A bit too close – and the sound pans from right to left, the repeated sound of his panting becomes a regular pulse. And then he's gone. Some very distant gun shots.

Bang!>>>>>> an unidentifable gesture that cuts across without warning. But it's gone before you know it, and isn't very long. Perhaps a processed gun sound. The birds don't stop singing.

In the natural landscape, *almost* 'almost nothing' going on: one ear idly listening to the familiar natural landscape, the other noticing that distant gun shots have started. Perhaps they're shooting birds. Was that a cuckoo? Forty seconds later the landscape seems to have started tapping its feet – short gestures that sound a bit like the guns, bits of cuckoo and a little plink occasionally. Some of those timbres came out of the percussion cupboard. The texture is gradually getting more complicated and louder. Music.

BANG!>>>>>> an unidentifiable gesture cuts across without warning. And this time it's much louder and more disruptive. But the birds continue.

In the natural landscape, almost music going on: those fragmentary sounds have become less shy; louder and there are more of them. The 'musical' patterning they make is clearly distinct from the continuing natural landscape. Just then a fragment, suddenly, of a female voice 'mmm ...', speaking in the landscape.

———

The music travels through the landscape and we shift our listening view from one to the other, without too much confusion. These first two 'bangs' which curtail events and bring us back to the natural landscape are unexpected but not completely alien. They are different in 'shape' from what we are used to but, like the dog who padded past a while ago, we can allow them a surreal familiarity. But there is an underlying friction here: in Barthes's terms we move from externalised listening to the internalised listening we employ for music, and yet we are cheated. The way in which 'music' arises from the landscape might seem to allow us to hedge our bets, but in fact the slow refocussing encourages us to commit far more to musical listening than we might if the piece cut suddenly from birdsong to Beethoven, and back again. But the 'music', despite its implications of 'going somewhere', is repeatedly thwarted by a disruptive gesture. We are once more aware of the natural landscape, and unsure of how things will 'go on'.

We don't know where we are, and we look at our watches in frustration. We are aware of two ways of listening, and of listening in two ways at once, but we are not yet aware of the space between.

IN TRAIN

I am sitting in a train, at the back of the carriage, facing forward. The carriage is nearly empty – just four or five other people dotted about.

The walls are yellow, the seats are a deep blue. Even though it is mid-morning, the fluorescent strip-lights are on. All sitting in bright isolation, staring straight ahead.

Now I lean against the cold, greasy glass of the window – fingerprints and smudges show it for what it is. The world is outside: rain, trees, houses, office buildings, cars and people. A man is walking his dog across Walthamstow marshes, they are alone. Only we know this.

Then I turn away from the window to look directly down the train carriage again. The outside world exists only in peripheral vision as a blur of green and grey.

But then, for a moment, it seems as if the train carriage is a long tube of separate space – real, bright and stationary – travelling at speed through an equally stationary world. Both are perfectly in focus. Nothing moves except the difference between them.

———

Sometimes we transcend our normal interpretation of the facts: we manage to shift our narrative construction of experience and the invisible is made visible for a while. Perhaps Ferrari's offering of 'now it's music' and 'now it's landscape' is like being in the moving train and looking at the outside world. We can flit from observing one view to another – the train carriage or the outside world – and we can certainly apprehend both at once, but we do so by a process of comparison. This involves choosing one view or the other as our point of reference in relating the two. But the train is also *moving* through the world, just as the music 'moves through' the landscape of *Presque rien avec filles*. How would it be if, for a few moments, it was not music or landscape we listened to, but the *movement* of one thing through another.

When we followed 'the composer' around in the piece we accompanied, at his invitation, an audible narrator who himself moved through the landscape. We were walking around in the piece with him. But when we are walking in a landscape we do not perceive our movement as separate from ourselves and we do not, as a rule, perceive ourselves as apart from the landscape – like Ferrari, our feet are on the ground and we are 'doing' the moving. But when we listened to the distinctly musical textures that detached themselves from the landscape of natural sounds, it was as if we were sitting – motionless – in the train carriage; at these times we were listening *inside* a music that itself travelled forward through a surrounding sonic landscape that, like the blurred view outside the window, had retreated to the background.

It would take something extremely bizarre to refocus our perception so that we could be not only aware of both worlds at once, but be aware of being 'inside' both music and landscape – *at the same time*. A shift in our subjective narrative would have to occur that meant what we were listening in two different ways simultaneously, in a manner that what we perceived was beyond the point of moving from one state to the other.

In the natural landscape, almost music going on: those fragmentary sounds have become less shy; louder and there are more of them. The 'musical' patterning they make is clearly distinct from the continuing natural landscape. Just then a fragment, suddenly, of a female voice 'mmm ...', speaking in the landscape.

BANG! >>>>>>> *a very loud, very sudden and very surprising 'drum-kit' riff. Everything else stops while this is going on.*

As the cacophonous drum-kit clattering sears through the landscape we, along with the birds, fall off our listening perch. All we hear is movement. In isolation. The gesture is astoundingly unexpected – unpolished, unexplained and derivative of another world. It marks the point where the 'visible' narrative voices of music, of landscape and of the two together, are kicked out of view. Now there's yet another narrator – who smirks knowingly, sitting behind a drum-kit with both sticks poised – who reveals all that 'went on' before as fiction. Even the stuff we thought was real.

Female voices. One German, one Italian, one French – to left, right and centre. Their words are intelligible some of the time, but the phrases are fragmented and sometimes masked by the sounds of the natural landscape. Among them I hear *der Blick ... s'importante ... quasi remoto ...* This is not a conversation. There are intermittent loud percussive gestures. Fragments of speech – sibilants and parts of words – interspersed with wood-block plinks and fragmentary temple-block glissandi.

Ferrari presents us with a sound that is the least likely to 'succeed' as abstract music, and he uses this sound to build a musical texture – an obviously composed music. In normal circumstances we just cannot separate normal speech from the natural landscape of our experience – speech can be acted, made artificial in its rhythms and inflections, fragmented so that words become meaningless, spoken in a language we don't understand – but it is still speech and part of our world. Many composers have celebrated this fact and the effect on our listening when the normal role of speech is undermined.[11] And Ferrari does this too – the voices speak in different languages, together but in isolation. It is essential that they do not speak the same language, for even if their phrases were unrelated, we would attempt to make linguistic connections.[12] We hear intelligible speech, but for various reasons cannot quite make out what they're saying. Listening to these relaxed voices, speaking together within the natural landscape, we accept the sounds as phatic: expressions of human sociability – humans *being* – rather than carriers of narrative meaning. And this is a real achievement, since we generally grab hold of speech as a useful narrative lead – a while back, when 'the composer' spoke just one word to us, we followed him around for *ages*.

But we don't feel the same now. For a start, we're still reeling from a narrative bang that snatched away all points of comparison. Previously we had perceived a gentle friction between music and landscape, but then we stood on the cracks for a moment. Now perhaps we are mistrustful of what is going on – or *how* things are 'going'. We don't listen only to the words, we don't listen only to the music. We are ready to listen to the space between.

The texture grows more frantic – faster, and more rhythmically defined. Low pitched sounds – vocal? – start to contribute a tuned pattern. Small sounds – a whistle, percussion, voice.

This passage – for me, speaking subjectively – is where time, and movement in time, shifts a notch: listening, I hear the *presence* of the movement of one thing through another, and not the moving things themselves. There is something external to my perception of a music that uses the sounds of landscape and a landscape that *is* music. The invisible is apprehended for a while.

Perhaps we are made ready for it; we have been moving from one view to another, comparing, contrasting, wondering what might happen and entertaining certain expectations. Things might not have happened quite as we expected, but we managed to adjust our reading of this diverse narrative to incorporate the fictionalisation of Ferrari's scufflings, an over-heated dog, some musically inclined guns and a cuckoo that put itself about a bit too much. Even the percussive twangs made for interesting structural diversions that we, looking back, could relate to the kind of music that had bubbled up out of the sounds of the natural world. Everything had made sense until that big bang that recreated our listening universe. And now, in retrospect, one aspect of Ferrari's compositional 'simplicity' becomes apparent: if either the music – our view of the train carriage – or the landscape – our view of the world – had been too engrossing, we might have become too interested in the way things looked. It's OK to be bored.

Then there's the faint sound of human movement – inside a room, in another place. Just when recognisable birds begin to sing, everything stops.

For a moment.

Notes

1. I have chosen these specific pieces for several reasons: I like them and they interest me; they are both quite widely obtainable on CD; they are very different from one another, yet neither sits well in the 'tape music' concert tradition and both are concerned with issues markedly outside the preoccupations of abstract music or art. This chapter is deliberately written to offer interest without necessarily requiring the works to hand on first reading. Exact 'timings' are avoided, since this is not analysis, but an invitation to listen. The text of the first movement of Lansky's work is given below, for information only (the composer himself suggests that a knowledge of the text is not essential to listening).

    Things she carried:
    A comb,
    A fine comb,
    A broken comb,
    Three pens and two pencils,
    Things she carried.
    A cheap comb,
    A comb with several teeth missing,
    Five credit cards,
    Social security card,
    Library card,
    Three pens and two pencils,
    Change purse with one dollar and coins,
    Change purse with a dollar and 25, 35, 45 cents,

Things she carried.
Keys,
Calculator,
Lipstick,
Piece of gum,
Ticket stubs,
Supermarket coupons,
Blank checks,
Three pens and two pencils,
A bottle of pain killers,
Brown leather bag,
A packet of homeopathic insomnia remedy,
Receipts,
House keys,
Credit card case,
Emory board,
An address book,
Phone numbers,
Fax numbers,
Orange wood stick,
Rumpled kleenex,
Car keys,
Woollen knitted gloves,
One earing,
Piece of gum,
Things she carried.

(text by Paul Lansky and Hannah MacKay, reprinted by permission.)

2. In my opinion gallery concerts, in which music is commissioned 'to go with' an exhibition both recognise at some level this likelihood and fail to understand the importance of a silent auditorium.

3. Liner notes, *Things She Carried*, Bridge, 1997.

4. '*Trompe l'oeil*, by taking away a dimension from real objects, highlights their presence and their magic through the simple unreality of their minimal exactness. *Trompe l'oeil* is the ecstasy of the real object in its immanent form. It adds to the formal charm of painting the spiritual charm of the lure, the mystification of the senses. For the sublime is not enough, we must have the subtle too, the spirit which consists in reversing the real in its very place. This is what we have unlearned from modernity – subtraction is what gives strength; power emerges from the absence.' (Baudrillard, 1997, p. 9).

5. 'All the utopias of the nineteenth and twentieth centuries have, by realising themselves, expelled the reality out of reality and left us in a hyper-reality devoid of sense, since all final perspective has been absorbed, leaving as a residue only a surface without depth. Could it be that technology is the only force today that connects the sparse fragments of the real? But what has become of the constellation of sense? And what about the constellation of the secret?' (Baudrillard, 1997, p. 12).

6. I will come back to what fiction and non fiction in sound-art could mean in relation to Ferrari's *Presque rien avec filles*.

7. 'The writer moves from narrative to direct speech without the use of the usual markers (for example, *Mary approached John. Did the man see you yesterday? John looked away*).' Crystal, 1987, p. 77).

8. In certain genres that inhabit a world between dramatic play and epic narration there can be a narrative voice, of course – consider the chorus or messenger of Greek Tragedy.

9. For instance, the narrator of *Our Town*. And this 'cross-pollination' also extends back to the novel, the 'Private Dick' detective novel being a prime example of a genre that borrows back the knowing voice-over from the B-movie film. The sixth movement of *Things She Carried* – not discussed here – makes homage to precisely that.

10. Roland Barthes provides a useful reflection on two different kinds of listening, if one ignores the woeful generality in his musical references: '"listening" to a piece of classical music, the listener is called upon to "decipher" this piece, i.e. to recognize (by his culture, his application, his sensibility) its construction, quite as coded (predetermined) as that of a palace at a certain period; but "listening" to a composition (taking the word here in its etymological sense) by John Cage, it is each sound one after the next that I listen to, not in its syntagmatic extension, but in its raw and as though vertical *signifying*: by deconstructing itself, listening is externalized, it compels the subject to renounce his "inwardness"' (Barthes, 1985, p. 259).

11. I discuss this more specifically in my contribution to *A Poetry of Reality: composing with recorded sound* (Norman, 1996).

12. As with Glenn Gould's sound documentary, *The Idea of North*, which plays on the tension to be had from connected meanings in a contrapuntal texture and thereby *encourages* a dual appreciation of 'music' and 'speech'.

References

Barthes, Roland (1985), *The Responsibility of Forms*, Oxford: Blackwell.

Baudrillard, Jean (1997), 'Objects, Images, and the Possibilities of Aesthetic Illusion' in Zurbrugg, Nicholas (ed.), *Art and Artefact*, London: Sage Publications.

Crystal, David (1987), *The Cambridge Encyclopedia of Language*, Cambridge and New York: Press Syndicate of the University of Cambridge.

Norman, Katharine (1996), 'Real-world music as composed listening', in Norman, Katharine (ed.), *A Poetry of Reality: composing with recorded sound, Contemporary Music Review*, 15, Parts 1–2, London: Harwood Academic Publishers.

Phillips, Adam (1994), *On Kissing, Tickling And Being Bored*, London: Faber and Faber.

Recordings

Ferrari, Luc (1989), 'Presque rien avec filles', in *Acousmatrix 3 – Luc Ferrari*, BVHAAST: CD 9009.

Lansky, Paul (1997), 'Things she carried', in *Things She Carried*, Bridge 9076.

Index